Looking Back at Macroeconomics 101

Alok Sheel has over 30 years of public service and policy experience as a member of the elite Indian Administrative Service (IAS), with key assignments in the finance ministry, Prime Minister's Economic Advisory Council and as multilateral interlocutor in the G20 deliberations during the Global Financial Crisis. With a Masters (distinction) in Macroeconomic Policy from the University of Bradford, U.K., and a PhD in History from Jawaharlal Nehru University, New Delhi, India, he has written widely on issues relating to the global economy and finance, macroeconomic policy, development finance, the international monetary system and global economic governance. He writes regularly for several financial dailies. He is widely travelled, participating regularly in international conferences and workshops on global financial and economic crisis and governance.

Looking Back at Macroeconomics 101

A Ringside View of the Global Financial Crisis from Asia in Real Time

ALOK SHEEL

ACADEMIC FOUNDATION
NEW DELHI

www.academicfoundation.org

First published in 2015
by

ACADEMIC FOUNDATION
4772-73 / 23 Bharat Ram Road, (23 Ansari Road),
Darya Ganj, New Delhi - 110 002 (India).
Phones : 23245001 / 02 / 03 / 04.
Fax : +91-11-23245005.
E-mail : books@academicfoundation.com
www.academicfoundation.org

Disclaimer:
The opinions/views/findings expressed in this book are solely those of the author and do not necessarily reflect the views of the publisher.

Cataloging in Publication Data--DK
Courtesy: D.K. Agencies (P) Ltd. <docinfo@dkagencies.com>

Sheel, Alok, author.
Looking back at macroeconomics 101 : a ringside view of the global financial crisis from Asia in real time / Alok Sheel.
pages cm
Includes bibliographical references.
ISBN 9789332701700

1. Financial crisis. 2. Globalization--Economic aspects. 3. Monetary policy. 4. International economic relations. I. Title.

DDC 338.542 23

Typeset by Italics India, New Delhi.

Printed and bound by The Book Mint, New Delhi.
www.thebookmint.in

For
My father who introduced me to the joys of thinking,
and for my mother who helped me afford this luxury.

Contents

II
Lowering Skies Over the Global Economy:
The US Sub-prime Crisis

III
Apocalypse: Lehman and After

IV
The Coordinated Policy Response: Rise and Decline of the G20

Part Two: Thematic

V

Bail-out and Stimulus: Global Financial Crisis and Fiscal Policy

VI

Helicopter Ben: Global Financial Crisis and Monetary Policy

VIII
Making Next Time Different: Reforming Global Finance

Acknowledgement

A student of history and a professional civil servant attempting to write a book on economics and finance must necessarily accumulate a number of intellectual debts and mentors along the way in trying to wed the long term with the short. I was fortunate in having several such. They have all played a part in the making of this book in some manner without being complicit in its shortcomings.

From my teachers and classmates in the history centre at Jawaharlal Nehru University I learnt to value the critical role of the past in understanding and shaping the present. I would like in particular to mention Shirin Ratnagar who mentored me in understanding the ancient world, Harbans Mukhia the medieval world, Sabhyasachi Bhattacharya, Bipan Chandra and K.N. Panikkar modern India, and Madhavan Palat European History.

Jawaharlal Nehru University of the seventies was a very argumentative institution. Even student union elections revolved not on water supply and the running of hostel messes, but on the positions on major intellectual debates. The finer points were fiercely debated in tutorials, outside the library and extended well into the small hours on sprawling lawns outside the hostels, sustained by endless cups of tea. I learnt a great deal together with my fellow students. I would in particular like to single out Vijay Tata, T.C.A Raghavan, Radhika Singha, Peter Ronald D'Souza, E. Sreedharan and Janakiraman Sriraman. Three of them went on to become distinguished academics, two (including myself) civil servants, and the remaining two professionals. It is my hope that this book is of interest to all these three categories. Alas, I am the only one who came anywhere close to becoming an economist!The credit for developing an enduring fascination with economics and finance, subjects that I was fearful of in the University because I considered myself a social and not a rocket scientist, goes in good measure to the stimulating approach and patience of Y. Venugopal Reddy, P.J. Nayak, Montek Singh Ahluwalia, R. Krishnamurthy and R.Sridharan with whom I worked in the union ministry of finance in the mid nineties.

During my maiden full time academic (masters) course in economics at the University of Bradford Colin Clarke gave me the confidence to negotiate my pathological fear of advanced mathematics and calculus through a state-of-the-art weapon, the computer, while Colin Kirkpatrick set me on the path to navigating major debates in macro-economics.

My appreciation of the global financial crisis was greatly facilitated by frequent interactions with Duvurri Subbarao, Eswar Prasad, M.R. Anand, the outstanding real time coverage and commentaries in the Financial Times, and several hours of deliberations sitting around the high table of G20 finance deputies and Sherpas. C. Rangarajan helped me hone my analytical skills at the Economic Advisory Council to the Prime Minister.

Kaushik Basu gave me the self-assurance that I could actually write a book on economics, and Patricia Ann Grey-Beddoe, that some people may actually want to read it, even as she helped smoothen awkward constructions and design the cover. I am grateful to Sona, Sanu and Uma Kapila of Academic Foundation for their efforts in transforming a clumsy manuscript into what I hope is a readable book and for reposing their confidence in me by agreeing to publish it.

I wish to acknowledge the magnanimity of *Business Standard*, *The Economic Times, Financial Express, Mint* and the *Indian Express* for permitting me to reprint opinion pieces originally published in these financial dailies in this book.

Finally, I cannot end before acknowledging the indulgence and patience of my loving wife for her understanding as I tapped the computer down to pursue sudden epiphanies without even an ' if you please.' She has played a greater role that she can imagine as I found it useful to address some of her down to earth skepticism of complex economic reasoning, such as inflation, over which spouses often spar, in my writings.

Preface

What Went Wrong with Macroeconomics 101?

I

This work comes from a historian by training, a civil servant by profession, an economist more by accident, and an irrepressible writer by inclination—of whom it could be said, like Oliver Goldsmith's village school master of *Deserted Village*, "in writing, too, the author owned his skill; though sparingly read, he would scribble still"—so it will inevitably bear the imprint of all four avatars. Being posted for several years in positions that called for well-defined skills in economics and finance, including their international dimensions, I segued into learning just smoothly enough to start writing about the subject. A little knowledge, says the Bard of Avon, is a dangerous thing, but even a substantial knowledge can be equally hazardous when one speaks of finance.

I was working in our Indian Prime Minister's Economic Advisory Council just as the storm clouds of the global financial and economic crisis were gathering. As the storm broke, with the collapse of Lehman Brothers, I was drafted into that wing of the Indian Treasury Department that engaged with the G20. This gave me a ringside view of the co-ordinated international response to the crisis. One could not hope to get closer than that.

My book is intended as a perspective from Asia on the global financial crisis as it unfolded in real time, and in the process redefined several prevailing macroeconomic paradigms. It is a collection of opinion based on fact submissions written for various financial dailies over almost a decade.

In retrospect, the decade turned out to be a highly interesting one indeed.

Considering where I am coming from, the work is addressed primarily to the interested layperson, including students who feel that their textbooks do not adequately explain the real world,[1] although I hope subject specialists would see some value in it as well, written as it is by a participant observer keen to understand, from scratch, goings on in the global economy and finance that are reshaping our lives in a fundamental manner. I have had to intensively research my way online to several basic precepts of advanced economics on my own while trying to understand the real world. The anomalies that I found in the process of fitting fact to theory are littered liberally across the articles.

The 'macroeconomics 101'[2] subtext in the title might appear intriguing, ambiguous and ambitious in its intent to the reader at best, and foolhardy at worst. There is in any case a thin line between ambition and foolhardiness, and I may well have transgressed this line because I never did an undergraduate course in economics and was admittedly econometrics and Samuelson-challenged. I am not proposing any new theories on macroeconomics, but simply drawing attention to what I found to be anomalies in applying received wisdom or theories to the real world. Is there a difference between theory and received wisdom? The reader must judge, as the case may be, and in the end if I am pretentious, I would stand guilty as charged. It is possible that I have not used the right word for the sub-text. But on deeper reflection, I decided that only a lesser good can emerge by limiting the level of one's ambition. I cannot claim to be the 'new conscience keeper of economics', but I am working towards it!

II

I have never considered a full length book before, and that too on such a topic. One could ask whether I have been lazy in not rewriting

1. Student activism in this regard is forcing Universities to make changes in the economics curriculum. See Jones (2014).
2. A metaphor for the basic mandatory course on macroeconomics at the undergraduate level in economics.

the original opinion pieces compiled over several years into a tightly organised full length book. I must confess that although I have a few hundred thousand words in print to my name, I was daunted by the prospect of writing a full book with separate chapters following on one from the other. Overlap and repetition may arise as the reader ploughs through a book of this nature.

If torpor and daunt are combined with an abiding belief in never letting the proverbial good come in the way of the best, all good projects would be banished to the back burner. There were however also three substantive reasons that reduced me to quibbling and oscillating between what was good and what was best and set me on a course that can so easily be confused with torpor and daunt.

First, the deep impression made on me by an article on writing books (Robinson, 2013) that cited the rather depressing statistic that 81 per cent Americans felt that they had a book in them! I am sure people in other countries are not too far behind. The logical, sober advice? The world would be better off if most of them kept the book where it belonged—inside them.

How many persons have the patience to read a book anyway in the much vaunted age of information? Today information has given way to ideation, especially when everybody is busy writing. Yet another book on the global financial crisis, by now a heavy industry in its own right! Give us a break! The author went further to put out another depressing statistic from the *New York Times* survey: few persons had the attention span to negotiate a book. Just one in four had actually read a book in one year. Constant distractions and reduced attention spans are the flipside of the age of information that has made half an hour of uninterrupted reading a luxury that few can afford (Parks, 2014).

Yet, how can one explain the fact that the book publishing industry continues to flourish? So, books still need to be written even though with the growing popularity of e-books, the younger generation may be moving away from printed works altogether.[3]

---

3. According to the Pew Research Centre, while they were effectively non-existent prior to 2010, now one in two Americans has an e-reader or tablet. In the UK, book sale monitoring data put out by Nielsen shows that e-book sales rose rapidly within five years from one in

The demand-supply equation between writers and readers has also changed vastly since the time up to the Middle Ages when a determined scholar could aspire to read in his lifetime most, if not all, books that had ever been written. How the world has changed! Till recently people paid to buy books, and authors could earn a reasonable living. Now only celebrated authors can hope to do so. In future, people may have to be paid to read by authors. According to the doom and gloom group, it needs a very 'muscular' self-belief, bordering on the delusionary, to write a book these days. In my need to write and my optimism, I opt for *Book Lovers anonymous*. What the Canadian book store, Book City describes as the "Bio Optic Organized Knowledge" device—'book'—and a revolutionary breakthrough retains several of its comparative advantages even in this Age of Information.

It is my hope that this book will sit easy on the reader. Indeed, this doesn't even count as an "original" work, as it is a compilation of my opinion pieces written over almost a decade. In the good old days, these would have been read as a collection of essays. It is not meant to be read from beginning to end, or even one chapter at a time. The author's recommended recipe is not to set aside any time dedicated to reading this book. It consists of several self-contained pieces, mostly comprising some 1000 words each, that can be read one at a time when there are blocks of about five awkward minutes to fill in that are otherwise spent twiddling one's thumbs. This could be while waiting for public transport, for a visitor, boarding a flight, for the seat-belt sign to go off after take-off, just before falling asleep (hopefully the essay will not accelerate the process!), served in a restaurant, over a cup of coffee, or whenever, wherever. In this sense, this book is a halfway house between a printed book and a 'Kindle e-book': both can be flipped out for short periods and put away. If the reader finds the articles even slightly interesting he should be able to complete the book this way without breaking into a sweat, in a fit of absent mindedness, as it were. If the interest of the reader is not stoked, the

five consumer titles to one in four in 2013. They no doubt continue to rise at the expense of printed books, as it may be difficult to 're-kindle' interest in printed books in the electronic age. See Baggini (2014).

book does not deserve to be read. There! I've said it and you are off the hook.

The big picture in its full detail should gradually fall into place frame by frame. If I were to draw an analogy, it would have to be with one of those gigantic jig-saw puzzles depicting a bafflingly complex picture where you work on one small part in a single sitting. Consider each opinion piece as locking together a few adjoining blocks of the big picture. I am confident that even if finance and economics are not your 'thing,' you will be interested. Money, as they say, makes the mare go. You, my reader, need to know, need to read the signs of the times and plan accordingly.

The second reason why I decided against rewriting the pieces into a regular book was that I felt some of the multidimensional weft and warp of the rich tapestry contained in the articles would be lost in trying to weave them into a single fabric of central themes and arguments. This book is not primarily aimed only at economists; and while its central theme is the recent global financial crisis, its overarching objective is to locate the crisis amidst the contours of a changing world. While analysing these contours the author goes as far back in time as each of the antecedents warrant. It therefore also aspires to be a work of 'contemporary economic history', in the sense the phrase was used some time ago by Barraclough (1964). The test of time will be the judge as to how far I have succeeded.

The historical craft is predicated on the view that it is impossible to understand the present without some, nay, even a thorough, knowledge of the past. In the words of William Faulkner, 'the past is never dead. It's not even past.' It is the door through which the present emerges. While history is usually divided into three periods—leaving out what is sometimes referred to as pre-history and proto-history—namely the ancient, mediaeval and modern worlds, contemporary events which become history in the making, or contemporary history, endeavours to trace issues of current relevance and interest as far back as on a 'need to go' basis. The themes *inter alia* of globalization, inequality, demography, global imbalances, macroeconomic policies, inflation, central banking and money, all central to the global financial crisis, have been handled in this manner.

Globalization takes us back to early modern history when the dawn of the Industrial age spawned technologies that facilitated the mass transportation of people, goods and information and also the demographic transition without which we cannot understand growth and fiscal dynamics. Human migration has always been associated with growth and takes us as far back as to the origin, or emergence, of *Homo sapiens sapiens* as they migrated out of Africa and his spread to practically every part of the globe. The export-led strategy of economic growth that underlies large global imbalances can be traced back to mercantilism that preceded the industrial revolution—the big difference between the two lying in the nature of money in the two eras. Money itself takes us further back still, indeed even beyond history to social anthropologists who studied the use of cowry shells in contemporary primitive societies. The origin of income inequalities compels us to look at the Neolithic Revolution that first facilitated the accumulation of surpluses, and accelerated by rapid productivity shifts in the industrial era; inflation is basically a problem of the fiat money era that began in the early 1970s when money ceased to have a nominal anchor like gold; modern finance with its periodic bubbles and crises goes back to the invention of banks and the joint stock company towards the end of the Middle Ages that transformed physical surpluses into financing savings that could be aggregated for investments on a large scale.

None of these historical asides is central to the main argument, but is nevertheless conducive to a deeper understanding of the forces at work that has made the present what it is, and may also be interesting in its own right to the general reader. These details would almost certainly have been excised in a rewritten book dedicated to the global financial crisis and the dismal science. When the full jigsaw puzzle is assembled, there will be a number of details, such as the squirrel in the corner nervously clutching a nut in its fore claws, engaging in their own right but only of incidental interest to the main action—which may well be a hunter in a thick equatorial forest gingerly taking aim at a hornbill high up in a tree with his primitive bow and poison arrow.

The third reason has also to do with where I am coming from, the discipline of history. If the past is the door that leads to the present, the present is also a window opening into the future. This is why the discipline of history is embedded in the human DNA, and is amongst the oldest disciplines. I saw value in an unexpurgated analytical response to events as they happened in real time—anomalies observed during the great moderation (Section I), the dark clouds (the sub-prime crisis) gathering in the run up to the Lehman Brothers apocalypse (Section II) during which the damaging effects of several fault lines in the form of a loose monetary policy, global imbalances and lax financial regulation were already apparent, and finally the aftermath of Lehman when sub-prime morphed into the global financial crisis (Section III), and the G20 coordinated a policy response by systemically important countries to pull the global economy back from the brink of an abyss (Section IV). It was during this period that the debates on extraordinary macroeconomic policies (Section V on fiscal policy and Section VI on monetary policy), the international monetary system and global spillovers (Section VII), and on a new regulatory framework to guard against a repeat of such a devastating financial crisis came to occupy centre stage (Section VIII). The book is consequently divided into two parts, with the first part (Sections I-IV) based on the timeline, and the second part dealing with the thematic debates (Sections V-VIII), that may be of greater interest to subject specialists and policy makers. I have no doubt that this work would also be of some interest to future economic historians as an outsider's account of what began as a Trans-Atlantic crisis in real time. I, for one, have learnt a great deal about my own country and its past from the accounts of periodic overseas visitors—most of all from observations of the great Persian scholar from Khwarizm, Al Beruni, who accompanied Mahmud of Ghazni on his predatory forays into India in the 11th century AD.

The lurking danger in an unexpurgated ringside view in real time is that it may expose the author's occasional flip flops and contradictions! It is my hope that the reader will find that I have been reasonably consistent and prescient[4] through the entire timeline—before, during

4. In "Restructuring Structured Finance" (chapter 23), written full seven months before the collapse of Lehman Brothers, I anticipated several of the problems with financial regulation that later came on the G20 and FSB reform agenda. See also Sheel and Ganguly (2008).

and in the wake of the crisis—even when I may have misread some current trends. In chapter 26 ('Life after Greenspan'), written in early October 2008, I was sceptical about the US escaping recession at a time when International Monetary Funds (IMF's) own projections did not indicate any recession going forward. It is true that in chapter 30 ('Asia: The Aftermath of Crisis'), I was somewhat misled by the smart recovery of 2010, as this was actually followed by the dreaded 'double-dip'. However, at a time when both China and India were witnessing a robust recovery, going against the prevailing decoupling hypothesis, I foreboded in the same piece that "Asia may have to live with lower trend growth." My reading of a subsequent outcome was at least spot on.

Or take the big 'I'—Inflation. While drawing attention to the decline in inflation, the disinflationary impact of productivity shifts in China and India on the global economy, the disconnect between consumer and asset prices, and between core and headline inflation, I initially underestimated the impact of financial markets on commodity prices as a source of 'agflation'. I had my finger on the button by August 2008, as the puzzle as to why commodity markets were moving north as the economy moved south seemed to lie in liquidity flows. I should have connected the dots earlier. Also, my fears at this stage (May 2008) regarding the return of stagflation proved to be unfounded. By October of the same year, within a couple of weeks of the Lehman debacle, I was complimenting Ben Bernanke for having presciently set his eyes on the deflationary threat even as the European Central Bank (ECB) was still fighting inflation.

Let's take a look at monetary policy. As early as August 2006, I wrote that "globalisation is leading to increased dissociation between domestic growth and employment. This threatens the soundness of monetary orthodoxy, such as the Taylor Rule". But in October 2006, I was still recommending John B. Taylor for the Nobel Prize, which he no doubt still richly deserves. At this time however, I did not quite appreciate that the Taylor Rule was being compromised from yet another direction, the dissociation between consumer prices and asset prices. In its present form, a straightforward application of the Taylor Rule could endanger financial stability.

The mighty dollar! While drawing attention to the continuing puzzle of a strong dollar and ingenious theories to explain its continuing strength in the face of mounting imbalances, when the sub-prime crisis hit, and the dollar declined and commodity prices rose, I thought that the dollar had at last met its comeuppance and was succumbing to macroeconomic logic, an event I had been awaiting for several years. I however underestimated the inherent strength of the global reserve currency, which strengthened as the US financial system all but collapsed following the Lehman debacle. The lesson was well learned. When there were renewed fears of a dollar collapse because the US Congress threatened not to revise the debt ceiling upwards, I argued in the *Financial Times* of 1 August 2011 ('Default would ignite Debate about Dollar's Global Role') that global uncertainty caused by such a wilful default would only serve to strengthen the dollar. As things turned out this prediction was never put to the test because the US debt ceiling was revised upward just in time, but the hypothesis stands for now. So does my rather pessimistic prognosis regarding the future of fiat money.

Finally, the ubiquitous Nation State. Having long been arguing about the growing economic and political irrelevance of the Nation State, I saw—and the optimist in me still sees—the gradual but irresistible march towards European Union and the emergence of first the G7, and more recently the G20, as evidence for this belief. But I obviously underestimated the power of nationalism, which continues to strengthen in emerging economies even as it has started to flicker in advanced economies. The crisis in Greece is putting globalizing forces to test. The short and medium term however is not to be confused with the long-term. In the 1930s, it may well have seemed that the tide of globalization had been reversed, whereas it resumed its triumphal march in the 1970s. Whatever be the direction of history, its course is rarely linear.

On balance I am willing to take the risk of being faulted but with hind sight. As a student of history I see some value in an unfiltered account, and I hope others will do so too. While all history may indeed be contemporary history, as each generation rewrites it in accordance with its world view, contemporary accounts never lose their relevance as they are also a source of history, coming closest to describing the past as it really was. What separates history from pre-history and proto-history is the record of what was on human minds as they lived through historical events. A contemporaneous record is even more credible. Therein lies the enduring importance of Thucydides' account of the Peloponnesian war, especially when compared to *The History* of his more distinguished contemporary, Herodotus of Halicarnassus, often hailed as the 'father of history', or the first historian to apply critical evaluation to his material.

Finally, I also try to peer prophetically into what lies in store for the future—something historians who deconstruct the past from hard facts rarely do, and what social scientists are ill-advised to attempt. But if the present can only be understood through the prism of the past, surely the present is at least a window of opportunity opening into our future? However, while the past may have determined the present in some sense, the present can only shape the future but not determine it. It is decisions taken by us today that transforms the frame of this window, and then the direction in which we pass through the door that leads us there. Current policies, therefore, will profoundly shape our future. This is a truism.

III

As the world slowly recovers from one of the worst economic downturns since the Great Depression, both economists and policy makers still appear to be in a state of shock over what still works and what does not. These are not my words. I have simply paraphrased, admittedly in a somewhat dramatic fashion, the words of the chief economist of the IMF.[5]

The various chapters capture some of the anomalies with respect to macroeconomics 101 that were already apparent to economists well before the global financial crisis. Let me try and list these for convenience of the reader who may lose the laundry list while following my recipe for negotiating the book.

5. Blanchard *et al.* (2010; 2013; 2015). See also Caballero (2010).

First, capital account flows no longer mirrored the current account in the balance of payments, as gross flows kept rising relative to net, trade related flows. As a result, some emerging market economies, such as India, that ran persistent deficits saw their currencies appreciate rather than depreciate on account of large capital inflows.

Second, large capital inflows into advanced economies meant that the chief instrument of monetary policy, namely the short-term policy rate, was not impacting long-term yields in the expected manner in what has come to be known as the Greenspan Conundrum. The Federal Reserve was losing control of long-term interest rates through which it was expected to stabilise economic growth (Greenspan, 2007). As a result, real interest rates in advanced economies started falling despite falling saving rates.

Third, on a net basis, capital started flowing out from emerging markets to advanced economies instead of the other way around. Ever since the days of the classical economists it was assumed that as countries developed, the rates of return on capital would decline. Capital would consequently seek higher returns in countries that were growing faster. However, defying gravity and economic orthodoxy, capital now started flowing uphill instead of downhill (Bernanke, 2005; Prasad *et al.*, 2007).

Fourth, the structure of international trade itself was fundamentally changing, with global production chains sharply increasing the trade in intermediates, making conventional trade metrics based on bilateral trade balances that netted off exports against imports, and tariff based trade policies increasingly irrelevant.[6] As trade metrics centred on difficult to measure value addition came to occupy centre stage, protectionism started taking on insidious non-tariff forms such as phyto-sanitary rules, geographical origin, exchange rates, etcetera, which are equally difficult to measure and quantify (Evenett, 2013).

Fifth, as customs tariffs approached the zero-bound, the political economy of trade shifted from tariffs on goods and services to trade in

6. "World Trade Organization, Measuring Trade in Value-Sdded and its Implications for Understanding Global Imbalances". Background note prepared by the WTO Secretariat for the G20 Framework Working Group, 29 August 2011.

technology. Technological innovation has been the engine of growth ever since the industrial revolution through the process of what Joseph Schumpeter described as 'creative destruction'. The *de facto* intellectual property regime of the industrial revolution was open and liberal, conforming to the principles of free trade that maximised welfare through minimal entry barriers. The new regime now protected rent-seeking transnational companies (TNCs) at the cost of infant industries, instead of the other way around as postulated by trade theory (Bhagwati, 2002). As globalization expanded the reach of markets, reducing the time for recouping investments, not only did patent protection time not adjust downwards, but rent-seeking TNCs used their clout to evergreen them. It is consequently difficult to tell whether the current regime is consistent with the principles of free trade, or whether intellectual property rights constitute the second (after infant industry) major exception to free trade.

Sixth, budget deficits and high debt levels in heretofore 'unstable' emerging markets started declining as their growth accelerated, while these started rising in the more fiscally disciplined mature economies as they aged and trend growth declined (Samuelson, 2010; Kay, 2012). Long-standing social democratic compacts put in place in response to the radical left critique of capitalism started pressuring extant monetary and fiscal frameworks, although these were temporarily muted by increasing cross-border spillovers. The pressure has however intensified in the wake of the global financial crisis, with public debt in advanced economies rising to levels that are impossible to grow out of, without an extended phase of financial repression or renegotiation of long-standing social compacts based on moderate tax rates and generous state funded welfare. This fiscal instability is *inter alia* undermining the independence of their monetary policy framework (Tanzi, 2011; Cecchetti *et al.*, 2011; Carmen and Sbrancia, 2011) and redefining the concept of 'risk-free' financial instruments (Tett, 2011).

Seventh, rising trade and structural budget deficits in a number of advanced economies were not leading to rising interest rates, higher inflation and currency depreciation. Unlike what Lord Keynes had assumed, there appeared to be no market pressure on the US, a behemoth that comprised one-fourth of the global economy with chronic and growing internal and external deficits, to adjust because it printed the world's premier reserve currency for which there was a bottomless global appetite (Prasad, 2014; Jen and Dreisin, 2013).

Eighth, macroeconomics 101 has long drawn a strong positive correlation between financial deepening and economic growth (Levine, 1997), assuming that the former simply intermediated for the latter. However, even as emerging markets with 'repressed' and regulated financial systems were setting new Guinness Book records in growth, trend growth started declining in economies with deep, sophisticated and open financial systems (White, 2014), even as their financial markets scaled new highs.

Figure 1

US Real GDP Growth: 5Y Moving Average

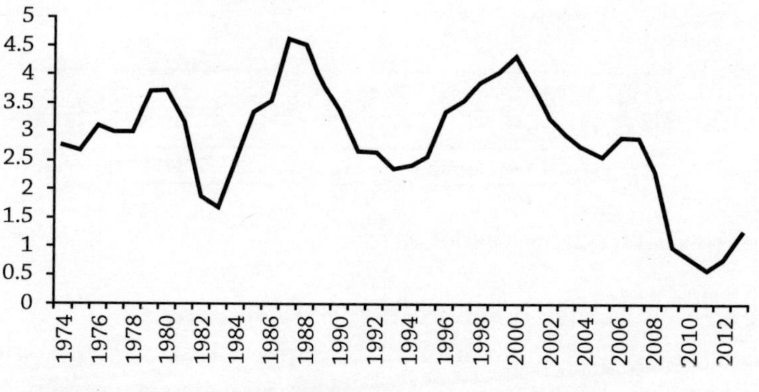

Source: US Department of Commerce: Bureau of Economic Analysis.

Ninth, real wages in the US started stagnating, and the labour participation rate started falling,[7] as returns to capital rose and those to labour declined, leading to sharp increases in income inequality. This was possible because restraints on cross-border capital flows were dismantled, but those on labour remained intact. This improved the

7. The US labour participation rate, or the percentage of the working age population gainfully employed, peaked at 67.3 per cent and started declining thereafter. It was 66 per cent in 2008 when the global financial crisis broke. The decline has accelerated thereafter, with the rate touching 62.8 per cent in May 2014, the lowest since February 1978 (US Bureau of Labour Statistics).

bargaining power of capital relative to labour, as it scoured the globe to invest and therefore create jobs in places where productivity gains were greatest, driving down wage growth (Spence, 2011). The much acclaimed Kuznets curve, which predicted that income inequality would rise in the early stages of growth and development, but then decline after crossing a certain threshold, was breaking down (Piketty, 2014).

Figure 2

US Average Weekly $ Earnings

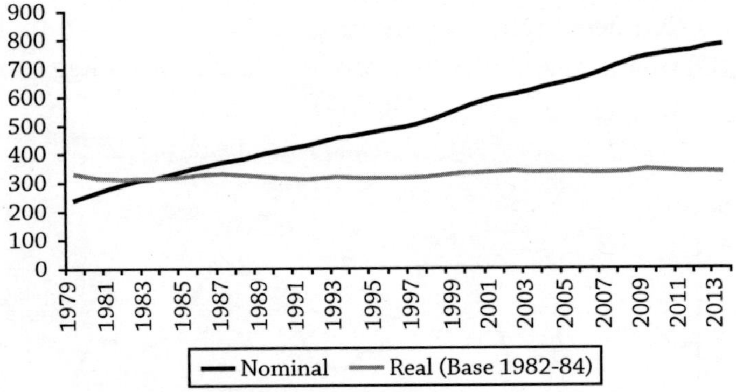

Source: US Bureau of Labour Statistics.

Tenth, consumer demand in the US somehow boomed despite stagnant real wages and a falling labour participation rate, converting it into the global consumer of last resort that drove global growth to unprecedented highs.

Eleventh, notwithstanding record levels of consumer demand, and global growth, the standard measures of overheating—rising consumer price inflation and real wages, and lower unemployment, were in little evidence. Both the Philip's curve, that linked inflation to employment, and Okun's law, that linked employment to growth, were either breaking down or flattening out (International Monetary Fund, 2013) in advanced economies. Consumer price inflation seemed remarkably stable everywhere by historical benchmarks. This sent monetary policy in advanced economies, based on inflation targeting, off course, as it turned very loose when measured by metrics of the widely used Taylor Rule (Taylor, 2010; Bishkek *et al.*, 2012; Sheel, 2014; Jen and Yilmaz, 2014). Central banks had long used inflation as the canary in the gold mine to gauge economic temperature of the economy. Defying macroeconomic textbooks, the canary now grew resistant to overheating, as globalization plugged into the rapid productivity growth in large, low income agrarian societies like China and India, unleashing disinflationary pressures that kept consumer inflation in advanced economies within central bank targets, even while output was at or above potential.

The excessive liquidity deriving from loose monetary policy had to find some outlet. It did so by inflating asset price bubbles that endangered financial stability and provided the powder keg ready to be ignited by the US sub-prime crisis. To clean up after the bubble burst, central banks veered off standard economic textbooks altogether, making the fiat currency system itself look vulnerable. The deviation from the Taylor Rule has only sharpened in the post crisis period and is again fuelling asset bubbles (Taylor, 2012). Both the fiscal and monetary frameworks seem to have broken down within the space of 40 years of abandoning the gold standard.

Twelfth, both economists and policymakers thought that they had finally stumbled upon the macroeconomic Holy Grail by abandoning the nominal anchor to a scarce commodity like gold. Money could now be created by sovereign fiat at will to stimulate economic activity. Unfettered, without any checks or balances, freedom can lead to excesses, and frequently does. Within a decade of going off the gold standard, growing structural fiscal deficits led to the debasement of paper money and the first major episode of breakdown of the Philip's curve through stagflation. It was evident that government treasuries could not be trusted with this new toy called 'discretionary fiscal policy.' In the post-Depression Keynesian world, governments did not have to be prodded to stimulate in a downturn. They however failed to run countercyclical surpluses during booms to finance these deficits. Dependence on market funding also exposed them to market revolt that drove up borrowing costs. As the fiscal framework threatened to collapse, an implicit consensus evolved by which the responsibility for stabilising economic cycles was entrusted to independent central banks, who in turn moved towards rule bound monetary policies such as the widely popular Taylor Rule.

This new framework restored macroeconomic stability for some time. Paul Volcker (US Federal Bank Governor between 1979 and 1987) used the monetary policy sledgehammer to drive down hyper-inflation. By the early years of the new century, consumer price inflation was no longer an issue on account of disinflationary forces emanating from globalization of trade and labour markets. By the last decade of the 20th century consumer price inflation was brought down, on average, to below 3 per cent in advanced economies, although it still averaged between 40-50 per cent in developing countries. By the opening years, average consumer price inflation in developing economies was down to a single digit.

These disinflationary forces however lulled central banks, that by now mostly followed variants of the Taylor Rule for monetary policy, and in which consumer price inflation was a major indicator, into pumping excessive liquidity into the economy. Symptomatic of this was the 'Greenspan Put', through which the US Federal Reserve opened its purse strings at the first hint of a downturn but never fully withdrew the punch bowl as the party got going. This excessive liquidity found its way into asset markets. Both stock markets and housing prices[8] entered an unprecedented long-term boom disproportionate to both economic growth and consumer price inflation. The Dow Jones Industrial Average (DJIA) that stood at around 50 at the turn of the 20th century, at around 380 just prior to the Great Depression of 1929, a level exceeded only in the early 1950s and scaled 1,700 by the early 1980s, went ballistic thereafter. It now hovers around 17,000. The S&P-Case Shiller real housing index for the United States similarly, with its base at 100 in 1890, and peak of just over 120 in the 1890s—a level not touched again till the 1970s—rose spectacularly from the beginning of the current century to peak at above 200 in July 2006.

The extant monetary framework, already under pressure prior to the global financial crisis, now seems to have fallen into a liquidity trap

8. In a recent comment in *Financial Times*, Adair Turner (2014) has drawn pointed attention to the global boom in property prices. While Adair Turner attributes this to rising wealth to income ratios, an additional reason is the tide of liquidity unleashed by central banks.

and is arguably being further debased through quantitative easing. The million dollar question is whether bad money (read debased paper currency) will once again drive good money (read gold) out of the market according to the age-old Gresham's Law. If this were indeed to happen, macroeconomic policies that are already in disarray would need to be reworked from scratch.

References

Baggini, Julian (2014). "E-books vs Paper", *Financial Times*, 20 June.

Barraclough, Geoffrey (1964). *An Introduction to Contemporary History*. London.

Jones, Claire (2014). "Universities to Revamp Economics Courses", *Financial Times*, 22 September. *http://www.ft.com/intl/cms/s/0/c0fe9722-4245-11e4-a9f4-00144feabdc0.html#axzz3Fe8OIHmZ*

Bhagwati, Jagdish N. (2002). *Patents and the Poor: Including Intellectual Property Protection in WTO Rules has Harmed the Developing World.* Council on Foreign Relations. 17 September.

Bishkek, Warsaw, Kyiv Tbilisi, Chisinau Minsk, Boris Hofmann and Bilyana Bogdanova (2012). "Taylor Rules and Monetary Policy: A Global "Great Deviation"?", *BIS Quarterly Review*, September.

Blanchard, Olivier, Giovanni Dell'Ariccia and Paolo Mauro (2010). "Rethinking Macroeconomic Policy, *IMF Staff Position Note* SPN/10/03. 12 February.

———. (2013). "Rethinking Macro Policy II: Getting Granular", *IMF Staff Discussion Note* 13/03. 15 April.

Caballero, Ricardo J. (2010). "Macroeconomics After the Crisis: Time to Deal with the Pretence-of-Knowledge Syndrome", *NBER WP* 16429. October.

Cecchetti, Stephen G., M.S. Mohanty and Fabrizio Zampolli (2011). "The Real Effects of Debt", *BIS Working Paper* No. 352. September.

Bernanke, Ben S. (2005). *The Global Savings Glut and the U.S. Current Account Deficit.* Remarks at the Sandridge Lecture. Virginia Association of Economists. Richmond, Virginia. 10 March.

Evenett, Simon J. (2013). *Protectionism's Quiet Return: The GTA's Pre-G8 summit Report. Voxeu.org.* 13 June.

Greenspan, Alan (2007). *The Age of Turbulence: Adventures in a New World.* Penguin Books.

International Monetary Fund (2013). *World Economic Outlook, April 2013.* Chapter 3.

———. (2015). *Rethinking Macro Policy III: Progress or Confusion?* Conference 15-16 April. *www.imf.org/external/np/seminars/eng/2015/macro3/*

Jen, Stephen L. and Alexandra Dreisin (2013). *The USD's Hegemonic International Currency Status.* SLJ Macro Partners. 11 September.

Jen, Stephen L. and Fatih Yilmaz (2014). *Is Inflation Global or Local?* SLJ Macro Partners. 22 January.

Kay, John (2012). "The Welfare State's a Worthy Ponzi Scheme", *Financial Times.* 25 September.

Levine, Ross (1997). "Financial Development and Economic Growth: Views and Agenda", *Journal of Economic Literature* 35(2): 688-726, June.

Parks, Tim (2014). "Reading: The Struggle," *The New York Review of Books, Blog* dated 10 June.

Piketty, Thomas (2014). *Capital in the Twenty-First Century*. Translated by Arthur Goldhammer. Harvard University Press.

Prasad, Eswar S. (2014). *The Dollar Trap: How the U.S. Dollar Tightened its Grip on Global Finance*. Princeton University Press.

Prasad, Eswar S., Raghuram G. Rajan and Arvind Subramanian (2007). "Foreign Capital and Economic Growth," *Brookings Papers on Economic Activity* 1.

Reinhart, Carmen M. and M. Belen Sbrancia (2011). "The Liquidation of Government Debt", *NBER WP* 16893. March.

Robinson, Colin (2013). "Writers should Take a Year Off, and Give us all a Break", *The Guardian*, 16 August.

Samuelson, Robert (2010). "The Welfare State's Death Spiral", *Real Clear Politics*. May 10. *http://www.realclearpolitics.com/articles/2010/05/10/the_welfare_states_death_spiral_105503.html*

Sheel, Alok (2014). "The Unravelling of Inflation Targeting", *Economic and Political Weekly* 49(20), 17 May.

Sheel, Alok and Meeta Ganguly (2008). "The Rise and Fall of Securitized Structured Finance?", *Economic and Political Weekly* 43(16): 44-51, 19-25 April.

Spence, Michael (2011). "The Impact of Globalization on Income and Employment: The Downside of Integrating Markets". *Foreign Affairs* 90(4), July/August.

Tanzi, Vito (2011) "The Return to Fiscal Rectitude After the Recent Escapade", *Rivista di Politica Economica* 3: 253-77, July-September.

Taylor, John B. (2010). "Does the Crisis Experience Call for a New Policy Paradigm in Monetary Policy?", *CASE Network Studies and Analyses* No. 402.

———. (2012). "Monetary Policy and the Next Crisis", *The Wall Street Journal*, 4 July.

Tett, Gillian (2011). "Sub-prime Moment Looms for 'Risk-Free' Sovereign Debt", *Financial Times*. 3 November.

Turner, Adair (2014). "High Tide for House Prices is Engulfing our Economy", *Financial Times*. London. 25 July.

White, William R. (2014). "Credit Crises and the Shortcomings of Traditional Policy Responses", in Deepak Mohanty (ed.), *Monetary Policy, Sovereign Debt and Financial Stability: The New Trilemma*. Foundation Books and Reserve Bank of India.

PART ONE

Timeline

I
Brave New World
Macroeconomic Anomalies and Premonitions of Crisis

The big bed was too hard. The middle-sized bed was too soft. But the wee little bed was oh, so nice! So Goldilocks lay down and went to sleep.

Goldilocks and the Three Bears (English folktale).

1

A Brief History of Globalization

Globalization involves the interplay of markets, technology and state, which are amongst the oldest and most distinctive human innovations. Exchange, the fundamental principle on which markets are organised, is known to exist in the most primitive human societies. Man is not the only living creature with the ability to store surpluses and live in complex societies controlled by chiefs—consider the industrious ants and bees—but he *is* unique in his ability to socially redistribute these surpluses through increasingly complex divisions of labour under the authority of the state.

The saga of globalization is that of an unbound Prometheus, who represents the free and progressive spirit of man—Life, Love, Joy and Victory, as the poet Shelley signified HOPE—with surges in productivity and growth unparalleled in history as markets, technology and states are progressively freed from local demand and supply constraints. Although the term 'globalization' has gained currency only recently, the forces driving this trend can be traced back to the end of the Middle Ages in Europe.

Pre-modern societies were above all else defined by localism and decentralisation. Most never moved. Migration was a one-way street to resettle in virgin territory in response to conquest, calamity or local demographic pressure. Religious experience was mostly limited to the local parish, with pilgrimages undertaken by an interested few. Empires meant mostly march of armies over land, and were never transcontinental, with the notable exception of North Africa adjoining the Mediterranean. State power was a coalition of the local power elite owing allegiance to a monarch who never had access to centralised administrative machinery.

With universal poverty a structural constraint on demand, markets were neighbourhood-trading places, with long distance trade mostly limited to luxury goods for the small power elite. New ideas, information and technology spread slowly since transportation and communication were based on yoked animal traction, be it oxen, horse or camel.

Four distinct phases of globalization can be discerned in modern history. The first phase began in the 16th century with the passing of pre-modern localism. Improvements in maritime technology led to the great age of maritime exploration, discovery, mercantilism, and the European Renaissance. It also facilitated centralising tendencies associated with absolute monarchy and the emergence of modern nation states following the Peace of Westphalia of 1648. It was also associated with the spread of the ideals of liberty and the American and French Revolutions from the 18th century.

The second phase from the late 18th century was marked by the spread of the Industrial Revolution and vast improvements in human technology, inanimate traction, productivity and demand. This led to mass production and conveyance of merchandise goods and people, cross-border integration through bulk long-distance trade, colonial plunder, investment flows and empire during a phase of European imperial expansion which saw the flag follow trade across the globe. The Industrial Revolution opened up a rapidly widening productivity and income gap between Europe and America on the one hand, and the rest of the world on the other.

The globalising trend was halted by the two great wars of the 20th century, and an 'autarchic' anti-imperial 'nationalist' interlude, which actually saw a decline in international trade and capital flows as a per centage of global GDP. Even as trade and flags disengaged, the per capita income between developed countries and the erstwhile colonies continued to diverge.

During the third phase, merchandise trade resumed its triumphant march as the engine of hyper growth in East Asia from the 1970s. International trade/GDP (gross domestic product) ratios recovered to their late 19th century level by the last decade of the 20th century. But whereas the globalization thrust in the second phase in the 19th century involved, in the main, the export of mass-produced merchandise to the colonies, this time round the export dynamism came from the erstwhile colonies. This globalization thrust was led by transnational corporations (TNCs) that endeavoured to disseminate international trade and modern technology to every flag on earth.

Globalization arguably entered a frenetic fourth phase from the end of the 20th century, in which developed and developing countries are becoming more equal partners in the flow of cross-border trade and investment, as per capita income between the developed world and the developing world rapidly converge, galvanised by the awakening of the ancient sleeping giants, China and India.

Merchandise trade is being swamped by 'invisible' trade in services led by rapid technological advances in information technology, and volatile capital flows, that have become new engines of growth redefining human interface and old nation-state based economic, social, cultural and political paradigms. Contradictions between TNCs and sovereigns are growing in several areas such as trade, investment, labour, agriculture and infrastructure policies. Nation states, in the form they emerged in the early modern period, are losing their *raison d'etre* as they are increasingly constrained in the conduct of foreign policy in a unipolar world where conventional war is yielding to stateless conflict and terror; in resolving the intertwined energy-food-security crisis; in freeing resources for the intertwined ageing-health-welfare crisis; in further extending the welfare benefits of trade; and in the use of time-tested macroeconomic fiscal and monetary tools to manage external shocks.

The globalising impulse can be seen as ever-widening circles trending towards greater homogeneity, from locality, to nation states to regional identities like pan-European, pan-Asian, pan-Arab and pan-American, the long-term logical corollary of which is a unified market, a unified culture, a unified language, a unified liberal-democratic state, or what V.S. Naipaul famously termed a "universal civilisation." Rapid strides in information technology (IT) are spawning new virtual relationships, cosmopolitan identities and communities that compete and conflict with those forged within the confines of the nation state. The interesting issue, however, is whether this process of 'cultural entropy' would, over the long run, abate the clash of civilisations underscored by a long line of eminent historians from Herodotus to Arnold Toynbee to Samuel Huntington.

The Economic Times, New Delhi, 25 July 2008.

2

Inequality and the Nation State

Curiously, globalization is a four-letter word for several intellectuals in both the developing and developed worlds. In the former, globalization has long been linked to imperialism, or more fashionably, neo-imperialism/liberalism. Seen as a continuation of colonisation of the 18th and 19th centuries, it supposedly not only left developing countries worse off than what they were before, but also indeed made them structurally 'underdeveloped.' In the developed world, globalization is blamed for the export of jobs and consequential prosperity to the developing world. Globalization would, therefore, appear to be a global threat.

The fact of the matter is that the prosperous Asian economies of China and India, with higher per capita incomes than western Europe as late as the beginning of the 18th century, had started falling behind well before they were colonised. It is, therefore, moot to discuss whether colonialism was the cause or consequence of backwardness. The per capita income divide with western Europe, including its white settler offshoots, and the colonies continued to widen during the 'enforced free trade' of the colonial period. India's per capita income growth during the colonial period was very nominal in the aggregate, a continuation of the preceding trend. However, there was a burst of growth between 1880-1910, largely as the result of agricultural expansion and commercialisation following infrastructural investment and integration into the world system.

Per capita income growth declined between the two World Wars, which also coincided with a retreat from globalization. While per capita income growth resumed modestly in the immediate aftermath of colonialism, when several former colonies retreated into autarchy and dirigisme, the per capita income gap with the developed world continued to widen despite conscious attempts at 'de-globalization.' The gap started converging only after erstwhile colonies, first in east Asia, followed by China and India, re-entered the globalization process.

The Asian countries' experience with globalization shows, firstly, that periods of globalization coincided with periods of accelerated growth. Secondly, the first phase of globalization coincided with widening income disparities with the west, while the (current) second phase is tending towards per capita income convergence.

Why should the two phases of globalization have had differing outcomes for developing countries? There are two possible explanations. The first phase of growth was based largely on agriculture which, as Kaldor postulated several years ago, has a much more modest growth impact than manufacturing. The second phase of globalization was based on manufacturing and services (as in the Indian case) in the former colonies, with higher attendant growth rates, while developed countries show signs of post-industrial growth fatigue.

Secondly, it was not free trade *per se* but imperialism that was the villain of the piece. Free trade was controlled and regulated by developed nation states. Whereas the first phase of globalization saw the flag of advanced nation states follow trade and markets, the second phase has seen trade, through the instrument of trans-national corporations (TNCs), follow markets across various flags. The globalising impulse today is multilateral, controlled and regulated by TNCs. Perfectly willing to relocate production and services, including the transfer of technology and capital overseas in search of higher profits, the interests of TNCs are frequently in conflict with those of the nation states. The latter often actively pursue policies as though they feel threatened by globalization.

The rise of absolutism and the nation state in the early period of modernisation was a major factor in the market integration of decentralised and fragmented feudal societies. In the current phase of globalization, however, it is a major force hindering global integration of markets. In any case, the nation state is being rendered increasingly ineffective in its two main functions of national defence and macroeconomic policy. While the first is threatened by the growing technological gap between the US and all other countries, globalization is rendering sovereign macro economic levers increasingly ineffective. Most other functions of the state, such as welfare and policing, can be performed by local and regional governments and markets. Taxpayers may realise sooner than later that the combination of increasingly modest outcomes and high overheads make nation states more predatory than benign.

The logic of globalization in continually relocating production and services to cheaper locations raises incomes in poorer countries. Consequential efficiency gains lead to higher returns to capital (through greater profitability). Returns to labour are rising faster in developing countries than in developed ones, and within developed countries, faster for skilled knowledge labour than for unskilled labour. Globalization rewards knowledge skills, both human and technological. It has reduced inequality between nations but increased it within nations. As per capita incomes in some developing countries rise, poorer developing countries get the chance of becoming more competitive. It is entirely possible that the logic of globalization will relocate production and services away from Asia to African countries in future provided issues of governance, infrastructure and human capital are sorted out.

Although widening inequality is a corollary of globalization, purchasing power has nevertheless risen all round in both developed and developing countries through universal access to a wide variety of cheap (Chinese) goods and (Indian) services. In that sense, globalization has been 'inclusive' as the standard of living of even the poorest has improved through efficiency and productivity gains deriving from globalization. Widening Gini coefficients may well be acceptable as long as equality of opportunity can be assured through universal access to knowledge.

Globalising forces are driven by efficiency gains deriving from trade on the one hand, and productivity gains deriving from technological improvements on the other. There were periods of widening global contact in the past, driven by humongous empires such as the Roman, Mongol and Ottoman, through dramatic long distance movements of peoples such as Vikings, Huns and Visigoths, and through long distance trade, such as the overland silk and Indian ocean routes linking the east and west. Until fairly recently, however, technological advances were few and far in between, and disseminated very slowly. The movement of goods and people was consequently limited until the Industrial Revolution let the genie of technology out of the bottle, leading to rapid mobility of all factors of production (other than land) and services on an unprecedented scale. The globalization process has been relentless since, although non-linear. For instance, the period following the First World War witnessed a retreat from globalization because stakeholders in the erstwhile colonies felt that they had been short-changed. The current phase of globalization that began with the east Asian surge in the 1970s could well witness another retreat if some stakeholders feel that they are being left out. History, however, tells us that this retreat is unlikely to be permanent. Goodbye nation state?

Business Standard, New Delhi, 29 April 2007.

3

The Population Conundrum

The 'population explosion' in developing countries was till recently considered a severe constraint on growth and development. China's mandatory one-child norm and India's 'sterilisation' drive were predicated on this view. Population control policies still exist, but hardly anybody talks about the population time bomb any more. Focus has quietly, but swiftly, shifted to addressing issues arising out of an ageing society: decline in the number of workers, pension and welfare reform, migration and decline in growth rates. The population time bomb has yielded to demographic bonus, with babies elevated to the status of future growth drivers. China's one-child norm now seems growth threatening while India's failed 'sterilisation' drive seems fortuitous.

The population scare in developing countries generated by the Club of Rome and scholars like Paul Ehrlich was centuries ago by something similar in Europe. As Europe entered the first stage of demographic transition, characterised by a sharp fall in death rates consequent on rapid improvement in public health, Thomas Malthus argued that human population growth would soon outstrip food supply, leading to catastrophic adjustment through war, famine and pestilence.

This did not happen. Out-migration to white-settler colonies provided a partial 'safety valve,' but Malthus was eventually proved wrong because productivity growth exceeded population growth. Scholars like Ester Boserup turned Malthus on his head, arguing that population pressure provided the creative impulse that boosted agricultural productivity.

Population density from the dawn of human evolution never exceeded more than 2-3 per square mile right up to the Neolithic

Revolution about 10,000 years ago. Even as man began to grow his own food, human densities beyond fertile river valleys remained very low as agricultural productivity was low. It is difficult to imagine today that average European grain yields were around 1:4 right up to the end of the Middle Ages. They were slightly higher in the low countries, in the rice growing regions of Italy, and in southern Europe which relied less on meat, devoting more land to cereal cultivation. The predominantly cereal consuming rice-growing riverine areas of China and India, and maize-growing ones of Meso-America, were more productive, and hence more densely populated. The west European marriage pattern of late marriage and high celibacy and resultant lower birth rates underscored these differences.

Population density thus adapted to available energy levels, which did not vary greatly over long periods since technological improvements were few and far in between. The demographic pattern was characterised by high birth and death rates. Demographic upswings occasioned by a succession of good seasons were periodically audited by famine, disease and war since man had limited control over his environment. Indeed, 'Malthusian crises' better described pre-industrial societies where the sharply fluctuating death rate was the critical equilibrating force keeping population in check.

This equilibrator became ineffectual with increasing food security and improvements in public health that marked the first stage of demographic transition. While death rates respond to technological progress, birth rates adjust to death rates with a variable 'cultural' time lag. With rising living standards, life expectancy and literacy, especially female literacy and empowerment, birth rates have adjusted so drastically that most parts of the developed world face sub-fertility rates and declining populations in what is described as the second stage of demographic transition. The third stage, where population is expected to stabilise after adjustment, remains elusive.

Sharp declines in poverty, rising living standards and female literacy have also sent several developing countries hurtling towards the second stage of demographic transition. It is estimated that over the 20th century population quadrupled, while per capita GDP (gross domestic product) quintupled. Global growth has been unequal, but most parts of the globe have nevertheless seen a rise in living standards. However, most developing countries would grey at a far lower per capita income compared to Organisation for Economic Co-operation and Development (OECD) countries, constraining their capacity to transfer incomes to cope with ageing-related crises in welfare.

Poverty and population growth share more in common than simply positive correlation. Neither seems capable of direct targeting, except in non-democratic environments like China. Democratic India's sterilisation drive was quickly transformed into 'Family Welfare' following political catastrophe. Both poverty and population are however sensitive to 'indirect' targeting through policies that promote growth, human productivity and social welfare.

As food supply continues to outstrip population growth, the Malthusian case now rests on the environmental impact of population growth. But unsustainable growth has less to do with population *per se* than with consumption benchmarks set by rich countries. They also contribute more to global environmental change despite their declining population. Others argue environmental pressure would stimulate technological solutions for its own abatement.

As the ageing and welfare crises in the developed world unravel, migration can be expected to increase sharply, equalising the global demographic structure over the long-term. Human demographic structure has come full circle, beginning and ending with high dependency ratios with one crucial difference: while pre-industrial societies had more infants on account of high birth and low life expectancy, the dependants in post-industrial societies consist primarily of the elderly on account of low birth rates and high life expectancy. The long-term threat to the human species may well be de-population rather than overpopulation.

Migration, crisis in welfare, declining growth and rise in age of retirement are well-known consequences of ageing and depopulation. The more intriguing impact however could be through correctives to globalization which is exacerbating inequality and leaving some countries, especially those in Africa, behind. Ageing could reverse this equation, with asset prices falling as a growing number of retirees sell assets to a shrinking base of workers. On account of the strong positive correlation between affluence and ageing, poorer countries will age later and have a higher proportion of workers. They could become the new nodes of growth as more affluent ageing societies slow down.

The Economic Times, New Delhi, 8 August 2007 .

4

Migration, Growth and the Human Future

Migration is as old as the human species. The urge to migrate is possibly embedded in the human genome itself as it appears to give *Homo sapiens* some evolutionary advantage. Anthropologists believe that early man originated in the East African rift valley and then migrated from there to colonise all parts of the world. Ever since, migration has been closely associated with growth, development and productivity improvement. The growth impact has tended to be positive on both immigrant and emigrant societies. While the narrative has changed over time, it is astonishing how little the big picture has altered. Right through history, rulers encouraged migration as new settlements enhanced their revenue streams and military might.

This was because till the Industrial Revolution, technological and productivity improvements were few and far between. Aggregate production mostly increased by addition to the workforce through new settlements deriving from migration and natural propagation. The latter was, however, constrained on account of high death rates, and periodic famines and epidemics that wiped out surplus population. Nature did periodic demographic audit in red pencil. From a historical perspective, it is useful to divide migration into two basic types, long-term and short-term, while recognising that there were several intermediate forms.

However, what is common to both types of migration is that they contributed to enhanced human growth, productivity and welfare. From the migrant's perspective, long-term migration was impelled by the desire to increase current levels of consumption, or to make it more secure by exploiting differences in productivity over space.

Short-term migration was impelled by the desire to smoothen the consumption cycle by exploiting differences over space and time, such as during the agricultural off-season. Low levels of productivity and technology limited both the size of the surplus generated by human labour, as well as its use for future consumption. In the absence of sophisticated instruments of modern finance, it was difficult to convert labour surpluses into financial savings that could be exchanged for future consumption as is the case today. The period of rapid growth in both continental Europe and the US in the wake of the Industrial Revolution was associated with rapid, systematic and sustained immigration (the US) and emigration (Europe) on an epic scale unparalleled in human history. While short-term and long-term migration continues to be distinct, their distinctive outcomes have been blurred because of vast differences and rapid shifts in productivity in the aftermath of the Industrial Revolution, and also with greater sophistication in financial intermediation that enables migrants to use current savings for future consumption. As a result, even short-term migration can also now result in higher levels of consumption through 'remittances.'

Following the rise of modern nation states, the primary migration divide gradually shifted from being between long-term and short-term, to between internal and cross-border. Internal migration stimulated by productivity differences continues to be robust as it exploits productivity differentials across regions and sectors, as observed by Simon Kuznets and Arthur Lewis several decades ago. However, with vast differences in per capita incomes and living standards opening up between advanced and developing countries in the wake of industrialisation, and with the rise of nationalist sentiments, barriers to international migration have become rigid, spawning a visa and passport culture. Cross-border migration rules now have a strong racial and country bias that discriminates against movement of labour from low productivity areas to high productivity areas. History indicates that it is such radical shifts that maximise the welfare gains from migration. Thus, even as trade and capital have become more integrated and mobile across borders, labour mobility has become relatively limited. This is a relatively recent phenomenon.

Roman emperors, for instance, came from all parts of the Roman Empire.

Closer home, the ethnic origins of Indian rulers were also very diverse. The 18th and 19th centuries witnessed huge cross-border migrations. Capital mobility has reduced the pressure on cross-border migration to sustain aggregate global growth. Capital has migrated to areas where labour is abundant and cheap, and the consequential potential for productivity gains and profitability is higher. This has also facilitated outsourcing of production to low-income developing countries, the emergence of 'global imbalances' and rising structural unemployment in advanced countries. However, with demographic decline and ageing populations, international migration is now necessary to prevent growth rates from declining in advanced countries. It is essential to get growth back on track to generate the savings and revenue streams necessary to support ageing societies. Unless this is done, their fiscal positions may deteriorate to the point that they could lose market access to finance rapidly growing deficits.

There is an imminent threat they would not be able to sustain current levels of living standards. Consider the explosion of public debt in Japan, and similar projections made for other advanced countries, and the consequential turbulence this has generated in international financial markets. From the developing-country perspective, it may be recalled that out-migration at a critical stage of the demographic cycle in Europe was a major factor in the latter's successful industrialisation since it relieved some of the excess pressure on land. Such pressure on land, which acts as a drag on productivity growth, persists in countries like China and India because of limited out-migration possibilities.

This could well result in a middle-income trap. Initial concerns over the negative welfare effects of out-migration on account of brain drain have proved to be short-lived. Over the longer term, the network effect of this brain drain also laid the foundations of India's homegrown IT/services revolution that subsequently became its engine of growth. While the economic imperative seems clear, cross-border migration needs a conducive social and cultural environment. Social and cultural changes, however, tend to lag behind economic development, and take place in an apparently non-linear manner over the short- to medium-term. Thus, migration from young African and Asian societies had been occurring on a large-scale before the emergence of concerns relating to rising unemployment and international terror that applied brakes on this process. Even as nationalism and the nation state are losing their economic rationale in a fast integrating world, they continue to be binding constraints on civil society and policy making not only in respect of migration, but in other areas of macroeconomic policy coordination as well.

The million-dollar question is whether ageing, declining growth and fiscal problems will be the game changers that will moderate restrictions on cross-border labour mobility that has contributed to rapid growth and development in the past. Will the emergence of a global civil society through the World Wide Web (WWW) facilitate this process by moderating cultural constraints on cross-border migration? Also, as young societies age, will there be competition to attract young migrants in future? The trillion-dollar question for future generations may well be whether human survival itself is ultimately contingent on our ability to develop technologically fast enough to migrate to other parts of the universe before planet earth becomes uninhabitable, as forcefully argued by Stephen Hawking?

The Economic Times, New Delhi, 26 September 2011 .

5

For Freedom and Markets

Free Trade and markets, two sides of the same coin were the lynchpins of the global consensus on economic policy forged in the wake of the Cold War. The Index of Economic Freedom brought out for the last 20 years by the *Wall Street Journal* and the Washington DC based think-tank, *Heritage Foundation*, illustrates statistically that economic un-freedom is the cause of human misery, and the close fit between societies that have for years been economically free and high median per capita national income. The fastest growing economies in the world today started growing rapidly only after opening up trade and markets for factors and products. The removal of entry barriers to economic activity showed that Adam Smith's invisible hand works after all.

Reams have been written on the subject. There is nevertheless room for re-iterating the case for free markets succinctly within the constraints of an opinion piece because an irrational fear of markets still pervades civil society. This fear holds back this great country, which always performed well whenever and wherever trade and markets were allowed to operate effectively, from realising its true potential. At the turn of the century, *The Economist* described India as the world's greatest under-achiever. With globalization and information technology, in which India has a competitive edge, expanding the range and efficiency of markets, the description is even more apt now.

Although the philosophical case for trade and markets is usually traced to the fathers of modern economics, Adam Smith and David Ricardo, these are of course much older than both. Their origins are lost in antiquity. The 13th century Arab scholar, Ibn Khaldun, cautioned the King against crowding out private enterprise through excessive state intervention, as this would bring dynastic ruin through fiscal collapse. The Dark Ages in Europe and the rise, and subsequent decline, of feudalism are linked to the decline and revival of long distance trade. This trade was in existence for very long and until it was supplanted by Trans-Atlantic trade in the 19th century, centred in our own backyard in the Indian Ocean and over land through the Silk Road. India's putative opulence derived from this trade. It catered primarily to ruling elites till fairly recently in historical time as transportation technology constrained its scope, reach and volumes. Going further back to pre-history, exchange, trade and markets are a recurrent theme in the works of social anthropologists studying primitive societies.

Like trade and markets, the state is such an archaic institution that its origins and economic roles are still keenly debated. The State has both facilitated markets by providing public goods without which they cannot function efficiently, and has also been one of their arch enemies.

The state's role in regulating markets to address market failures is frequently underscored to prevent non-State actors from subverting free markets through monopolies that limit competition and erect barriers for new entrants. Adam Smith noted that participants tend to abuse the market, paving the way for state intervention. States also impede markets through war, taxes and sundry market interventions. The *reductio ad absurdum* was the socialist state which did away with markets altogether! But even free societies have tried to eliminate certain markets, especially for hallucinogens like alcohol, tobacco and other drugs, pornography, prostitution, etc., by criminalising them. These are thus market failures and state failures.

The compelling force of trade and markets can be compared to that of the ocean, whose boundless energy can be harnessed but never fully constrained. Wherever there is demand, human ingenuity will exploit the opportunity through supply response. Steering the Ship of State against such elemental forces merely generate 'grey', 'black' or 'illicit' markets that ultimately weaken the state because it loses its taxation power over the considerable income generated through these markets. Revenues falls into the hands of a powerful mafia that undermines the authority of the state. Thus high tariffs and prohibition generate widespread smuggling, capital controls lead to financial repression, visa and immigration controls spawn vast networks of illegal immigration, and an increasingly stringent IPR regime promotes technology piracy.

Attempts by the state to stifle these markets are ultimately self-defeating and relatively short-lived. The state has in the end acknowledged them and tapped their resource base to maximise the welfare of its subjects. At one stage, the state even sought to suppress exotic articles like tea, cocoa, coffee and chocolate. They were considered dangerous or subversive hallucinogens before becoming popular items of mass consumption. The list of banned items has shrunk sharply over the years, tariffs and capital controls have diminished, prohibition has mostly been given up as a lost cause, as the world moves towards higher planes of integration and globalization.

While all restraints on trade and markets reduce efficiency by increasing costs and widening the demand supply gap, and on the whole reduce human welfare, four kinds of restraints may nevertheless enhance it. The first is protection of infant industry by nation states in the early stages of industrialisation; the second safeguards the commons; the third regulates natural monopolies to simulate competitive markets; and the fourth taxes economic activity to provide public goods, including infrastructure, good governance and redistribution to underwrite a basic standard of living.

Such restraints however need to be judicious and market friendly. Domestic lobbies will seek to extend trade protectionism indefinitely to the detriment of consumer welfare. There will always be a market for criminal activities, and the state needs to come down heavily on them through the provision of good governance, which lies in the core domain of the state rather than markets. However, the state may set the bar too low by criminalising activities such as alcohol, drugs and obscenity, on the basis of majoritarian civil society views that impinge on individual liberty and minority rights. The state often tries to ensure equality of outcomes through redistribution. This is not possible under free markets and, as demonstrated by the experience of socialist states and the Index of Economic Freedom, only results in greater misery in the absence of markets. But free markets abhor indigent poverty as it depresses demand and stifles their growth. Public goods, including redistribution, can be provided most effectively when market grow. Redistribution should therefore lean towards equalising opportunity that builds social capital to equip individuals to optimise their own genius within the market framework.

Business Standard, New Delhi 24 August 2014.

6

Market Economies and the End of History

Two distinct models of socioeconomic organisation competed for global hegemony until recently. The western model hinged on free markets. The Soviet model eliminated markets. Following the collapse of the Soviet Union, Francis Fukuyama heralded "the end of history." However, scholars now began to notice significant differences within market economies earlier masked by the grand East-West ideological conflict.

Liberal market economies enjoy a less interventionist state, lower taxes and welfare; flexible labour markets are more open, productive, internationally competitive and have higher growth rates. America is the archetypal liberal market economy. But there are others: Canada, UK, Ireland, New Zealand and Australia.

Market economies in continental Europe are qualified as 'social market' economies. The state plays a greater role, they are more protectionist, have higher tax-GDP (gross domestic product) ratios, liberal state-funded welfare, inflexible labour markets, lower per capita productivity and growth, and are altogether less efficient.

Are liberal market economies better-off and social market economies destined to lead Europe into economic decline? Moot point. First, social market economies score better on equity. Second, neither unemployment rates nor per hour productivity is markedly different between the two. Demographic decline and protectionist labour laws create a mirage of low unemployment in Europe. The unemployed, however, do stay unemployed longer. As for productivity, continental economies have chosen to work less and devote more time to leisure.

Therefore, while their per capita incomes are lower than their American cousins, Europeans may well be happier. After all, money and wealth are not ends in themselves but means to attaining what Aristotle described as 'something else.'

It would be wrong to conclude that continental economies are welfare-oriented, while liberal market economies are not. The welfare state forms the bedrock of all modern democracies. Differences lie in the funding of welfare. Europe relies more on tax-funded welfare. In America, much of the burden has traditionally been on corporates and private charities, although this may be changing.

If European economies are stuttering under the burden of tax-funded welfare, the American model is coming unstuck with the emergence of the new open economy based on rapid technological change, outsourcing and shorter employment tenures. Companies also baulk at rocketing health insurance premia. More Americans are now without health insurance and other welfare benefits.

'Defined contribution' health and pension accounts, where the contribution of the employer and/or contribution of the state is fixed in nominal terms, rather than open-ended under 'defined benefit' schemes, are touted as the fiscal solution to ageing and associated rising health care costs and looming budget deficits. However, a shift to 'defined contribution' could also starve state-funded welfare. Ageing also effectively means that an increasing proportion of retirees would be selling assets to fewer workers, thereby lowering asset prices and compelling workers to save more and more for retirement.

A rising retirement age, migration from younger societies and cross-border capital flows can postpone but not avert the crisis. Other societies would eventually age, too. Workers would, therefore, need to save even more during their working years to smoothen the consumption curve over their life cycle. If they fail to do so, the state may have to step in through enhanced tax revenues to cover the deficit, *á la* the social market model. Either way, enhanced savings or taxes would make young couples even more averse to having children, further compounding the ageing crisis.

While the liberal market system appears more viable than the social market one at present in the brave new world of open economies and ageing societies, the differences may not be at first glance so stark.

Market economies need to evolve a viable welfare model before proclaiming the end of history. This denouement is of profound significance for emerging market economies like India and China, as they struggle to cobble together their own welfare systems. India is currently Janus-faced. Its liberal attitude to foreign investment and low public outlay on social security points in the American direction. However, its conservative stance on labour and privatisation, and an interventionist state with aggressive taxation policies, point towards Europe.

The Financial Express, New Delhi, 10 May 2006.

7

Dark Matter

Keeping Global Finances in Place?

One of the great macroeconomic mysteries of the past decade is the remarkable resilience of the US dollar in the face of mounting US current account imbalances. To put this imbalance in perspective, consider that the total current account deficit (CAD) of the US is at present (2006) roughly equal to the combined current account surplus of the rest of the world.

CADs are financed through external capital flows in the form of foreign equity and debt. Large unsustainable deficits over the years result in foreigners accumulating huge financial assets, which need to be serviced.

The twin demands of funding CADs and servicing ever-growing financial assets held by foreigners should, according to macroeconomic wisdom, lead to a rapid depreciation of the national currency against other currencies, and capital flight. Given the dependence of global growth on American demand, this could lead to a global meltdown. This shows no signs of happening.

It has been observed that US deficits have, in the past two decades, been funded by mopping global savings from current surpluses generated in the rest of the world. Two natural corollaries follow. Both, America's share of global financial assets and its net income from these assets (the difference between what Americans earn from financial assets in other parts of the world, and what the rest of the world earns through ownership of American assets) should have dipped sharply and turned negative.

While the first corollary holds, the second is not supported by data. Like the matter-energy constant, the net income from America's financial assets has remained constant, the sharp decline in its share of global assets notwithstanding. This indicates that Americans earn much more on their financial assets than what the rest of the world does from its dollar assets.

How is this possible? In a recent paper, Harvard economists Ricardo Hausmann and Federico Sturzenegger provide a startling answer: dark matter. Physicists have long held that matter visible to the human eye, aided or unaided, cannot fully explain the stability of the universe. What arguably holds it together is some kind of 'dark matter.' Using this analogy, they argue it is 'dark matter' that keeps the global financial firmament in place. It consists of the net provision of knowledge, liquidity and insurance services by the US.

Knowledge-based dark matter, quantitatively the most significant, assures a return on American FDI overseas in excess of its nominal/book value on account of the 'knowledge,' technology, intellectual property right (IPR) and brand premium embedded in multinational corporations (MNCs) like Disney, MacDonald's, Microsoft, etc.

The liquidity-based dark matter derives from the eagerness of the rest of the world to hold liquid assets, earning nil interest, in dollars. The insurance-based dark matter derives from the role the dollar plays as the universal reserve currency, with individuals, organisations and sovereigns, eager to park savings in low-yielding, risk-free, US treasury bonds. The liquidity and insurance avatars of dark matter enable the US to obtain cheap funds to purchase higher yielding assets abroad.

Hausmann and Sturzenegger conclude that if dark matter is taken into account, far from running deficits with the rest of the world, America is running a modest and remarkably constant surplus. This explains the stability of the dollar and the global macro-economy, since America is not really a debtor nation.

There are problems with this intrepid explanation. First, there is too much reliance on rule-of-thumb and back-of-the-envelope calculations in projecting surpluses, returns and capitalising net current incomes. Second, even if US net financial assets have remained constant in absolute terms, their size relative to the economy has reduced. That leads to a third question mark over the accrual of dark matter, and whether it has prevented Armageddon or simply deferred it.

Fourth, are there other kinds of dark matter waiting to be unearthed, even more difficult to measure and quantify? For instance, America's unique position as the world's only superpower generates global demand for the dollar and financial gravity like the three other avatars.

Finally, on its own admission, the dark matter theory disregards conventional accounting rules. But how helpful has grey matter based on old rules been in explaining the real (globalised) world anyway?

The Financial Express, New Delhi, 15 February 2006.

8

How About a Taylor Rule for India?

According to a universally acclaimed rule for monetary policy, the central bank should increase or decrease interest rates by a margin slightly exceeding, or lower than, the current inflation rate to stabilise GDP (gross domestic product). The Taylor Rule was formulated through a *post facto* analysis of US Federal Reserve (Fed) monetary policy, culminating in a statistical relationship that best fitted past 'successful' monetary policy. John B. Taylor, the architect of the rule, is a professor of economics at Stanford University.

Data show that other developed countries' central banks have also, implicitly or explicitly, followed a similar rule. Taylor felt the Rule was also relevant for developing economies with flexible exchange rates. Ajay Shah (*Business Standard*, 19 April) was critical of Reserve Bank of India's (RBI's) 2006-07 annual policy statement since it did not abide by the Taylor Rule. Despite two subsequent hikes, the reverse repo—effective signaling—rate of 6 per cent was significantly lower than the 8.25-9 per cent warranted under the Taylor Rule predicated on an inflation of 5-5.5 per cent, GDP of 7.5-8 per cent and potential GDP of 8 per cent.

Whether such a policy was optimal for the US or other economies is moot. Moreover, it is known that correlations cannot determine the direction of causation, which can only be established through argumentation. Taylor made no claim that the statistical relationship was based on economic theory, or that policy makers should follow his rule mechanically. He also acknowledged the difficulties in determining output essential to his equation: interest rate = last quarter inflation rate + 0.5*(last quarter GDP minus potential GDP) + 0.5*(last quarter inflation rate minus inflation target) + inflation target. The inflation target for the US was 2 per cent.

Keynesian economics predicated a positive correlation between GDP growth, inflation and employment, and monetary policy rested mainly on fixing money supply. Stagflation sounded the death knell of Keynesian economics because it had no answer to it. Sovereigns have since largely desisted from inflating their way out of deficits, preferring to borrow from markets instead. Monetary policy now mostly targets inflation by fixing interest rates.

Riding on the back of manufacturing and service outsourcing, and robust cross-border financial flows, globalization is leading to increased dissociation between domestic growth and employment. This threatens the soundness of monetary orthodoxy, such as the Taylor Rule, because global growth, inflation and monetary policy are converging. As domestic policies become less relevant to outcomes, central banks look over each other's shoulders, and especially at the US Fed, while formulating monetary policy.

With 25 per cent of global GDP, the US economy is the prime mover of global economic trends, and the Taylor Rule works well for it. Given the global appetite for the US dollar, central banks must respond to periodic US Fed shifts or open up huge arbitrage opportunities and consequential capital flight. The obverse does not hold, since monetary shifts in any single country—with the arguable exception of Japan, China and the Euro area—do not significantly impact financial flows into the US.

Should central banks continue to fix benchmark interest rates when they are losing control of key domestic variables? Their days of 'fixing' interest rates are gone. Now, they simply determine interest rates at which they lend and borrow money. Their capacity to influence interest rates derives from their dominance of the domestic currency market. In a situation of full or virtual capital convertibility and resultant huge financial flows, their market power and ability to influence rates will continue to diminish.

Left to market forces, both exchange and interest rates would adjust to global demand and supply. Since long-term interest rates are market determined, the issue is whether central banks should desist from setting short-term rates.

Such withdrawal would concede 'policy space' to the US Fed and independent credit rating agencies. The former has a major impact on domestic interest rates. Rating agencies, at arm's length from government, are less likely to get interest rates wrong. Market-based sovereign borrowings would continue to be domestic risk-free benchmarks for rating purposes. But central banks would now concentrate on catering to government's banking needs, supervising financial markets and keeping financial institutions robust.

The Financial Express, New Delhi, 2 August 2006.

9

Wanted: Economists for the 21st Century

The 2006 Nobel prize for economics went to Edmund Phelps for his work centred on the Phillips curve. Simply stated, the Phillips curve postulated a stable, inverse relationship between inflation and unemployment. Derived from a 100-year statistical study of the British economy from 1860, the trade-off meant that when unemployment was high, an expansionary monetary and/or fiscal policy was the *mantra*. This was in step with Keynesian thinking. What Phelps did was to take a dynamic view of the relationship between prices and wages and conclude that this trade-off was illusory and that every economy had a permanent, or slowly changing, unemployment rate through which governments and bankers cannot inflate their way out. In this sense, the 2006 Nobel was a victory for fiscal prudence over Keynesian profligacy as well as monetary excess.

Stagflation in the 1970s alerted economists to the fact that all was not well with either Keynesian economics or the Phillips curve. The simultaneous occurrence of high rates of inflation and unemployment consequent to low growth was contradicted by both Keynes and Phillip. Milton Friedman led the charge for free-market economies based on fiscal and monetary prudence.

But, surely, a central bank could still use a monetary policy to stimulate and stabilise the economy through interest rate changes. The seminal works of John B. Taylor (Stanford University) and Edmund Phelps (Columbia University) demonstrated the limitations of monetary policy. Through his statistical study of US Federal Reserve (Fed) policy, Taylor deduced an equation, the Taylor Rule, which closely fitted the Fed's successful interventions. Taylor's work demonstrated that monetary policy needed to be rule-based rather than discretionary to be effective. The rule is based on current and expected inflation and growth rates.

Phelp's work brought fiscal and monetary policies further down to earth as they could do little to lower unemployment. The economy soon reverted to its long-term equilibrium or 'natural' rate of unemployment. This rate is often called NAIRU, the non-accelerating inflationary rate of unemployment. When unemployment falls below this rate, inflation tends to accelerate, and *vice versa*.

Phelps arrived at this conclusion by taking a dynamic view of the relationship between prices and wages, with the latter chasing the former without actually catching up. When the unemployment rate was low, employers enticed workers with higher wages. Keynesian economists had assumed that workers could be fooled by higher money wages into working for lower real wages in a tight labour market. According to Friedman and Phelps, workers soon grasped that employers passed on the cost of higher wages through higher prices that raised the cost of living. Such rational expectations caused the jobless rate to fall back to its natural state.

If both fiscal and monetary policies have severe limitations, how is the monster of unemployment to be tamed? Phelps tried to look at other explanations, like savings, for workers' current incomes came from both wages and returns on past savings. NAIRU itself has long been under attack, with economists pointing to economies like Hong Kong and Switzerland that had low rates of unemployment and inflation for long spells.

The definition of 'unemployed' keeps changing from time to time, as politically sensitive data are often fudged. Concerns regarding 'jobless growth' indicate that there is ample room in Nobel's Hall of Fame to accommodate a future monster slayer. What is certain is that we need to look beyond fiscal and monetary policies of states and central banks. The works of 20th century economists were based primarily on closed-economy models. In an open, integrated and fast globalising economy, these entities are losing their efficacy, anyway.

Friedman undermined the role of fiscal policy in stimulating the economy. The works of Phelps and Taylor point to the limitations of monetary policies in attaining the same objective. By exposing the limitations of fiscal and monetary policies, all three economists have strengthened the case for a free-market economy. Friedman and Phelps have been awarded the Nobel for their endeavours. Will it be Taylor's turn in the foreseeable future?

The Financial Express, New Delhi, 25 October 2006.

10

The End of Macroeconomic Policy?

Robust growth lowers unemployment. Huge trade and budget deficits lead to currency depreciation, rising interest rates and inflation. Higher input costs fuel inflation. Natural resources are a source of comparative advantage. Standard economic textbook stuff is no longer true, as multi-layered global integration and open economies are redefining old relationships and challenging established economic paradigms.

The link between merchandise trade balance and currency strength is weakening with the increasing importance of invisible trade and capital flows. Thus, America's burgeoning trade deficit has not dented the dollar. In India, despite the worsening merchandise trade balance in relation to the GDP, the rupee is stable against major currencies, even as the share of invisible trade in the current account has gone up from about 15 per cent to almost 40 per cent, and the share of foreign investment in capital flows from nil to over two-third within the last decade.

The predominance of financial over physical flows means faster market adjustments, for financial market characteristics are distinct from products and other services. There is no 'J curve effect' of physical investment and infrastructure lagging policy, environment and price changes. In financial markets, supply-demand adjustments are immediate, at the click of a mouse. Such volatilities also threaten sovereign tax bases, still geared to tax goods rather than services.

Rich mineral deposits in Newcastle, the Loire, Ruhr and Alsace-Lorraine were critical to the early industrialisation of Europe. With the growth of international trade, the lack of natural resources ceased to be a constraint on growth, Japan being the classic example. Deepening international trade now meant that discovery of new natural resources, or a sudden spurt in their price (as in oil), transmitted 'positive' external shocks, with an adverse fall-out on global competitiveness, diagnosed as the 'Dutch Disease'. Further, in the face of collapsing institutions and failing states, local militias and mafias milked resources like diamonds, oil, opium and timber by plugging into a seamless global economy with few trade barriers. The curse of diamonds and oil now contributed to the comparative disadvantage of nations.

Weakening of the relationship between domestic growth and employment has fuelled a lively debate on 'outsourcing' in the US. 'Jobless growth' is possible because the economy can outsource both manufacturing and business processes overseas. This has seen corporate transactions and profits boom without commensurate addition to the domestic workforce or assets and greater convergence of global business cycles. While multilateral institutions like the World Trade Centre (WTO), Multilateral Investment Guarantee Agency (MIGA), the World Bank and the International Monetary Fund (IMF) have contributed greatly to policy convergence, it is transnational corporations (TNCs) that constitute the motor force of convergence in the real economy.

Global price inflation has remained low despite rocketing commodity, especially oil, prices driven by Chinese demand. In a departure from past trends, however, continuing productivity gains, thanks to rapid advances in information technology (IT), have combined with cheap Chinese exports to counteract the spurt in commodity prices. The Chinese fiscal and monetary system has absorbed much of the oil price shock and insulated its economy—also the global workshop. The Chinese stance drives global price inflation far more than commodity prices, just as the US Federal Reserve (Fed) drives global interest rates.

The greatest culture shock, however, is reserved for economic policy makers. Convergence has reduced the effectiveness of domestic public policy in macroeconomic management and muted the deleterious effects of acts of commission. Policy makers, other than key players in dominant markets, are now less relevant to outcomes. Aided by a global savings glut and invisible 'dark matter,' America can run high imbalances without macroeconomic penalties of higher inflation and interest rates and lower growth.

Conversely, falling growth rates in America are likely to dampen growth globally, despite sound macroeconomic management elsewhere. Global capital flows, and *ipso facto* the cost of capital, are more influenced by US Fed announcements than by the monetary policies pursued by central banks. The European Central Bank (ECB) and our Reserve Bank of India (RBI) both keep one's weather eye open on Fed policy while fixing interest rate benchmarks. Those who argue that the central banks should respond mainly to domestic business cycles ignore the fact that the latter are now more aligned to global cycles.

Sovereigns still formulate domestic fiscal and monetary policies. There is always headroom to influence investment flows and growth, by creating a world-class infrastructure and investment environment. It is also a moot point as to what would happen if sovereigns were to monetise their way out of deficits, something no longer fashionable. However, the tolerance threshold of poor domestic policy is rising. India can sustain fiscal deficits over three times the Maastricht 3 per cent norm without adverse macroeconomic fallout.

It is tempting for the government of the day to take credit for good macroeconomic fundamentals that are not of its making, despite acts of commission, such as high budget deficits. But having done so, it becomes difficult to escape blame for adverse developments, to wit lower growth, falling asset prices and rising interest rates, over which their control is diminishing. As macroeconomic parameters become increasingly insensitive to domestic policy, it is arguably better for public policy makers to openly acknowledge the constraints of an open economy in which they operate and concentrate more on nurturing institutions. They would do well to heed the findings of the World Bank's survey of the 1990s, which concluded that robust institutions impacted growth much more than right policies.

The Financial Express, New Delhi, 17 April 2006.

11

The New Mercantilism

Mercantilism, or the belief that the strength of nations hinges on accumulating gold through persistent trade surpluses, was the prevailing economic orthodoxy just before the dawn of the golden age of classical economics. According to the classical economists, however, although trade could make nations wealthy on account of its ability to promote efficiency—through the theory of comparative advantage—trade surpluses were not an end in themselves. They took a neutral position on whether international trade or domestic demand should be the engine of growth.

Classical economists postulated that as countries developed, the rate of return on capital declined, leading capital to flow to developing countries. In the pre-1914 phase of globalization, this is exactly what happened. The fact that the bulk of capital flows subsequently were between developed countries did not disprove these assumptions: the size of developing economies was just not big enough to absorb such large flows. On balance, there was, as predicted, net outflow of capital from the developed to the developing world. In the post-colonial period, this was initially mostly in the form of debt, though more recently equity flows have become predominant.

Trade deficit was the mechanism through which capital flowed to developing countries. Developing countries were expected to run trade deficits, which would be funded through external capital flows that supplemented domestic savings to enhance growth.

This formulation was rendered increasingly complex on account of changes in the international monetary system that classical economists could not have anticipated. Neo-classical economists have, however, fleshed in the details. If a developing country ran trade surpluses, *ceteris paribus*, its currency would appreciate, reducing its export competitiveness and transferring purchasing power and demand from external to domestic residents. The external account would consequently move back closer to balance.

But what if the domestic currency were not allowed to appreciate by the central bank? Developing countries today are piling up huge reserves through a combination of persistent trade surpluses and managed floats. These reserves constitute net capital outflows from developing countries, contrary to the formulations of classical economists. These flows finance consumption in the US, whose trade deficit is equivalent to the combined trade surplus of the rest of the world.

Why would developing countries prefer overseas demand over domestic demand as their engine of growth? One reason could be the size of the domestic economy relative to the world economy.

Many East Asian economies that started industrialising from the 1970s using international trade as their growth engine were small-sized economies. But why continental economies like China and India should show a similar preference is not entirely clear. Are we seeing a return to mercantilism, with hard currency reserves taking the place of gold? This mercantilist logic enables developing countries like India and China to register high rates of growth despite muted domestic demand on account of low per capita incomes and pervasive poverty.

But the new mercantilism has costs beyond depressing local demand. Large-scale hard currency acquisitions release huge amounts of equivalent local currency in the domestic market that can be inflationary if the absorptive capacity of the economy does not increase proportionately. This hazard has been in part neutralised through 'sterilisation,' where the central bank buys back the excess local currency through sovereign bond issues. This, however, has a huge negative fiscal impact, since the interest paid out on domestic bond issues is significantly higher than what the central bank earns on its foreign currency assets that are typically parked in low-yielding risk-free hard currency sovereign bonds.

Large-scale sterilisation operations also put an upward pressure on interest rates that can both compromise growth through reduced international competitiveness and attract even more capital inflows. Continued appreciation of the domestic currency can also lead to capital losses in the central bank's accumulated stock of hard currency assets.

While several reasons have been attributed to the recent emergence of sovereign wealth funds, that invest part of the sovereign reserves in higher yielding but riskier equities, they should *inter alia* be seen as a response to the fiscal dilemma associated with sterilisation on an epic scale which is a logical corollary of the new mercantilism.

The Financial Express, New Delhi, 29 August 2007 (print version).

12

The Failure of Currency Floats

When India floated its currency in the early 1990s and moved to a relatively market determined exchange rate, the expectation was that the exchange rate would keep the current account in equilibrium: a widening current account would lead to currency depreciation, compress imports and boost exports. Conversely, a current account surplus would appreciate the currency, diminish export competitiveness and make imports cheaper. In either scenario, the current account would be nudged back into balance.

This belief was based on the conventional wisdom that floating rates were sensitive to current account balances. This view may have had merit in an age when capital flows into developing countries consisted mostly of debt and foreign aid that basically financed the current account deficit (CAD). However, even as early as the mid-1990s, capital flows to developing countries were far in excess of what was required to finance CADs. During 1994-1996, the cumulative CAD of developing countries averaged $86.05 billion, while the net addition to their foreign currency reserves—the net excess of capital inflows over what was required to finance the CAD—was $99.16 billion.

The dwarfing of the current account by the surge in the capital account continues unabated. In 2003-2005, the cumulative current account surplus of developing countries averaged $356.13 billion. In a trade-led global economy, this would have been balanced by equivalent outflows from the capital account in the overall balance of payments (BoPs). However, there was a net addition of $453.19 billion to the reserves of developing countries that year.

Exchange rates are determined by the demand and supply of different currencies at any point of time, just like any other commodity. It is the combination of trade and capital flows—including the demand for arbitraging real interest rate differentials—that determines exchange rates. The strategy of 'sterilised intervention' currently followed by several developing countries is an acknowledgement of the new reality that market determined exchange rates can no longer be expected to nudge the current account balance back to equilibrium.

It is pertinent to note that the rupee appreciated faster than the currency of several other developing countries despite India's substantial CAD. Between October 2006 and October 2007, the rupee appreciated twice as much against the US dollar as the Chinese yuan, despite the fact that China ran a current account surplus of about 9-10 per cent of GDP (gross domestic product), compared to India's deficit of 2-3 per cent.

The current account equilibrium should not, of course, be read as zero. Indeed, it has been long believed that developing countries should run CADs to augment domestic savings in raising investment and growth. As with a fiscal deficit, though, the desirable level—the figures usually cited are 2-3 per cent of GDP—is arguable. If developing countries are able to leverage (which they are currently able to) and absorb (which unfortunately they are not, since their huge reserves end up financing US consumption) much larger levels of foreign savings, much higher CADs can be sustained. The US has been able to sustain CADs of 4.5-6.5 per cent over the last five years without an adverse macroeconomic fallout in the form of high inflation and interest rates, or low growth.

Back when capital flows to developing countries were modest, market-determined exchange rates could be used as an effective policy instrument to stabilise external imbalances. However, with capital flows dwarfing trade flows, there is now no effective marker for what an appropriate exchange rate should be, or indeed what new policy instrument can take the place of a currency float. In practice, developing countries try to ensure that the real effective exchange rate, which takes account of differences in inflation in different countries, remains more or less constant over time. However, it is not clear whether this would push the current account towards equilibrium over the long term.

The Financial Express, New Delhi, 21 November 2007.

13

Inflation in a Globalizing World

Recessionary and stagflationary fears in the wake of the US sub-prime credit crisis notwithstanding, the opening decade of the 21st century was characterised by remarkable macroeconomic stability, combining record levels of output growth and low rates of inflation. According to International Monetary Fund (IMF) estimates, global output rose from an average of 3.2 per cent per annum in 1989-98 to 4.4 per cent in 1999-2008. This was driven by a dramatic increase from 3.8 per cent to 6.4 per cent in emerging and developing economies, even as advanced economies grew steadily at around 2.7 per cent.

Consumer price inflation in advanced economies fell from an average of 3.3 per cent in 1989-1998 to 1.7 per cent in 1999-2008. The decline in emerging and developing economies was dramatic, falling from an average of 50.3 per cent to 6.2 per cent. While Asia saw a drop from 9.7 per cent to 3.1 per cent, the decline in putatively hyperinflationary developing economies in the western hemisphere from 134.2 per cent to 7 per cent was truly epic. Not only does supply appear to have kept pace with the record expansion in output, but rapid and increasing globalization, in particular the integration of huge labour markets in China and India, also resulted in price deflation across the globe in tradable goods and services over the past decade.

Sustained levels of high global growth, especially in China, has nevertheless resulted in supply side constraints on the supply of commodities, as a result of which commodity prices—particularly oil—are currently enjoying an unprecedented boom. *The Economist* commodity index shows an increase of 15 per cent in commodity and 30 per cent in food prices over the past year (2008 over 2007).

In the past, high oil prices fuelled inflation, but not so this time around. As a result, there is presently a major disconnect between consumer prices and commodity prices, which is reflected in an emerging gap between headline and core inflation in developed economies, and between whole price index (WPI) and consumer price index (CPI) in India. This is because headline inflation indices are mostly insulated against volatile commodity prices. It is widely believed that major emerging economies, such as China and India, have absorbed most of the increase in oil prices in the fisc and through productivity increases.

Globally, monetary policy, generally based on the widely accepted Taylor Rule, typically targets headline inflation (WPI in India) to stabilise output growth. The recent trend, therefore, has been for central banks to follow a loose monetary policy since headline inflation has been low. Asset prices, on the other hand, have been unusually exuberant over this period of low inflation. Thus, the US Real Home Value Index that fluctuated within a relatively narrow range of 90-120 over the last century from 1890 (base 100) to 2000, except during the Great Depression, rose sharply over the last 4-5 years so as to touch 200 in 2006. The Dow Jones rose at an annual average 8 per cent between 2002 and 2008. This pattern was replicated in developing economies such as China and India.

According to received wisdom, excess money supply fuels inflation. According to Milton Friedman's famous dictum, "Inflation is always and everywhere a monetary phenomenon."

While the common sense meaning of inflation is consumer price inflation, there is nothing in monetarist logic to suggest that excess money supply can leave some kinds of inflation relatively unaffected while being mostly transmitted to particular classes. On account of the disinflationary effect of globalization on tradable goods, excess money supply has mostly impacted non-tradable assets such as real estate or partially tradable financial assets like stock prices.

One of the reasons underlying this excessive liquidity was cross-border financial flows deriving from huge current account surpluses of developing countries (Bernanke's "savings glut"), and financial innovations such as credit derivatives that are widely believed to have inflated the sub-prime credit bubble. There were apparently no limits to this asset exuberance because they were not even on the radar of central banks that were targeting consumer prices. Yet, the changing nature of inflation in a globalising economy may well herald a change in the basket of goods and services used for price indices—and inflation—and arguably for monetary policy.

The Financial Express, New Delhi, 13 February 2008.

14

Petrodollars Ahoy!

Why are commodity and oil prices rising...and rising? The most commonly cited reason is sustained unprecedented global growth rates in recent years and, in particular, the demand from China and India. Speculation is cited as a secondary reason. Following the financial crises in Organisation for Economic Co-operation and Development (OECD) countries and the sharp slide of the dollar, commodities, particularly oil, are considered a relatively safe haven. But why commodity markets are scaling historic highs well after recessionary fears have crystallised, and quite out of proportion to the fall of the dollar, are mystifying. Even as economists animatedly debate the issue, and global stock markets seem to have emphatically rejected it, some segments of the market appear to have bought into the decoupling hypothesis.

Rising oil prices are making biofuels increasingly attractive, leading to a strong linkage between oil and food prices. Since oil-exporting countries are also major food importers and *vice-versa* part of the oil boom surplus may ultimately be delusory. The net financial windfall is nevertheless likely to be huge. A back of the envelope calculation indicates that at the current global oil consumption of 86 million barrels a day, a price increase of $60 per barrel translates into a windfall of roughly $1.9 trillion. This amounts to over 10 per cent of global exports of goods and services, or more than twice the current account deficit (CAD) of the US. To this must be added the relatively small windfall in other natural resources, such as coal, gas, iron ore, copper, aluminium and so on.

A tsunami of petrodollars has been generated and the first waves are already striking global financial markets. Where will this money be invested? Since the absorptive capacity of oil-rich economies is limited, booming oil prices have in the past vastly inflated global liquidity, laying the seeds of subsequent financial crises. While the US Federal Reserve (Fed) shares part of the blame for driving excess liquidity by keeping short-term interest rates low, as Alan Greenspan pointed out in his memoirs, *The Age of Turbulence*, the Fed has little control over long-term interest rates which are now mostly driven by massive cross-border capital flows.

During the oil boom of the 1970s, petrodollars were recycled through the banking system by extending cheap debt at low floating rates to Latin American countries. When floating interest rates rose, Latin American countries went bust over a decade of lost growth. The Latin American debt crisis has an eerily familiar parallel to the excessive liquidity-driven sub-prime housing mortgages at teaser rates. The villain of the piece this time around is the double whammy of rising interest rates and falling housing prices.

Oil surpluses were only partly responsible for the excessive liquidity associated with the sub-prime crisis. The major portion was accounted for by trade surpluses of east Asian countries, especially China, on the back of manufacturing exports to OECD countries, and excessive leverage associated with financial innovation. With oil hovering above $100 a barrel, and showing no signs of declining, and asset securitisation on the wane, petrodollar surpluses are overtaking manufacturing exports as drivers of global liquidity.

During the first oil price boom, petrodollars were mostly invested in the currency in which payments were made through the banking system. How and where will the surplus be invested this time around? Past experiences of oil boom indicate that petrodollars have always been controlled by a handful of risk-averse entities that parked money in dollars, and which appreciated over the years despite growing US CADs. The recent sharp decline of the dollar and also the current financial turmoil in western financial markets have made the dollar lose much of its past lustre.

A defining characteristic of the current boom is the important role likely to be played by mostly authoritarian regimes that control much of the foreign hard currency reserves. These sovereigns have also moved to increase their direct control over natural resources over the past few years. The investment decisions, therefore, are likely to be more strategic, often ignoring risks that ordinarily deter commercial investors.

China, for instance, is channelling huge amounts into resource-rich but conflict-ridden countries in Africa. Some of the surplus is being recycled to acquire stakes in the western financial system by bailing out troubled western banks through sovereign wealth funds. However, the likely resistance of OECD governments to such takeovers, and also the sliding dollar, may well mean that emerging markets could be the likely final destination of much of these surpluses. Since debt markets are less well-developed in emerging markets, equity would appear to be the natural choice. Since emerging market stocks are currently in the tight grip of a bear hug sparked by fears of a global recession, the imperative of parking huge oil surpluses could well trigger a bull charge in the foreseeable future.

The global imbalance generated by the oil price hike of the 1970s eventually had a calamitous fallout on Latin America, where the surpluses were recycled. The global imbalance created by developing country trade surpluses is at least indirectly linked to the current financial turmoil in America, where most of these surpluses eventually ended up.

The impact of the debt crisis was particularly severe and protracted in Latin America because the borrowed money did not result in any productivity gains. Continuing technology-led productivity improvements may partly offset the damage arising out of the sub-prime crisis in the US.

It is difficult to divine how the emerging global imbalance deriving from the current oil price and commodity boom will play out, but if much of it flows to Asia, we may be reasonably certain where future financial bubbles and crises might occur. Investment and productivity are of course rising in Asia, but domestic savings are rising even faster, making huge external injections destabilising and an invitation to financial crisis *via* the familiar route of asset price inflation. This asset price inflation could, of course, fuel a consumption boom in developing countries, as it did in the US, which could help unwind global imbalances.

However, given the extent of financial exclusion in both China and India, where only a thin upper crust invests in such assets, the social gains from such a consumption boom may be limited. The social gains from a tradables-led consumption boom are likely to be more widespread, but few emerging markets are inclined to overcome their mercantilist mindset so as to let their currencies appreciate.

Business Standard, New Delhi, 6 April 2008.

15

The Comeback State

Sovereign wealth funds (SWFs) remain much in the news with Brazil announcing a new $200 billion fund, equivalent to just under 40 per cent of its annual GDP (gross domestic product) at the turn of the millennium.

Given that 'sovereign wealth' appears almost like an oxymoron, as governments are known far better for their deficits than for their wealth, when we consider the long march of history, state deficits are a relatively recent phenomenon. The pre-modern state always had a balance, or surplus, on the current account because, small city states with strong merchant classes excepted, there was no way to fund state expenditure other than through domestic taxes and the spoils of war. The former risked domestic rebellion because taxes were one-way extractions without pretence of welfare, while war was a dangerous zero sum game. The state was primarily predatory, with few commitments other than defraying the costs of war and upkeep of the royal family and the local elite.

Sovereign wealth, consequently, has a long history. It was the rise and establishment of modern finance and banking that enabled the state to 'borrow' against future tax receipts and run huge deficits. State expenditure and functions expanded enormously as laissez faire-led capitalism accommodated socialist concerns, constantly nudged by competitive electoral politics, all post-1850 phenomena. Over the last three decades, there have been attempts by governments to balance their budgets, but without significant liquid assets. All of a sudden a number of sovereigns have accumulated substantial liquid assets, and threaten to become an influential international investor group. Morgan Stanley and the International Monetary Fund (IMF) estimate that about a dozen countries, mostly in the Middle East, China,

Singapore and Norway, have SWFs aggregating $3 trillion, equivalent to half of official global reserves. SWF holdings are projected to swell to $12 trillion by 2012 (IMF) or 2015 (Morgan Stanley), equivalent to 1.5 times official reserves.

The ultimate source of most of this new found sovereign wealth is the fundamental global imbalance deriving from the current account surpluses of developing and oil-exporting countries whose cumulative surplus from 2000 to 2006 alone totalled $1.43 trillion.

Also, private capital flows deriving from the trade surpluses of developing countries were bought up by central banks loathe to letting their currencies appreciate as part of their strategy of export-led growth. The falling dollar and rising sterilisation costs are now pressuring sovereigns to seek higher returns by transferring a portion of these reserves, currently parked in risk-free highly liquid hard currency instruments (US treasuries) to special purpose vehicles seeking higher returns. According to a recent Indian Council for Research and International Economic Relations (ICRIER) paper, India's opportunity cost of holding excessive reserves is equivalent to 2 per cent of GDP.

The shift from creditor to owner increases returns and risk. The sub-prime crisis is a cautionary tale of how liquidity risk, not captured in credit ratings, can be ignored only at one's own peril, since a good portion of this sovereign wealth has counterpart liabilities in the form of relatively high cost domestic debt. The exchange rate transactions of developing countries have had the result of vastly inflating money supply that may have to be reversed to keep inflation in check.

Secondly, in countries like India, big current account deficits (CADs) are worsening by the day. Foreign currency reserves have been largely built through volatile capital flows such as short-term debt, non-resident and foreign institutional investment. These can reverse in the event of worsening macroeconomic conditions or shifts in US monetary policy.

Coming after decades of privatisation, SWFs are widely perceived as a form of backdoor re-nationalisation and the primacy of strategic over commercial objectives, especially since authoritarian governments control the biggest SWFs. But for the same reasons, they also have longer horizons and are arguably the answer to the capital crisis in Western banks, the looming ageing crisis, and the huge infrastructural requirements of developing countries.

The Financial Express, New Delhi, 11 June 2008.

16

On a Self-destructive Mission

The earth's geological past has seen violent climate shifts. The extinction of the dinosaurs, the Neolithic Revolution that followed the retreat of the last ice age, and the sudden demise of ancient civilisations have been linked to climate change. While mankind has been altering the planetary environment ever since the Neolithic Revolution, it is only after the Industrial Revolution that it has attained the weight of numbers and technological capacity to alter the climate through its own activities in any major way.

The origins of the anthropogenic environment change debate can perhaps be traced back to the 18th century English mathematician and parson, Thomas Malthus, who predicted that unconstrained population growth would outstrip man's ability to feed itself. In case the carrying capacity was exceeded, war, pestilence and famine would descend, like the four horsemen of the apocalypse, to wipe out the surplus population.

Malthus has been repeatedly proved wrong by history, as cereal production outstripped population growth on account of continuing technological progress, and mortality actually declined sharply through improvements in public health. Indeed, the Malthusian perspective was turned on its head by Esther Boserup, who postulated that population pressure acted as a catalyst for technological progress. As a result, the global population, which had inched its way upwards since Neolithic times to some half a billion by 1650, doubled by 1820 and doubled again to touch the 2 billion mark in 1930. Then the doubling to 4 billion took only 44 years. Current projections are alarming enough to trigger major environmental concerns regarding the ability of planet earth to sustain such vast numbers. Currently, there are close to 7 billion people on the planet.

The neo-Malthusian school continues to have a wide following as it is feared that the speed and rate of population growth, combined with rapid economic advancements and per capita consumption, presage a Malthusian catastrophe that would wipe out not just the surplus population but the entire human species through catastrophic climate change.

The Malthus-Boserup paradigms saw population and technology as independent prime movers, virtually glossing over distributional issues that are vital for understanding the way in which population impacts the environment. On one hand, poverty, in tandem with rapid population increase, pushes poor people to encroach on forests and rely on firewood for fuel, which is a major reason for deforestation as well as soil and water quality degradation.

On the other hand, there is an even stronger nexus between affluence and the environment that can be measured by multiplying the total population by the degree of affluence (or per capita consumption) and the level of technology (Ei = P x A x T). While populous, underdeveloped societies affect the environment more by the sheer weight of numbers, the impact of such degradation is mostly local. But it is the less populous but highly developed affluent societies that have the technological capability to impact the global climate by plundering the planet's resources.

The link between affluence and environmental change is complicated by the 'environmental Kuznet's curve (EKC)' identified by World Bank studies on Organisation for Economic Co-operation and Development (OECD) countries. This postulates that environmental hazards are an increasing function of GDP (gross domestic product) when GDP per capita is low, but a decreasing function when GDP per capita is high as environmental consciousness increases. Clearly, technology can be a force for both environmental damage as well as mitigation, although the applicability of EKC to greenhouse gas (GHG) generation is less clear.

The relative weights of population and affluence can be gauged from the following statistics: between 1850 and 2002, the US, Canada, EU-25, Russia, Germany, Japan, France and the UK contributed 85 per cent of the stock of GHG. Despite the surge in growth in developing countries, the developed world contributed over 50 per cent of global greenhouse emission in 2000, even though it accounted for just about 20 per cent of the population. Moreover, much of the environmental degradation in least developed countries (LDCs) is due to the demand in industrialised countries that leads to a significant transfer of resources *via* trade flows. Thus, rainforests in Southeast Asia and the Amazon have been destroyed to supply Americans with ground beef for their burgers.

The distribution of world population has already shifted heavily towards poorer countries. Consumption levels of today's poor will increase absolutely, if not relatively to rich countries. The interaction of these two factors can be used to illustrate how consumption and waste generation will increasingly shift to developing countries, greatly increasing their share in global environmental degradation. It is estimated that by 2015, developed and developing country contributions to GHG flows would be about equal.

The convoluted knot tying population, poverty, affluence and technology is perhaps best illustrated by four paradoxes that together constitute a classic catch-22 situation:

(a) At present, the major contribution to global environmental change comes from developed countries where population growth rates are near zero or negative.

(b) There is a close association between poverty and population growth. However, even as poverty generates environmental hazards of its own, such as deforestation, soil degradation, etc., it nevertheless effects economy in resource use. Poor people are not wasteful: per capita emissions of GHG was 3.9 tonnes of CO_2 equivalent in China and just 1.9 in India in 2000, compared to 24.5 in the US.

(c) While the process of economic development may mitigate under-developmental environmental hazards and stabilise the population, replicating the consumption behaviour of developed societies would only exacerbate the environmental problem. Potentially therefore, the populous 'South' could contribute much more to future global environmental change than the North, if we were to go by the equation P x A x T.

(d) By the time major developing countries cross the inflexion point on EKC, the stock of GHG may be too large to save the human species.

There is a fear that if vast areas of the developing world escape from the net of poverty and population explosion, they would simply end up adopting the wasteful lifestyles of the developed world, while simultaneously stabilising the global population at twice the present level. It is unlikely that the planet would be able to sustain such high levels of aggregate consumption.

The inescapable conclusion is to redefine 'development' in such a manner that the developed world adopts sustainable lifestyles which could be replicated by the developing world. This is perhaps the essence of what is sometimes termed the 'third (great) revolution' in man's evolutionary history. While the Neolithic and Industrial Revolutions facilitated quantum demographic jumps through technological breakthroughs, the ultimate outcome in both cases was a quantum leap in aggregate consumption. What is required now is an attitudinal change to use technology so as to limit aggregate consumption to environmentally sustainable levels.

Business Standard, New Delhi, 16 August 2009.

II
Lowering Skies Over the Global Economy
The US Sub-prime Crisis

17

Sub-prime, Leverage and Contagion

While the current turmoil in international financial markets has multiple roots, it can perhaps be traced to the global glut of savings relative to investment and the easy-money policy of the US Federal Reserve (Fed) after the dot-com bust of 2001-2003. The monetary tightening from June 2004 onwards was very measured, with the US Fed too narrowly focused on stable consumer prices even as there was unprecedented exuberance in asset prices. Asset bubbles and falling yields fuelled a shift to risky high yielding assets such as sub-prime housing loans and structured products like collateralised debt obligations (CDOs), leveraged buyouts (LBOs) and other derivatives. A good measure of this 'disintermediation' was the sharp fall in the share of banks in household borrowing, which fell from 95 per cent in 1973 to just 56 per cent in 2007.

Years ago, when banks made loans and held them until maturity, credit analysis was their essential skill. But as loans turned into tradeable securities, credit analysis standards fell. Investors began to rely on credit ratings. Because rating agencies were also associated in designing complex structured financial instruments and bundling cash flows of varying risk, including sub-prime housing loans that proliferated since 2003, there was a possible conflict of interest in objectively assessing risks.

The proximate cause of the financial turmoil was rising interest rates and falling house prices. Sub-prime borrowers found it impossible to refinance backloaded 'teaser' adjustable rate mortgages, such as 2/28 and 'interest only' loans, through softer home equity (the difference between the net present value (NPV) of the mortgage and house valuation) second mortgages. Since many mortgages are now worth more than the underlying asset, increasing defaults and foreclosures may be expected. These systemic shocks could trigger defaults in prime segments as well. Resets of mortgages this year (2007) are estimated to occur at rates about 4 percentage points higher than the current rate on 30-year home loans.

Defaults to date have been relatively modest and sub-primes comprise a very small segment of the housing mortgage market. The real problem lay in the fact that investment in structured products was mostly leveraged. While losses from fully funded investments could have been contained (being limited to some investors), contagion spread because investors found that they could not refinance their cheap short-term commercial paper invested in high yielding long-dated securities. They were forced to sell off assets at knockdown prices.

The value of even high-quality mortgages fell because the market could not pinpoint where repayment risk resided in view of information asymmetries arising out of the global dispersal and complexity of structured products with sub-prime exposures. The liquidity crisis was transmitted to banks managing these 'conduits' and underwriting the commercial paper. Forced to take off balance sheet exposures on their books, they became reluctant to extend credit as they now faced capital adequacy problems. Although Europe does not have a sub-prime problem, financial integration transmitted the contagion instantaneously to Europe since, unlike product markets, adjustments in financial markets are immediate.

The new model of financing, in which debt is repackaged and risk dispersed through a web of leveraged derivative contracts, has much merit. It has deepened financial markets and enabled those with modest incomes, including minorities, to buy homes. But it plainly has had an unhappy consequence: when a problem emerged (in this case, in sub-prime mortgages), it was harder to work out whom it was safe to do business with. Banks became wary of even lending to each other, leading to a flight-to-quality that raised credit cost across the board. Symptomatic of this is the widening spread between US Treasuries and Libor, which reached a 20-year high.

While central banks have stepped in to slash benchmark rates and inject liquidity into the banking system, the underlying crisis in the real estate market remains unresolved, making a taxpayer funded bail-out likely.

The Financial Express, New Delhi, 26 September 2007.

18

Sub-prime and Monetary Policy

The central bank, as we know it, evolved in the wake of the financial panic of 1907 in the US when a private banker, J.P. Morgan, was called upon to bail out the financial system by injecting liquidity in financial markets. The US Federal Reserve (Fed) was consequently established to maintain orderly conditions in financial markets.

Central banks subsequently acquired a second objective, namely, to ensure macroeconomic stability across business cycles. They lowered benchmark short-term rates and injected liquidity when the economy was expanding, and sucked out liquidity through monetary tightening and higher reserve requirements when demand surged ahead of supply, leading to inflation ('overheating').

More recently, the resurgence of mercantilist beliefs has added a third objective, namely a competitive exchange rate. Central banks in developing countries now mostly juggle the twin objectives of inflation control and exchange rate management on a regular basis. Since globalization makes it virtually impossible to control cross-border capital flows even where the capital account is regulated, central banks have struggled unsuccessfully to tame the legendary, triple-headed monster called the 'impossible trinity,' none more than the Reserve Bank of India (RBI).

But there are other conflicting objectives as well. Central banks are every now and then rudely reminded of their *raison d'etre* when a crisis of epic proportions, such as the Great Depression over a quarter century ago, or the sub-prime threat today, presages financial Armageddon.

The legendary Milton Friedman's explanation of the Great Depression, reiterated not too long ago by the current Fed Chairman Benjamin Bernanke, was that it was mostly a monetary phenomenon. The Fed apparently did not heed the sage advice of Walter Bagehot, the founding father of central banking theory, to lend freely in a liquidity crisis.

The ghosts of 1907 and 1929 have haunted the boardrooms of central banks ever since. Benjamin Bernanke's predecessor, Alan Greenspan, pumped liquidity into markets during the stock market crash of 1987, during the banking crisis associated with the collapse of the Long Term Capital Management Hedge Fund in 1998, and again during the dot-com bust of 2001-2003. The Fed and European Central Bank (ECB) also moved quickly to pump liquidity to stabilise financial markets in the wake of the current sub-prime mortgage crisis. Indeed, the central bank's propensity to cut rates when bubbles burst has now come to be known as the 'Greenspan put.'

The irony this time around is that central banks have been constrained to pump liquidity into markets that they have put on inflation watch for possible benchmark short-term rate increases. While central banks may dither between the conflicting objectives of demand and exchange rate management, the trade-off between demand management and financial apocalypse is a no brainer, the attendant moral hazard of encouraging future risky behaviour notwithstanding. And rightly so, for protracted turmoil in financial markets will sooner or later spill over into the real economy.

The danger lies in the liquidity overhang once the crisis is past, which can either lead to a liquidity trap (what happened in Japan in the 1990s following repeated rate cuts by the Bank of Japan in response to the collapse of the real estate bubble) or a buildup of the same exuberance that creates financial bubbles in the first place. The Great Depression, it may be recalled, was preceded by an easy money policy. Greenspan has been faulted not for his 'put,' but for the excessively slow monetary tightening after the dot-com crisis, and which may well be the long-term cause of the current sub-prime imbroglio. According to some observers, the tightening was more measured than what the Taylor Rule for monetary policy predicated.

The real problem, however, is that monetary rules currently followed by central banks are too narrowly focused on consumer prices as benchmarks for inflation targeting. In view of rapid globalization and trade liberalisation, consumer price indices based primarily on baskets of internationally traded commodities are arguably becoming a less reliable measure of domestic overheating than asset prices. The US Urban Consumer Price Index has remained low and stable between 2-3 per cent since 2000. However, the US Real Home Value Index that fluctuated within a relatively narrow range of 90-120 over the last century from 1890 (=100) to 2000, except during the Great Depression, rose sharply over the last 4-5 years to touch 200 in 2006. This unprecedented real estate bubble does not seem to have had a major influence in shaping the Fed's monetary policy, Greenspan's occasional references to 'irrational exuberance' in asset prices notwithstanding.

Perhaps the most enduring lesson of the sub-prime financial crisis may well be the need to revisit the rules informing monetary policy.

Business Standard, New Delhi, 14 September 2007.

19

Unwinding of Global Imbalances?

For a long time, the behaviour of the dollar seemed to defy macroeconomic gravity. It kept strengthening despite a growing US current account deficit (CAD). Several inventive theories were postulated to explain this anomaly. Perhaps none was more inventive than the 'dark matter' that enabled the US to earn higher returns on its overseas assets than what the rest of the world earned on dollar assets. The dollar was perceived as the 'primus inter pares,' a singularly strategic and relatively risk-free reserve currency that found universal favour with central banks despite its low returns.

Unlike most countries, the US seems to be perfectly happy with a strong dollar. Cheap Chinese imports counter the political backlash stemming from greater global integration that increases domestic inequality by rewarding capital and penalising labour. Much of the increase in inequality in the US over the past two decades is attributed to the entry of a vast pool of cheap labour from developing countries into the global market.

At the heart of the current global macroeconomic imbalance is the burgeoning US CAD that is roughly equal to the current account surplus of the rest of the world, mostly deriving from the trade surplus of developing countries. What this means is that the US over-consumes—relative to its domestic production—by roughly the same amount that the world overproduces.

The expanding US trade deficit is widely seen as the engine of growth for developing economies. A strange new mercantilism informs their economic policy. The recipe for high growth is to tap export markets through managed exchange rates. Undervalued exchange rates, however, suppress domestic demand as they erode the purchasing power of domestic residents by keeping the price of tradable goods high. China consumes only about half its national income.

The long-term outcome of neo-mercantilist policies has been to push developing countries as a group from a cumulative CAD of around $100 billion in 1990 to a huge current account surplus of over $600 billion in 2006. This flies in the face of conventional wisdom that developing countries should run CAD to leverage foreign savings to supplement domestic savings and enhance growth and development.

Far from leveraging foreign savings to boost development, developing countries have been exporting their own surplus savings so as to finance excess consumption in the US, even as their median per capita incomes remain low. Household savings in developing countries are unusually high by western yardsticks because there is no credible tax-funded social security or pension system in place for the vast majority of people.

One of the relatively unsung corollaries of the sub-prime crisis and financial turmoil in the US is that the dollar at last appears to be succumbing to macroeconomic logic. While the trade-weighted dollar index has been declining steadily since its peak of 2002, until recently the decline was much sharper against the euro and yen, than against Asian currencies from which the US sources much of its imports.

The decline in 2007 has been precipitous with the dollar falling to its lowest level in decades. The fast declining dollar is now lowering the US trade deficit and the US draft on developing country surpluses to finance consumption.

As the dollar weakens, the value of the international reserves of developing countries, currently heavily over-weighted in dollars, is declining. Unless this is compensated through higher interest rates/monetary tightening by the US Fed, sovereigns could seek to park reserves elsewhere, thereby aggravating the dollar decline. The dollar may be America's currency, but it is other countries' problem.

The Economic Times, New Delhi, 3 December 2007.

20

Macroeconomics of Agflation

Global wheat and corn prices have doubled over the last two years. Stocks appear to be at historic lows despite good harvests. Indeed, the rise in food prices has been universal across the globe, affecting the prices of practically all food items, including meat, eggs and milk. Fears that food demand may outstrip supply have kept surfacing every now and then since Thomas Malthus' celebrated essay on population was published in 1798. The last big scare was in the 1960s and 1970s, largely fuelled by the Club of Rome's doomsday scenario that the population explosion in developing countries was not sustainable.

That fear was overcome with the development and propagation of high-yield varieties (HYVs) of food grains generated through crossing different strains, and more recently, genetically modified strains, that raised productivity dramatically. While the human population continues to increase, for the first time since the Industrial Revolution the rate of growth is declining, and so the population is projected to peak sometime in the middle of the current century. The pressure on food supplies is not on account of population growth, but on account of shifts in the food grain usage away from direct human consumption.

Food demand is rising fast as large numbers emerge from poverty. The use of grain for bread is linked to the world's population, but this has been flat for decades on account of the slowing population growth. The demand for meat, however, is linked to economic growth, which has been rising globally over the last decade. Per capita meat consumption in developing countries has risen by about two-third since 1990, given that the average annual per capita consumption of meat in China has increased from 20 kg in 1985 to over 50 kg today (2008). It takes 5-7 kg of grain fodder to produce 1 kg of meat.

Changes in dietary patterns, however, are slow and incremental, and cannot explain the dramatic price movements of the past year. Increasing diversion of corn for biofuels, which has a cascading effect on the price of wheat through diversion of wheat acreage, and for feeding cattle, probably can. According to World Bank estimates, the grain needed to fill up a sport utility vehicles (SUV's) tank can feed one person for an entire year.

The use of maize for producing ethanol in America has increased from 15 million tonnes a year in 2000 to 85 million tonnes presently. It is estimated that up to 30 per cent of the entire American corn crop could be diverted for biofuel by 2010. America accounts for some 40 per cent of the global corn production. The sharp spike in oil prices, as well as generous subsidies given by governments, is making biofuels an increasingly attractive option.

Commodity analysts believe that heavy agricultural subsidies in recent decades had deflated global food prices and made investment in agriculture unprofitable in many developing countries. Although Organisation for Economic Co-operation and Development (OECD) countries were formerly exporting agricultural deflation, they are now exporting 'agflation.'

It is entirely possible that the current food supply scare may eventually subside through a robust supply side response. New farmlands could be ploughed up, and technological advances made, to ratchet up production. In the short-term, however, foodgrain prices may hinge on oil price trends and subsidies. High oil prices could also depress the use of oil-based fertilisers—and hence productivity—that have greatly contributed to the increase in farm productivity over the past half century.

Agflation also has a less talked about monetary fallout. Since food has a major share in the consumer price index (CPI) in developing countries, they have tended to tighten monetary policy to control inflationary expectations, even as OECD countries are moving to lower short-term rates in response to the financial turmoil arising out of the sub-prime housing mortgage crisis. This is widening the interest rate differential between rich and emerging markets and exacerbating the surge in capital flows from the former to the latter.

The Financial Express, New Delhi, 16 January 2008.

21

Inflation as a Tradable Commodity

Inflation has traditionally been seen either in terms of supply-demand imbalances or as a monetary phenomenon, and largely in terms of consumer prices. According to Milton Friedman's famous dictum, "Inflation is always and everywhere a monetary phenomenon."

Globalization is, however, changing the way inflation is viewed and transmitted. It is increasingly becoming an "internationally tradable virtual commodity" over which governments and central banks have little control. A gap has also opened up between consumer, commodity and asset prices.

Current inflationary expectations need to be seen against the backdrop of the remarkable macroeconomic stability that has characterised the opening decade of the 21st century, combining record levels of output growth with low rates of inflation. According to International Monetary Fund (IMF) estimates, global output rose from an average of 3.2 per cent per annum in 1989-1998 to 4.4 per cent in 1999-2008, driven by a dramatic increase from 3.8 per cent to 6.4 per cent in emerging and developing economies.

Consumer price inflation in advanced economies fell from an average of 3.3 per cent in 1989-1998 to 1.7 per cent in 1999-2008. The decline in emerging and developing economies was epic, falling from an average of 50.3 per cent to 6.2 per cent. While Asia saw a drop from 9.7 per cent to 3.1 per cent, the decline in putatively hyperinflationary developing economies in the western hemisphere from 134.2 per cent to 7 per cent was truly heroic. This deflation occurred despite the Goldman Sachs broad commodity index jumping by 288 per cent over the 6 years to February 2008. This led to a major disconnect between consumer and commodity prices, reflected in an emerging gap between core and headline inflation in developed economies, and between whole price index (WPI) and consumer price index (CPI) in India where there is currently a 2 per cent difference. This is because core inflation indices are relatively insulated against volatile commodity prices.

It is widely believed that increasing cross-border movement of goods and services has muted demand-supply imbalances, while productivity gains and integration of the huge labour markets in China and India exported price deflation over the past decade, despite the huge demand generated by record growth. At the same time, inflated Organisation for Economic Co-operation and Development (OECD) subsidies exported agricultural deflation.

On account of the disinflationary effect of globalization on tradable goods and services, excess money supply mostly impacted non-tradable assets such as real estate, or partially tradable financial assets like stock prices. Thus, the US Real Home Value Index that fluctuated within a relatively narrow range of 90-120 over the last century from 1890 (=100) to 2000, except during the Great Depression, rose sharply over the last 4-5 years to touch 200 in 2006. The Dow Jones rose annually on average by 8 per cent between 2002 and 2008. This pattern was replicated in developing economies such as China and India.

Globally, monetary policy, generally based on the widely accepted Taylor Rule, typically targets core inflation to stabilise output growth. The trend therefore was for central banks to follow loose monetary policy since core inflation was low. The lax monetary policy of central banks was, however, only the proximate reason for the surge in global liquidity that inflated asset bubbles, including the sub-prime crisis. Alan Greenspan, the erstwhile US Federal Reserve (Fed) Chairman, confessed to the Fed's helplessness in influencing long-term interest rates that responded more to huge cross-border capital flows. The ultimate cause therefore lay in humungous cross-border financial flows deriving from huge current account surpluses of developing countries (Bernanke's "savings glut"), and financial innovation such as credit derivatives. These surpluses tended to be deflationary since they generated huge demand for dollars on account of emerging markets' unwillingness to let their currencies appreciate, thereby appreciating the currency in which international trade, including oil, was mostly priced.

The recent surge in commodity prices, particularly oil, would seem to indicate that supply side constraints have at last caught up with record levels of growth. Emerging markets now threaten to export inflation through their unquenchable demand for commodities, even as OECD countries export 'agflation' by diverting food grain for biofuels. *The Economist* commodity index has risen by 45 per cent, and the food index by 70 per cent, over the past year ending 4 March 2008. The falling dollar is also fuelling inflation.

But why commodity and oil prices continue to scale historic highs well after recessionary fears have crystallised is mystifying. While Asia's contribution to global growth and trade has increased significantly in recent years, as has intra-Asia trade, the US share in Chinese exports has remained constant at just over 20 per cent over the last decade. Since much of intra-Asian trade feeds this continuing global imbalance, the decoupling hypothesis seems weak, and stock markets certainly seem to think so. If that is indeed the case, commodities are hardly likely to provide a medium- to long-term hedge against asset deflation in OECD countries and the dollar's sharp slide. The proceeds of continuing global imbalances, now bolstered by a fresh surge in 'petrodollars' and 'commodollars,' would however need to be parked in assets somewhere—in America, Europe or emerging markets.

The dollar may well be the bellwether currency indicating which way the wind blows and how inflationary expectations crystallise.

The Financial Express, New Delhi, 12 March 2008.

22

A Brief History of Inflation

The movement of prices over the last few decades can be broadly divided into three distinct phases. The 1970s and 1980s were a period of hyperinflation. By way of illustration, US consumer price inflation averaged at 8.7 per cent between 1973 and 1982, and 6.6 per cent between 1973 and 1990. This was followed by disinflation in the 1990s and first half of the current decade. US consumer price index (CPI) inflation fell sharply to 2.7 per cent between 1991 and 2002, before rising slightly to 2.9 per cent between 2003 and 2007. Globally, consumer price inflation declined from 3.3 per cent in advanced economies between 1989 and 1998 to 1.7 per cent between 1999 and 2006. In emerging and developing countries, it declined from an annual average of 50.3 per cent in between 1989 and 1998 to 6.5 per cent between 1999 and 2006.

It now appears that we are entering a new inflationary, and according to some, potentially hyperinflationary phase. This was initially insidious, not fully captured in CPI data since the price of commodities rose even as the price of manufactured goods declined consequent to productivity gains arising from the integration of China and India in the global market for goods and services. The price of non-fuel primary commodities that showed an average annual decline of 2.7 per cent between 1989 and 1999, rose by 9.4 per cent annually between 2000 and 2006. Oil prices that declined by 1.2 per cent annually between 1989 and 1998, rose on an average by 20 per cent annually between 1999 and 2006.

This sharp increase in commodity prices was fuelled by hyper growth in emerging and developing economies whose real GDP (gross domestic product) growth spurted from an average of 3.8 per cent between 1989 and 1998 to 6.2 per cent between 1999 and 2006. Advanced economies continued to average annual growth rates of below 3 per cent over both these periods. Commodity price inflation was exaggerated by the steep fall in the international value of the dollar, the currency in which commodities are traded internationally.

It is only over the past year that the sustained upswing in commodity prices is being rapidly transmitted to headline inflation. According to *The Economist*, CPI inflation over the past year has risen from 2.6 per cent to 3.9 per cent in the US, from 1.3 per cent to 3 per cent in France, from 3 per cent to 8.5 per cent in China, from 7.4 per cent to 13.3 per cent in Russia, and from 3 per cent to 5 per cent in Brazil, as of mid-May 2008.

The hyperinflation of the 1970s can arguably be explained in terms of monetary and fiscal excesses, since Keynesianism and the associated Phillips curve were the prevailing intellectual orthodoxy. From the 1980s, however, under the intellectual influence of the great monetarist, Milton Friedman, the general perception was such that both governments and central banks largely eschewed excessive monetisation of government deficits and followed a rule-based monetary policy based on variants of the Taylor Rule. Paul Volcker, erstwhile Chairman of the US Federal Reserve (Fed), is credited with taming the monster of inflation by sucking excess liquidity out of the financial system through repeated rate increases. Why then is inflation rising again?

Excessive monetisation was inherent in the manner in which the fundamental global imbalance, which saw developing countries run huge current account surpluses, has played out. Emerging market and developing economies taken together, but excluding the newly industrialised Asian economies, still ran a current account deficit (CAD) of $21.2 billion as late as 1999. This deficit was turned around dramatically into an annual surplus of $544 billion by 2006. Their cumulative surplus in the 7 years from 2000 to 2006 was $1.43 trillion. These surpluses led to counterpart capital flows to developing countries; but instead of letting their currencies appreciate as a consequence, their central banks bought up these flows as part of their strategy of export-led growth. This released a tsunami of domestic currency into the system, only part of which could be sterilised. The weighted average of broad money growth in emerging and developing economies consequently rose from 15-16 per cent between 2000 and 2003 to about 20 per cent in 2005 and 2006—way above their average nominal GDP growth of 13 per cent.

A loose monetary policy in emerging and developing countries was supplemented by a loose monetary policy in advanced countries, especially the US, which accounts for about one-fifth of global demand. The growth rate of M3 in the US, on average, exceeded nominal GDP growth by about 3 per cent between 1998 and 2006. For advanced economies on the whole, broad money growth exceeded nominal GDP growth by about 1.5 per cent between 1999 and 2006.

Monetary tightening did not take place in the US despite growing external deficits on account of, firstly, the tendency of developing countries to park their growing foreign currency reserves mostly in low-yielding but risk-free US treasuries. This enabled the US to seamlessly fund rising external deficits—and falling domestic savings—in the US by dampening interest rates. The effective US Fed funds rate fell sharply from an average of 5.6 per cent between 1989 and 2000 to a low of 1.13 per cent in 2003.

Secondly, the changing nature of inflation in a fast globalising world was also conducive to a lax monetary policy. Disinflation was largely limited to tradable value-added goods and services. The relative prices of mostly non-tradable assets, as well as commodities—including agricultural commodities—actually rose because of hyper-growth in developing countries, another by-product of globalization. Inflation consequently had a 'non-core' bias, whereas disinflation had a 'headline' bias on account of the predominance of tradable manufactures. Even as headline inflation was low, commodity and asset prices were entering a period of unprecedented boom. The Schiller index of real home prices (1890=100), which fluctuated within a relatively narrow band on either side of 110 between 1970 and 1997, rocketed to a peak of 200 in 2006. This insidious inflation lulled central banks into following a loose monetary policy since the US Fed, in particular, targeted core inflation that excluded commodity and food prices. A loose monetary policy also facilitated hyper-leverage, especially in the unregulated non-banking segments of the financial sector, which further amplified liquidity and demand.

If the above diagnosis of the resurgence of global inflation is correct, the prescriptions for addressing emergent hyperinflation over the short to medium term are self-evident. Developed countries need to look beyond core and headline inflation, and also target commodity and asset price inflation while formulating monetary policy. Developing countries need to follow a more market-based approach to exchange rate management. Price and market signals should not be tampered with, so that supplies of commodities, including oil and food grain, can rise and efficiency gains effected to equate demand and supply over the medium to long term.

Business Standard, New Delhi, 25 May 2008.

23

Once Old Certainties Collapse

Following the Keynesian Revolution and the established Phillips curve, it was widely believed that there was a trade-off between price stability and growth. Since inflation and unemployment (a proxy for low economic growth) were negatively correlated, the use of fiscal and monetary policy appeared simple: countercyclical during inflationary episodes and expansionary when growth dipped.

This simplistic Phillips curve relationship was undermined by the 'stagflationary 1970s' that opened up the possibility of a positive correlation between unemployment and inflation, and through the work of Nobel laureates, Edmund Phelps and Milton Friedman. Following the expectations-augmented Phillips curve, authored *inter alia* by Edmund Phelps, policy makers do not see a long-term trade-off between price stability and growth, as inflationary expectations can push up wages even when unemployment rates are high. Following Milton Friedman, it is now recognised that inflation can increase even when there is an output gap if money supply is excessive. Countercyclical macroeconomic policies are now tempered with concerns over inflation, which is now the new target of central banks. Governments and central banks have moved away from discretionary to rule-based fiscal and monetary policies to stabilise growth. The Taylor Monetary Policy Rule and the European Union Maastricht Treaty norm of containing the fiscal deficit within 3 per cent of the GDP (gross domestic product) are now widely accepted as conducive to macroeconomic stability.

Although possibly inspired by neo-Keynesianism, in retrospect the response of the US Federal Reserve (Fed) under Paul Volcker to stagflation in serially raising the Fed funds rate, until the effective rate crossed 19 per cent in 1981, is also consistent with the monetarist assumption that there is no Phillips long-term trade-off. It was only after the monster of inflation was tamed that the problem of low growth was addressed through easy monetary policy.

There are now widespread fears that the world may again be headed for stagflation. In sharp contradistinction to the Volcker era and the expectations augmented Phillips curve, the US Fed and Bank of England have relaxed monetary policy to counter the systemic sub-prime financial crisis and attendant recessionary fears, overriding inflationary expectations. There has, however, been no such pump-priming in Europe, also reeling under recessionary fears but with the European Central Bank (ECB) steadfast in its focus on inflation.

Arguably growing above potential over the last few years, the Indian economy has lost momentum in recent quarters (May 2008), which is partly the result of Reserve Bank of India's (RBI's) relatively tight monetary stance to dampen demand. Wholesale price index (WPI) inflation has, nevertheless, crossed the 7 per cent mark, with consumer price inflation running a good 150 basis points above the WPI. India cannot be insulated against stagflation—were it indeed to occur—in an increasingly integrated world.

While there is unanimity that primacy should be accorded to containing inflation, there are differences of opinion on the effectiveness of monetary policy in combating the emerging stagflationary circumstance. Many analysts argue that since the current spurt in inflation is cost push—the outcome of global short supply—rather than demand pull, monetary tightening would simply end up hurting growth without significantly reducing inflation. The burden of dealing with agflation in particular, which has a disproportionate fallout on the poor, would mostly fall on fiscal rather than monetary policy in any case.

There are, however, several problems with the argument that tight monetary policy is ineffectual in dealing with the current stagflation threat.

First, short supply is simply the flip side of excess demand. The distinction between demand-pull and cost-push inflation is essentially neo-Keynesian. The neo-Keynesian view of stagflation is that it is caused by cost-push inflation, and its strategy for dealing with it is to cut off money supply to bring down inflation to manageable levels before increasing money supply to spur economic growth. This 'disinflationary' neo-Keynesian policy was pursued to good effect by the US Fed under Paul Volcker during the Carter administration.

Second, although most of the inflation in tradable goods over the past year, in India and abroad, has been in oil, commodities and food, where global demand-supply imbalances have emerged, domestic money supply can nevertheless impact the rate of inflation on the margin. Indian inflation has been relatively benign by global benchmarks over the past year, partly the result of rupee appreciation and RBI's tight monetary stance. Nevertheless, money supply growth of over 20 per cent during the last 3 years substantially exceeds nominal GDP growth, which is mostly the outcome of large capital inflows and hence inherently inflationary.

Third, even as the IMF has given confusing signals to developing countries to use contractionary fiscal policy to counter the expansionary impact of large capital inflows on one hand, and expansionary fiscal policy to bolster growth on the other, India's fiscal stance following the recent Union Budget is expansionary and needs to be counteracted through a tight monetary policy. This is indeed the current stance of the central bank that hiked mandatory reserve money requirements even as it kept key policy rates unchanged in its 2008-09 annual policy statement of 29 April 2008.

Following continuing serial Fed rate cuts, there is the danger that widening spreads between US and Indian real interest rates could induce more foreign capital to flood the country. However, the ongoing financial crisis in Organisation for Economic Co-operation and Development (OECD) countries and the resultant flight to treasury bonds may have stalled this danger for now. Besides, a slight appreciation of the rupee might in fact help moderate inflation.

The Financial Express, New Delhi, 1 May 2008.

24

Restructuring Structured Finance

The current credit storm in western financial markets, with its roots in the US housing market, threatens to bring down the entire edifice of structured finance that has in recent times become the high priest of the Anglo-Saxon financial system. It is fuelling fears of a deep and sustained recession, pressuring panic-stricken central banks to serially lower benchmark short-term rates even as inflationary expectations abound, inducing governments to throw fiscal prudence to the winds, and exacerbating the steep fall in the value of the US dollar on one hand and destabilising surge in capital flows into developing economies on the other.

Driven by complex mathematical engineering, securitised structured, finance is a modern financial marvel that has deepened capital markets through greater dispersal of risk, contributed to higher growth by intermediating access to large amounts of low-cost funds generated by global imbalances, and made development more inclusive by giving previously excluded groups access to assets like residential property. It has also spawned a new breed of highly paid graduates well versed in mathematics and calculus, but alas, quite divorced from the real world of old-fashioned finance with its putative sixth sense of sniffing out risk through a deep appreciation of human psychology, market sentiment and moral hazards.

In *A Short History of Financial Euphoria*, John Kenneth Galbraith advanced the rather depressing theory that finance did not lend itself easily to innovation, since at the end of the day all credit is secured on some asset—no matter how much it is repackaged and sliced. If asset prices are volatile—dependent on rapid ebbs and flows of liquidity rather then on the capitalised value of future income streams from the asset—financial instability is the logical corollary.

This artificial increase in money supply was not created through regular money-creating banking, but through financial innovation that mimicked fractional banking and exposed the system to new risks. Is the collapse of the market in complex structured products merely another manifestation of Galbraith's dictum, especially since investors are currently eschewing complex structured financial products in what is termed as a 'flight to simplicity,' or can the gains of the credit revolution be sustained through highly nuanced regulatory oversight and reform that does not price credit derivatives out of the market?

First and foremost, it is widely felt that the Basel capital adequacy norms need to be tweaked to cover the loophole opened up by escalating off-balance sheet exposures since these norms pressured banks to take these liabilities off their balance sheets in the first place. While this move is likely to result in a sharp shrinkage of liquidity underlying the credit revolution, it may be desirable where contingent risks remain with the originating bank through guarantees or underwriting of short-term asset-backed commercial paper.

Secondly, the originating bank could be required to retain a 'fraction' of the original portfolio, mirroring the logic of fractional banking. This would not only take care of cases where the default risk has been permanently taken off the originating balance sheet, but also address the moral hazard inherent in the 'originate-to-distribute' lending model where there is little incentive for the loan originator to adhere to prudential lending and monitoring standards with the risk being 'distributed.'

Thirdly, Basel norms also need to be tweaked to address liquidity risks arising from maturity mismatches. Conventional (money creating) banking will always face this risk since it borrows short term and lends long term, and runs the mother of all Ponzi schemes through 'fractional banking' by which it keeps recycling the major portion of deposits. The liquidity risk arising from conventional bank runs is presently handled through state-funded deposit insurance and central bank/government bail-outs.

In the post-Glass-Steagall era, universal banking also faces liquidity risks arising from positions taken in (non-money creating) investment. The sub-prime financial crisis was not escalated by large-scale loan defaults, but because assets became illiquid as credit markets simply froze. Banks became wary of even lending to each other. Short-term debt raised to fund long-term investments could not be rolled over. The Ponzi-like structure of fractional banking was replicated in the investment banking segment both in maturity mismatches, and bundling and recycling of loans and investments several times over, without prudential norms in place as in the case of money-creating banking.

Liquidity risk residing with the banks' investment business is also effectively borne by central banks/governments because the collapse of individual banks would have a knockdown effect on conventional money-creating banking, leading to bank runs as in the case of Northern Rock recently.

Fourthly, the structural asymmetry in the banking industry, where traders get a good share of the annual profits but the losses are borne entirely by shareholders, tended to magnify the moral hazards encouraging risky behaviour. The business model of the supposedly far more exposed private equities and hedge funds seems to have weathered the credit storm far more effectively since their traders and managers had a big direct stake and moved nimbly to cover losses.

Bank bonus schemes need to be more long-term oriented with only part of the bonus disbursed in the profitable year. The balance should be adjusted against shortfalls, if any, in subsequent years.

Fifthly, there may be need to review the list of financial products that only qualified investors can buy. Spreading of risk proved delusive since it was ultimately foisted on borrowers who did not quite understand the complex product they were buying into.

Sixthly, hedge funds, structured investment vehicles (SIVs) and credit default swaps may need to be brought within the regulatory framework. It is not entirely co-incidental that the most exuberant players in the sub-prime boom were such unregulated entities.

Seventhly, the time has perhaps come to let structured products be traded in regulated exchanges. Collateralised debt obligations (CDOs), collaterlised bond obligations (CBOs), etc., are presently traded over-the-counter, making it impossible to mark such products to market because trading in these has virtually ceased. Exchange-based trading would make price discovery in difficult market situations easier. A financial system that can be embroiled in a major crisis without substantial defaults actually taking place requires some tweaking of the mark-to-market mechanism.

Lastly, the regulators too may need to be regulated, although it is not at all clear by whom. The sub-prime crisis has, in particular, brought credit rating agencies and central banks under the lens. Since the former have been arraigned for not maintaining arms-length distance from the products they rated, thereby under-pricing risk, they may need to be brought within the ambit of the Sarbanes-Oxley Act.

Central banks have been criticised for practicing loose monetary policy, narrowly focused on consumer prices even as asset prices were rocketing. Rapid globalization is creating a disinflationary impact on the prices of tradable goods, on which the consumer price index (CPI) is mostly based. Overheating pressures in the economy are, therefore, more likely to be reflected in asset prices.

While rental prices can be included in the CPI, it is difficult to see how housing, stock and other asset prices can be similarly incorporated. Since asset value appreciation is the major source of funding, consumption and well-being for most people in developed markets, a monetary policy response to asset inflation is likely to be strongly resisted once the crisis is past.

The Economic Times, New Delhi, 18 February 2008.

25

Decoupled Globalization?

Globalization is binding trade and markets across the world closer together. This integration has raised all boats with countries across the globe, from China, America to war-ravaged Liberia and Sudan recording unprecedented growth and low inflation.

Much of this can be attributed to efficiencies deriving from international trade, which grew substantially faster than GDP (gross domestic product). Two-way merchandise and commercial services trade as a percentage of global GDP at market prices increased from 36 per cent in 1985 to 60 per cent in 2005.

It is consequently surprising that recent months (April 2008) have seen the emergence of a new counter-intuitive hypothesis, to which even *The Economist* has lent its weight, which flies in the face of this globalising trend. Asia is seen as the new engine of growth that could drive the global economy out of the recession induced by the sub-prime crisis in the US. How persuasive is this argument?

The argument runs roughly as follows. As Arthur Lewis pointed out in his Nobel Prize lecture three decades ago, economic growth in developing countries has historically been dependent on economic prospects in Organisation for Economic Co-operation and Development (OECD) countries that account for the major share of global GDP. In 2006, the US, UK, Japan, France, Germany, Italy and Spain still accounted for 58 per cent of global GDP at market prices, with the US alone accounting for 27 per cent. Their share at purchasing power parity (PPP) was 41 per cent.

Over the last few decades, however, developing countries, in particular those in Asia, have been growing much faster than OECD countries. Thus the combined share of China and India in global GDP increased from 5.7 per cent in 1971-1975 to 14 per cent in 2005 at PPP [according to the revised International Comparison Program (ICP) tables]. The share of the four largest developing (BRIC) economies was 20 per cent.

The Economist points out that BRIC nations are the least dependent on the US, with exports to America accounting for just 8 per cent of China's GDP, 4 per cent of India's, 3 per cent of Brazil's and 1 per cent of Russia's. Over 95 per cent of China's growth of 11.2 per cent in the current year (2008) came from domestic demand.

Asia's share in global trade has also risen significantly. While global exports of goods and services trebled between 1997 and 2007, Asia's exports increased almost 10 times. China's share in global exports has increased dramatically from 1.9 per cent in 1971-1975 to 8.2 per cent in 2000-2005.

Asia's intra-trade has also grown substantially over the past decade. Since 2000, the share of the US in regional exports has come down significantly (with the notable exception of China), even as exports to China have risen dramatically. India's trade with China now matches that with its long-standing biggest trading partner, the US. According to the International Monetary Fund (IMF), the impact of regional perturbations on domestic growth has consequently increased sharply over the last two decades.

The argument is sometimes more nuanced. A recent IMF paper argues, for instance, that while there is now closer coupling between so-called 'developing economies' and OECD countries, there is greater decoupling between emerging economies and OECD countries.

There are also other versions of the same basic argument. John Authers described, in the *Financial Times* of 29 February 2008, decoupling as "the notion that demand for raw materials in the developing world will allow emerging markets to grow even if there is a US recession." The decoupling sentiment is certainly implicit in the current boom in world commodity prices that are scaling historic highs, despite fears of recession in OECD countries, particularly America.

The decoupling hypothesis notwithstanding, the US share in Chinese exports has remained constant at just over 20 per cent over this period, even though half its exports are now to developing countries. Indeed, Asia runs a huge cumulative current account surplus of over $300 billion with the rest of the world, which is at the core of a fundamental global imbalance that keeps the global financial and real economies closely coupled.

Because of this continuing external dependence, it is difficult to see how Asia would not be significantly affected by a US recession ,unless China and other developing countries are able to expand domestic demand substantially. This would mean abandoning their current mercantilist mindset and letting their currencies appreciate, thereby increasing the purchasing power of their people.

India appears to be less vulnerable to the global downtown because it is much more dependent on domestic demand for growth, being unique amongst Asian countries in continuing to run a current account deficit (CAD). Even so, India's engine of growth is its booming services sector that is highly coupled with global, and especially US, markets.

The Economist points out that domestic demand constitutes by far the biggest source of GDP growth in China and India. However, the trend over the last 20 years actually indicates greater coupling. China's consumption has declined from two-third of the GDP in 1986 to just over half in 2006, and India's from 85 per cent to three-fourth.

China actually ran a CAD 20 years ago. GDP at PPP is also not the best measure for world trade because tradables involve international purchasing power. The combined share of Chinese and Indian GDP in 2005 was only about 8 per cent at market exchange rates, and the entire BRIC share was just over 10 per cent.

Decoupling sceptics are on even stronger ground when they draw attention to growing global coupling in capital flows and inflation. Between two-third to three-fourth of export revenues, remittances and foreign investment, and almost all cross-border syndicated loans in developing countries continue to be along the North-South axis.

US monetary policy is exercising stronger, indeed determining, pull on volatile cross-border capital flows. The huge hard currency reserves of developing countries, the flip side of the global imbalance, are also deepening financial integration, which may well be the ultimate root of the current storm in credit markets.

On balance, the decoupling hypothesis that growth in developing countries is increasingly decoupling from OECD countries does not appear to be very compelling. Stock markets, certainly, are far from convinced that some countries can continue to swim robustly even as others sink.

The Economic Times, New Delhi, 2 April 2008.

26

Caught the Second Time Around

When the sub-prime financial crisis broke out a year ago (August 2007), it did not affect developing countries directly on account of their limited exposure to derivatives. The expectation was that robust growth in emerging economies would rescue the global economy as they had 'decoupled' from Organisation for Economic Co-operation and Development (OECD) countries. However, it now appears that the second round effects of the sub-prime financial crisis, particularly through the associated spike in oil prices, is devastating for Asian countries at several levels since they are mostly commodity importers. Indeed, but for the cushion created by the reserves built up assiduously over the last few years, several Asian economies have the ingredients of a classic currency crisis: simultaneous sharp reversals in capital flows, current account balances and fiscal deficits.

By dramatically lowering interest rates in response to the credit freeze, the US Federal Reserve (Fed) set the stage for a sharp depreciation of the dollar—the currency in which oil is internationally traded. Plummeting real estate, stock and financial asset prices also redirected liquidity, earlier distributed amongst other asset classes, towards commodities, particularly oil, further intensifying the price rise even as growth prospects moved in the reverse direction. Thus, while oil and commodity prices had been rising steadily for a few years consequent to sustained high rates of global growth, especially in BRIC countries, they went ballistic—quite out of proportion to the underlying demand-supply imbalance—following the onset of the sub-prime financial crisis in August 2007. The six monthly moving average price of Brent crude which fluctuated within the range of $60-

70/barrel between end 2005 and mid-2007 rose steeply to cross $80/barrel by December 2007, $90/barrel by March 2008, breached the $100/barrel barrier by May and threatened to top $150/barrel in July 2008, before falling back recently.

One year on, the second round effects of the sub-prime financial crisis on emerging economies are apparent at several levels. Firstly, the spike in oil prices has sharply worsened the current account of several Asian countries, which are major oil importers, while strengthening that commodity-exporting emerging economies. This has split the BRIC economies down the middle, with the economic prospects of Brazil and Russia brightening and those of China and India dimming. In the aggregate, the global imbalances that inflated the sub-prime bubble are still intact.

While commodity prices, including oil, metals and food, appear to have peaked in mid-July 2008 and are now falling, they are still 20 per cent higher than what they were a year ago. It is therefore too early to judge whether this is simply a 'correction' or whether a 'commodity bubble' has been pricked. The long-term upward pressure on oil prices, consequent on sustained high rates of global growth, especially in emerging markets, needs to be separated from short-term liquidity-induced volatility. Oil prices are widely expected to remain firm for some time on account of the anaemic supply response and International Monetary Fund's (IMF's) current (July 2008) forecast of continuing robust demand expansion in the emerging economies.

Secondly, the belief that oil prices are likely to stay firm means that it is no longer possible for governments to insulate retail consumers in an open-ended manner. The consequential increase in retail oil prices, although modest in relation to international prices, combined with the spike in food prices that have become increasingly linked to oil prices through the biofuels link, has meant that inflation rates have increased much more sharply than in the advanced countries, since both oil and food have a greater weightage in the general price index in emerging economies.

Thirdly, the increase in retail prices notwithstanding, there is a sharp increase in fiscal deficits in emerging economies as governments try to absorb and stagger the commodity price shock. This has not only contributed to worsening the inflation outlook over the medium term, but has also led international credit agencies to consider downgrading credit ratings of some of the worst-affected emerging economies, including India. Should this occur, the rupee can come under greater pressure through rebalancing of currency portfolios.

Fourthly, the continuing credit freeze in western capital markets evident in wide TED (difference between 3-month treasury bills and 3-month Euro dollar Libor) and financial credit default swap (CDS) spreads notwithstanding, the deteriorating macroeconomic environment in emerging economies and the diminishing influence of the 'decoupling' hypothesis has sharply reduced capital flows, worsened the balance of payments (BoP) outlook and sharply lowered stock market valuations in commodity-importing countries. The reduction in capital flows may have made monetary management easier, but has put several Asian currencies, including the Korean won, Thai baht, Vietnamese dong, Indonesian rupiah and Indian rupee, under pressure against the US dollar, even as the latter has been depreciating against major international currencies. The reduction is so sharp that the rupee in particular has come under heavy pressure. While the current account deficit (CAD) is eminently manageable in view of large foreign currency reserves, rupee depreciation at this point will only feed inflationary pressures.

Fifthly, it is now clear that the asset wealth loss, including housing equity that was a major source of household demand in the US, and prolonged financial squeeze and deleveraging in international markets, is depressing global demand and growth. While the decline in US growth to date has not been as sharp as forecast on account of fiscal stimulus, easing of monetary policy and a surge in exports consequent on the depreciation of the dollar, the diminishing US trade deficit is weakening the country's role as global consumer of the last resort and recessionary clouds are growing darker over the Euro area and Japan. While India is not as dependent on external markets as several other economies, notably China, this cannot but have a dampening effect on its growth in the emerging world, since the US accounts for about a quarter of global demand. According to the IMF, this decline would be differential, with OECD countries showing a sharper and more protracted decline, followed by Asian countries like China and India that are commodity importers. Then again, commodity exporters like Russia and Brazil would be the least affected. Growth in oil exporting Middle-eastern countries is expected to accelerate slightly in 2008.

Business Standard, New Delhi, August 17, 2008 .

III
Apocalypse
Lehman and After

In life, my dear sir ... we have to distinguish between the unusual and the impossible. It would be unusual for a comparative stranger to lean out of a cab and soak you one, but you appear to have laid your plans on the assumption it would be impossible....

George Bevan in *Damsels in Distress* by P.G. Wodehouse.

27
Life After Greenspan

As the world faces what is clearly emerging as the greatest financial crisis since the Great Depression, attention is increasingly focused on the new master of the financial universe, Ben Shalom Bernanke, Chairman of the US Federal Reserve (Fed). How will he steer the closely inter-twined global financial armada through what is often described as the perfect 'stagflationary' storm? Low profile, plain speaking and democratic in contrast to his predecessor, Bernanke was initially seen as the poor man's Alan Greenspan, caught sleeping at the wheel as the sub-prime crisis imploded, and too doctrinaire and scholarly to don the mantle of a real world central banker. In recent months, however, as the Greenspan legend unravels in wake of the expansive sub-prime financial crisis, 'Helicopter Ben' has been widely credited for being ahead of the curve in anticipating the worst through dramatic rate cuts, liquidity injections and bank bail-outs to shore up a tottering financial system.

A self-confessed "Great Depression buff, the way some people are Civil War buffs," he appears eminently equipped intellectually to lead the battle from the front lines. He has indeed been doing so in a heroic fashion in close consultation with Hank Paulson, Secretary of the Treasury. The lessons he drew from the Great Depression probably explain why the US Fed response to the sub-prime crisis was so different from that of the European Central Bank (ECB) that was focused on the inflationary threat, even as Bernanke saw potential deflation as the greater threat. In retrospect, the professor may well have made the right call, for the US real economy appears to have held up relatively well so far, even as Europe stutters into recession.

However, as the oft-repeated one-liner from Bollywood goes, the movie is by no means over, indeed, we might simply be at the end of the beginning. The jury is still out on whether the US economy can hold out against recession, and whether tools honed through deconstructing the Great Depression and the inflationary 1970s are appropriate for taming a 21st century hybrid monster that appears to have combined elements of both on account of the excessive liquidity deriving from global imbalances and financial innovation.

Just as Greenspan was prescient in sniffing out productivity gains underlying the 'great moderation' that permitted both sustained high growth and lower inflation, Bernanke was amongst the first to draw attention to the global savings glut arising from the ballooning current account surpluses of emerging economies that drove interest rates down and may have, along with financial innovation, inflated the sub-prime bubble under the very nose of the master of the universe (retired). It is therefore surprising that Bernanke, apart from a predilection for 'leaning against the wind,' by and large goes along with Greenspan in not targeting asset prices while formulating monetary policy.

The Great Depression and the inflation crisis of the 1970s spawned what are perhaps the two great economic orthodoxies of the 20th century, namely Keynesian economics to tame deflation, and monetarism, along with the augmented Phillips curve to tame inflation. Even as fiscal policy is hostage to politics, the burden of stabilisation has increasingly fallen on independent central banks using monetary policy.

Bernanke apparently considers deflation deadlier than inflation, and that is perhaps why he seems to favour explicit inflation targeting, unlike his illustrious predecessor who nevertheless appears to have had an 'informal target' not very different from Bernanke's in the 1-2 per cent range. He however, recognises the limits of monetary policy, as interest rates cannot be pushed below zero. It is in such a scenario that Bernanke propounded perhaps his most controversial theory: a money-financed tax cut which is essentially equivalent to helicopter drop of money.

Yet, some difficult questions remain to be both asked and answered. How would such a helicopter drop fare in a turbulent open economy buffeted by robust cross-border capital flows? Despite deleveraging, the problem is not one of liquidity—ask sovereign wealth funds—but of pricing of risk, which is fast leading to a virtual nationalisation of the financial sector in the very heart of global capitalism. Nationalisation of risks means more regulation that could constrain the very financial innovation that lay at the heart of the great moderation. If the state resolutely refuses to bail-out the financial sector, how can the central bank do so on its own? Ben Bernanke has his task cut out to fashion the monetary tools for the 21st century.

The Financial Express, New Delhi, 5 October 2008.

28

Sub-prime Impact on India

The collapse of Lehman Brothers and the bail-out of Bear Sterns, Merrill Lynch, AIG and housing mortgage majors Fannie Mae and Freddie Mac is the latest wave of the sub-prime financial crisis that first hit international financial markets in August 2007. In August 2007, India was on a sustained growth path, close to 9 per cent—the rise in trend growth underpinned by a sharp increase in both domestic savings and investments from under 30 per cent of the GDP to over 35 per cent within a space of five years. Wholesale price inflation (WPI) was within the tolerance band of 5-7 per cent. Global optimism regarding India's future growth prospects, particularly that of its burgeoning information technology (IT) sector, was generating a tsunami of capital inflows that kept the central bank battling on two separate but interrelated fronts: mopping up excess dollars to prevent appreciation of the rupee and sterilising the monetary fall out of this reserve accumulation to keep inflation in check.

The sub-prime crisis did not affect India directly. Indeed, the initial expectation was that robust growth in China and India would rescue the global economy as emerging markets had 'decoupled' sufficiently from Organisation for Economic Co-operation and Development (OECD) countries. This resulted in an influx of capital, currency appreciation and a stock market boom. However, once the credit storm in western markets combined with the spike in commodity prices to coalesce into a 'perfect storm' of faltering growth and high inflation, the second round effects appear ominous.

The rise in oil prices dealt a severe terms of trade shock that sharply worsened the current account, increasing India's merchandise trade deficit by 50 per cent in April-July 2008 over the corresponding period last year. Although oil prices are now substantially below the July peak, they would need to fall much further to substantially abate the terms of trade shock in view of the sharp depreciation of the rupee. While the impact of the financial crisis on exports has been relatively muted so far, it must be recognised that while adjustments in the financial sector are immediate, adjustments in the real sector are lagged. It is becoming increasingly clear that the asset wealth loss, including housing equity that was a major source of household demand in OECD countries in recent years, combined with prolonged deleveraging and repricing of risk in international markets is leading to demand destruction in these countries.

Growth in the US has been surprisingly robust, registering an annualised expansion of 3.3 per cent in the second quarter of 2008. But this was mostly on account of the surge in exports consequent on the depreciation of the dollar and the fiscal stimulus of $150 billion that counteracted the fall in household demand. The diminishing US trade deficit is weakening the country's role as a global consumer of the last resort. It now appears that both the Euro area and Japan could be headed into recession by way of collateral damage on account of the credit crunch, falling housing prices and contraction of the US trade deficit and demand. It is these fears that seem to have turned the tide in favour of the dollar and against commodity prices. As the impact of the fiscal stimulus and the resurgence of US competitiveness on account of the appreciating dollar run out of steam, the decline in household demand and consumer confidence on account of the continuing housing crisis is widely expected to drive US growth lower in subsequent quarters. The real test of the 'decoupling hypothesis' would be if, given the downturn and crisis in the US, Europe and Japan, capital were to flow back into emerging markets instead of the traditional haven, namely US treasuries.

While India is not as dependent on external markets as several other developing countries, notably China, this cannot but have a dampening effect on export growth as the US accounts for 15 per cent of India's merchandise exports (compared to 20% in the case of both Brazil and China), while western Europe accounts for another 23 per cent. The dependence on OECD, and particularly on the US market, and on services exports, through which India mostly plugs its yawning merchandise trade deficit, is even greater. Of India's trade deficit of $90 billion in 2007-08, 40 per cent was covered by IT-related invisibles exports to the US and Europe. While the falling rupee could make non-import intensive Indian merchandise exports more competitive, since banking, financial services and insurance (BFSI) are at the centre of the credit storm in western markets, there is likely to be shrinkage in both job opportunities and export revenues in what is the largest outsourcing vertical of India's IT sector.

The combination of current account and inflationary pressures has put the Indian rupee under pressure since capital flows other than FDI (foreign direct investment) are drying up as a consequence of the credit freeze and repricing of risk in western capital markets. There was a net outflow of $3.7 billion of FII (foreign institutional investment) from India during April-August 2008. The reduction in capital flows may have made monetary management easier, but the reduction is so sharp that the rupee is coming under heavy pressure, dipping below ₹46 to the dollar, even as Reserve Bank of India's (RBI's) foreign exchange reserves fell by $20 billion between 31 March and 5 September 2008. The reversal in FII flows has sharply reduced market capitalisation on account of the stock market's dependence on FII flows. Although the current account deficit (CAD) is eminently fundable in view of the large stock of foreign currency reserves, rupee depreciation at this point will only feed inflationary pressures. Fiscal pressures have moreover led international credit agencies to consider downgrading India's credit rating from investment to speculative grade. Should this occur, the rupee would come under even greater pressure through rebalancing of currency portfolios.

Savings and investment, widely credited for the rise in trend growth over the last few years, are both likely to be adversely affected. The Economic Advisory Council to the Prime Minister estimated in July 2008 that the commodity terms of trade shock could administer an additional fiscal shock of up to 4.5 per cent, thereby sharply lowering savings. Although oil prices have fallen drastically since this estimate was made, it would undo only some of the damage in view of the depreciating rupee.

Although the domestic savings investment gap over the last few years was modest, ranging from 1 to 1.5 per cent of the GDP, Indian companies and public sector enterprises had become increasingly dependent on cheap overseas finance for investment, possibly as a result of monetary tightening at home and rupee appreciation. External commercial borrowings as a percentage of gross capital formation of the corporate and public sectors rose sharply from 3.2 per cent in 2005-06 to 12 per cent in 2006-07 and even higher in 2007-08. The dependence on foreign investment, net of portfolio flows, likewise rose from 2.8 per cent to 6.4 per cent. While foreign direct investment is unlikely to be immediately impacted by the credit crisis, the expected sharp increase in the cost and access to external credit could drive both investment and growth below trend.

Business Standard, New Delhi, 23 September 2008.

29

The Future of Globalization

With 13 letters, is it surprising that globalization has such a chequered lineage? It has entailed rapid intensification of cross-border trade, services and capital flows; greater to and fro movement of people and ideas; enhanced welfare through efficiency gains, greater equity and higher growth even though it may have increased income inequalities and undermined nation states.

Globalization, however, has also been linked to colonialism, underdevelopment and to external shock, along with a crisis in the US housing market threatening to bring down the global economy. How far, and in what directions, will the process go in future?

The emergence of nation states towards the end of the highly localised Middle Ages was critical to modernisation. They facilitated trade and market integration, centralisation and scale economies. The imperial extension of nation states was an important element of the globalization surge in the 19th century. In the 20th century, nationalist sentiment fuelled bitter conflict in Europe, as well as the anti-colonial movements that followed.

The post-colonial surge in globalization from the 1970s is led by TNCs (transnational corporations). Their individual assets now exceed the GDP (gross domestic product) of several countries.

Their objectives are also coming into sharp conflict with those of nation states as they endeavour to disseminate international trade, capital, labour, modern technology, transportation and communication channels seamlessly to every flag on earth. Nation states are recovering lost space in the wake of the ongoing global financial and economic crisis. But these attempts lack conviction and in any case they find it impossible to substantially influence events without greater co-ordinated action.

Historical trends are rarely linear either in space or time. There are parts of the world where nationalism is just fructifying through conflict emanating in new nation states, such as in the Balkans and Africa, even as it diminishes elsewhere through post-nationalist unions such as the European Community and Asean.

Indeed, civilisation itself has time and again teetered on the brink during interludes of barbarian dominance, only to surge forward at a higher plane after having seemingly regressed. Consider Europe following the collapse of the Western Roman Empire, or during the 1930s. Globalization, likewise, beat a major retreat with the outbreak of the First World War, before resuming its triumphant march from the 1970s.

Predicting the future is consequently fraught with hazards, since history is neither linear nor a natural science. Nevertheless, just as a study of the past is a meaningful way of comprehending the present, the present in turn is a creaky window opening into the future.

One of the immediate consequences of the 9/11 attacks on the US was to reverse the growing ease of cross-border labour mobility. However, global integration through trade in goods and services and capital flows, and at the level of ideas and interpersonal exchange, continued to expand geometrically.

In recent months, however, following the unprecedented global financial crisis, a number of renowned developed country economists, such as Joseph Stiglitz, Lawrence Summers, Paul Krugman, Martin Wolf and Dani Rodrik, have expressed scepticism regarding the globalization process. Its institutional basis is seen to be weak, and perceived losses seem to outweigh gains.

For the first time in modern history, per capita incomes in developed and developing countries are converging. Understandably, protectionist sentiment is currently stronger in developed countries, just as it was in developing countries during the anti-imperialist interlude when the divide was widening. Workers in developed countries seem to be losing out. The greatest gains seem to accrue to non-democratic countries like China, Russia and Venezuela, who are bent on pursuing geopolitical ends rather than enhancing welfare.

The recent surge in commodity prices rekindled nationalistic fervour and temporarily reversed the long-term trend in transportation costs that made globalization possible. There is also widespread fear that globalization may unravel in the wake of the ongoing turmoil in financial markets and global recession. Are these rising whispers of a retreat from globalization a turning point in history, or yet another interlude in a relentless movement forward?

A global recession, and possibly depression comparable with the 1930s, appears imminent, and with it a contraction in world trade and capital flows.

Unlike the 1930s, however, when the disastrous Smoot-Hawley tariffs only compounded the problem, the macroeconomic response to an impending global recession this time around is co-ordinated. This is reflected in the 15 November 2008 declaration of the Washington Summit of G-20 leaders representing over 85 per cent of global GDP. The disastrous consequences of uncoordinated action were immediately manifest in the unilateral steps taken by some European countries rushing to guarantee bank deposits, and in divergent monetary action by the US Fed and the European Central Bank (ECB).

A global super financial regulator is unlikely in the immediate future. However, co-ordinated multilateral action on the lines of World Trade Organisation (WTO) to address issues arising out of escalating global capital flows is now more likely than ever. The concept of a college of national regulators to enforce common regulatory principles and accounting standards is already on the table.

While globalization may well beat another retreat, it is nevertheless becoming clear that several emerging economic and political challenges cannot be meaningfully addressed within the nation state framework. The institutional structure that would succeed the nation state is, however, still unclear.

Firstly, a sustainable solution to the emerging energy-food (the two are becoming increasingly substitutable) imbroglio lies in greater integration of several predominantly poor agrarian countries stuck in a vicious cycle of poverty and low median incomes and developed economies constrained by fiscally damaging agricultural subsidies.

Secondly, an emerging demographic crisis is making labour mobility from young developing countries to ageing developed countries a categorical imperative.

Thirdly, the production and trade of technology, goods and services is increasingly becoming the domain of TNCs that are by definition global entities.

Fourthly, the global environmental and climate change that threatens the very survival of the human species cannot be meaningfully abated with the nation-state framework.

Fifthly, the efficiency of regional supply and production chains is constrained by market failure in funding and managing inter-operable cross-border networks like roads, railways and energy. This can be overcome only through greater integration.

Sixthly, sovereign macroeconomic tools are getting blunted as growth, inflation, tax, and now increasingly financial and monetary policies, become globally coupled, with the dollar as the global reserve currency. The dollar has emerged stronger than ever from the current financial turmoil, despite the financial crisis emanating from the US.

Seventhly, for the first time in modern history, the balance of military power in the world has become uni-polar. War between states is yielding to state-less conflict and dissent that cannot be meaningfully addressed with the nation-state framework.

Eighthly, at the sociocultural level, rapid advances in communications technology are fast creating a global culture through greater people-to-people contact. The logical corollary is diminishing nationalist sentiment, apparent in the declining lure of military service. A brave new universal civilisation is, of course, inconceivable alongside competing cultural pulls of strident nationalism and religious bigotry.

However, like nationalism, institutionalised religion (as distinct from individual spiritualism) also appears to be in long-term decline in the wake of science, reason, liberty and globalization. Christianity has come a long way from the days of heresy, inquisition and crusades. In the Islamic world, the twin deficits of democracy and socio-economic growth may have stalled social reform, but the rise of Islamic terror could hasten reform from within in the foreseeable future.

Evolutionary biologists might see this universalising trend as disruptive since robustness of the evolutionary process is premised on heterogeneity and hybrid vigour. Man, however, is by nature a restless and exploratory animal. The virtuous cycle of globalization, in particular rapid technological advance, would induce man to become more extra-terrestrial oriented.

Indeed, the tools of a global level organisation would serve him well in any future extra-terrestrial contact. This could both hasten and redefine globalization and the evolutionary scale.

Those who think the future reads like a chapter out of the science fiction serial *Star Trek* would do well to compare man's recent advances with the writings of Jules Verne and H. G. Wells, or compare the crew profile of the ill-fated space shuttle Columbia with that of Starship Enterprise. The only constraint on man's future is his own imagination.

The Economic Times, New Delhi, 9 February 2009.

30

Lessons and Red Herrings

The 'Great Moderation' preceding the current crisis turned out to be simply the proverbial calm before the storm. It seems odd, even appalling, that economists, policy makers and multilateral surveillance bodies like the International Monetary Fund (IMF) should not have seen the storm coming, especially since the calm was associated with several macroeconomic anomalies.

The dot-com boom and burst had shown, even prior to the housing boom, that asset prices were widely out of sync with consumer prices that remained remarkably stable. The latter were not responding as expected to rising liquidity, and even to rising input prices. The link between growth and employment was weakening. Mounting trade and budget deficits were not translating into inflation, higher interest rates and currency depreciation as expected. The need for bail-out of hedge funds, such as Long Term Capital Management, was a pointer to the build up of systemically critical risk and leverage outside the regulated financial system.

The Great Moderation was therefore an indication that rapid, multi-layered global integration was redefining acknowledged relationships and challenging established economic paradigms. Since macroeconomic policy did not adjust to changing winds, is it surprising that it found itself trapped in the approaching 'perfect storm' that is now widely believed to be the greatest threat to the international economy since the Great Depression of the 1930s?

The US sub-prime housing crisis was by consensus the proximate trigger of this perfect storm, whose ultimate genesis is attributed to a complex interplay of several factors such as global imbalances, monetary policy, regulatory failure, financial innovation and globalization. It is perhaps time to separate grain from chaff, or causes from distractive red herrings, if we are to put in place new structures to prevent similar crises in future.

The 'new mercantilism', where hard currency acquisition through exports is targeted as the conscious objective of national policy just as gold was a few centuries ago, no doubt has harmful consequences, including to other emerging market economies for which they create enormous competitive disadvantages. However, there have been global imbalances in the past, as the marginal propensity of countries to save and consume varies according to cultural preferences and their phase of development. The proximate problem was consequently the failure to manage the fallout of imbalances. The failure was both monetary and regulatory.

Global imbalances led to excessive liquidity that drove down long-term interest rates, particularly in the US. This encouraged excessive risk taking to increase returns. This should have raised regulatory red flags but did not. Why? Most central banks have over the years moved away from targeting monetary aggregates to targeting inflation. The red flag did go up, in the form of asset price inflation, but central banks were not looking in that direction.

This was because the conventional measure of inflation is consumer prices, which were remarkably stable on account of rapid globalization. Excess liquidity was re-directed towards non-tradable assets, particularly the housing sector, which witnessed an unprecedented boom. Alan Greenspan, once the doyen amongst central bankers, was of the view that central banks could not detect asset price bubbles and therefore were ill advised to prick them. They could only clean up the mess afterwards. It so turned out that the mess was too big for the Federal Reserve (Fed) to clean up. There was, consequently, a failure of inflation targeting on the part of central banks.

As Adam Smith observed long ago, a house generates no income of its own, and has to be ultimately paid out of current income earned in the real economy. When a huge gap opens up between income growth in the real economy and the financial sector, central banks need to take note. The problem is not that inflation targeting is ineffectual but that the measurement of inflation needs to change. The Taylor equation needs to be tweaked to accommodate asset price inflation.

Practically every financial crisis has been preceded by runaway credit creation. Recognising this, circuit breakers and liquidity buffers have evolved over the years, but proved both too pro-cyclical (as risks typically decline during booms) and too micro-regulatory (addressing only risks relating to individual lending institutions). We need to get back to basics by treating the financial system as a handmaiden of the real economy and should not allow it to run amuck through excessive leveraging.

Although sub-prime lending was risky, lenders were able to take the associated risks off their balance sheets through the securitisation route. The moral hazard inherent in this originate-to-distribute model is that lending standards can become lax since associated risks could be passed on. Securitisation, however, has long been an article of belief in the financial sector, with a trade-off between return and risk. And the solution does not lie in banning complex innovative products, but in ensuring that risky investments are conservatively leveraged with adequate equity buffers to cover losses, and in optimising trading mechanisms to make such products liquid through standardisation and centralised, mandatory market clearing mechanisms.

Since globalization amplified the crisis through monetary and regulatory arbitrage and through cross-border trade and investment linkages, it too has come in for blame and flak. But it is globalization that lies behind surges in productivity and unparalleled growth.

One of the lessons of the current crisis is that growing trade and investment linkages are fast blunting time-tested macroeconomic policy tools as fiscal, monetary and financial policies now need to be coordinated across countries in order to be effective. Yet the institutional framework for such global governance lags far behind economic reality. It would however be impossible to design such institutions without an inclusive global financial architecture of all systemically important economies through a radical reform of the Bretton Wood institutions. Only then can the subject of a global regulator, necessary to prevent monetary and regulatory arbitrage, and a mechanism for dealing with failed cross-border institutions be conceivable, as this involves ceding sovereign space. Until this happens, we can at best think in terms of national monitoring and implementation of globally agreed regulatory principles that is currently engaging the attention of the G20.

The Financial Express, New Delhi, 27 April 2009.

31

Asia: The Aftermath of Crisis

Now that the worst of the global financial crisis is possibly behind us, the time is perhaps opportune to reflect on where Asia stands at the current juncture. High levels of global integration initially saw double-digit quarterly declines in GDP (gross domestic product) in some small Asian economies induced by external trade shock. Recovery, however, has been equally remarkable. Asia seems on the whole to have weathered the financial crisis better than a decade ago, and also better than developed countries. Consequently, the crisis has only served to accelerate the recent trend in convergence in per capita incomes between the West and Asia. Why?

It would be a serious mistake to attribute the bounce-back to decoupling which is a contradiction in terms in an increasingly globalising world. There has no doubt been a robust increase in recent times in intra-Asian trade, but much of this is in primary and intermediate goods that feed final consumer demand in high-income Organisation for Economic Co-operation and Development (OECD) countries. Fiscal support measures and rebuilding inventories in western economies have aided this recovery that could be severely tested in the event of a double dip in OECD countries. Of course, the fact that the two fastest-growing major economies are located in the region also aided the recovery. Some of the smaller dynamic economies are recovering rapidly on their coattails.

Difference in policy response is a more plausible explanation. Both advanced and emerging markets resorted to aggressive monetary and fiscal policies to counter the unprecedented crisis. Transmission channels of monetary policy, for long the first line of macroeconomic defence, collapsed in OECD countries. Although monetary policy transmission has traditionally been weak in emerging markets on account of its unsophisticated financial markets, these channels never became impotent. Unlike western countries, there was no need to fall back almost exclusively on fiscal policy, as both orthodox monetary and fiscal policies worked in tandem. For the same reason, the crisis has not battered public finances in the fashion of western economies.

Being first off the block, it is also likely that exit policies would be implemented first in Asia. As elsewhere, the timing and sequencing of exit strategies is critical. Unlike western markets, where the IMF has advised that fiscal exit should precede monetary exit on account of the unsustainable accumulation of public debt, the sequence may well be reversed in Asia, for two good reasons. Firstly, sustained and unorthodox monetary easing in western markets is drowning emerging markets in liquidity through a surge in capital flows. Secondly, public finances are not as strained in Asia as they are in western economies.

The implementation of exit strategies in developed markets is likely to reduce the surge in capital flows to Asia. A decade ago, a sudden stop could have endangered growth. But this is no longer the case since Asian economies have since accumulated a huge war chest of hard currency reserves.

If anything, monetary tightening in western countries might ease the pressure on asset prices, monetary policy and exchange rate appreciation, and therefore, actually prove beneficial. Moreover, exit policies in developed markets would signal the revival of private demand, which is critical for the return to trend growth in Asia that has mostly been affected through the trade channel.

It is too early to tell whether the recent crisis would lead to fundamental structural shifts in Asia through a substantial unwinding of global imbalances. Mercantilist exchange rate policies in Asian countries have not fundamentally changed.

Weighed down by wealth losses, threat of default and high unemployment rates, the US consumer may be retrenching and returning to saving habits. This saving is, however, counterbalanced by the increase in government deficits. These deficits are unsustainable over even the medium term, unless surplus economies fund these with the same alacrity as they funded leveraged private consumption. Otherwise, there would be a permanent decline in global trend growth as it is difficult to envisage, on current trends, that Asian consumption would increase so much so soon to make up the entire slack. Consequently, there is a real threat that Asian trend growth could drift lower.

It is difficult to say at this point in time whether the recent decline in the value of the dollar is structural or simply on account of the revival of risk appetite in the aftermath of the global financial crisis. Arguably the crisis has only strengthened its safe-haven status, and the first whiff of crisis or monetary tightening by the Fed could easily reverse the declining trend. If global imbalances are to unwind, the dollar would need to depreciate in an orderly manner. However, if the Chinese renminbi remains effectively pegged to the dollar, Asian countries could suffer from the double whammy of a declining dollar and renminbi that would not only devalue their hard currency reserves, mostly parked in dollars, but also adversely affect the export competitiveness that is their engine of growth.

There is consequently a real danger that instead of unwinding, as the global economy recovers, both major surplus and deficit economies are tempted to return to old ways, as this could lead to a quick return to the former levels of high growth. Imbalances will not go away easily, as they are also partly cultural—Angela Merkel's thrifty 'Swabian housewife!'—and also structural, as fast-growing young societies have a marginal tendency to save, just as slow-growing aged societies have a marginal tendency to consume. Arguably, household consumption in Asian economies can increase if the compulsion of households to save for retirement and for episodes of unemployment is reduced by putting comprehensive social security systems in place.

Is it possible to mitigate the risks associated with global imbalances that brought the global economy to the brink of financial Armageddon? Much hinges on the retrofitting of the financial system that is currently underway under the watchful eyes of the G20. But therein lies a paradox. If the financial system is to be truly inoculated against risky lending practices and hyper leverage, it might be difficult to recycle surpluses to private consumption on anywhere near the scale seen in the recent past. The other alternative is to recycle them to emerging market stocks, or to developed country governments, who may otherwise have to inflate their way out of unsustainable debt.

What do ongoing reforms in the financial system mean for Asia? Its financial system held up well during the crisis because it was conservatively regulated on the assumption that it should be handmaiden to the real economy. Some of the more hotly debated regulatory issues within the Financial Stability Board (FSB), such as bank recapitalisation, liquidity buffers, extending the perimeters of regulation and compensation practices, have little immediate relevance for highly regulated deposit-based Asian financial systems that already operate as utilities. The major concerns at this stage are not regulatory but developmental, such as financial repression, financial inclusion, reducing the cost of capital, long-term finance for infrastructure and development of private bond markets that can make transmission of monetary policy actions more effective.

While being mindful of pitfalls that lie ahead, most clearly brought out in the animated debated within and without the Financial Stability Board, failure to move ahead with development of the financial sector could make their companies less competitive going forward. Globally competitive corporates in Asian countries kept capital costs low by accessing either subsidised finance at home or cheaper finance from overseas. To the extent that higher capital requirements in western banks will increase borrowing spreads on external commercial loans in Asia, this 'safety valve' could be partly shut. Higher capital norms at home, when not really required, would only further increase the cost of domestic finance.

To conclude, Asia's rapid recovery is not because of decoupling but because both fiscal and policy transmissions worked better. For the same reason, public debt has not risen as steeply. Exit policies will likely be implemented in Asia first, and monetary exit will likely precede fiscal.

Going forward, since global imbalances may not easily abate, Asia may have to live with lower trend growth. Finally, developmental, not regulatory, issues are more relevant for the Asian financial sector presently.

The Economic Times, New Delhi, 18 January 2010 .

32

Euro Zone's Impossible Trinity

The economic and monetary union of the European Union had a basic flaw: monetary integration without fiscal union. This flaw was derived from the 'impossible trinity' embedded in the Mundell-Fleming equation. According to this equation, a country can have only two of the following: an open capital account, a stable exchange rate and monetary independence.

While several developing countries, including India, have at times tried—with little success—to get around this impossible trinity, countries have mostly adopted different solutions to this equation. Thus, the United States (US) has an open capital account, independent monetary policy but a floating exchange rate (India's solution largely resembles this model with a big BUT). China has adopted a stable exchange rate, independent monetary policy but a closed capital account. The Euro zone solution to the equation was to have a fixed exchange rate and an open capital account, while it sacrificed monetary independence.

Given the solution adopted by Euro zone countries, fiscal balances needed to be kept in check because there was no lender of the last resort. This was done by setting a budget deficit limit of 3 per cent of the GDP (gross domestic product) for each country, and public debt limit of 60 per cent of the GDP. This was critical. Although countries are expected to keep fiscal deficits and public debt within prudent limits for sustainable growth, they can never be held hostage by the market because the central bank can always step in to buy government debt by printing money. It is for this reason that credit rating agencies assign the highest ratings to sovereigns for debt repayable in their own currencies, while they rely primarily on macroeconomic fundamentals in rating external debt.

Since Euro zone countries, including Germany, did not have this central bank backstop, it is intriguing that credit rating agencies assigned risk-free status to the sovereign debt of these countries, instead of basing them on macroeconomic fundamentals. Economists and the International Monetary Fund (IMF) also seem to have missed this fine distinction between domestic debt and external debt: the domestic debt of Euro zone countries had some features of external debt, as a result of which they could be held hostage by markets, as appears to be happening at present. Had such a distinction been made, the ratings assigned to the weaker Euro zone countries would have been so calibrated as to make it difficult for them to run up such high levels of euro-denominated public debt.

What also seems to have been missed was the 'impossibility' of the holy trinity attempted by the European Maastricht Treaty: a currency union with 'no bailout, no exit and no default' in the event of the public debt of a Euro zone country becoming unsustainable through a market revolt.

It is perhaps because this second, but related, impossible trinity was not highlighted by economists, the IMF and even rating agencies that markets were lulled into pricing the sovereign domestic debt of all Euro zone countries on an equal footing as risk-free, despite vastly differing macroeconomic fundamentals. In hindsight, it is now clear that:

(a) If there was to be no bail-out and no exit, a country might have to default on its debt since it could not inflate its way out through the printing press.

(b) If there was to be no bail-out and no default, a country might need to exit to regain monetary independence to enable it to honour its debt obligations through a depreciated new currency that its central bank could print at will.

(c) Finally, there was to be no exit and no default, a country would need to be bailed out through either budgetary support from other countries (such as through the European Financial Stability Facility) or the common central bank (the European Central Bank or ECB) acting as a lender of the last resort.

The impossible trinity attempted by the Maastricht Treaty now threatens to bring down not only the Euro zone but also the global financial system, unless one of the three nays is abandoned. This alone would rectify the fatal flaw in the Maastricht Treaty, short of full fiscal and monetary—which effectively means political—integration for which European civil society is not quite prepared yet. And Germany would not allow the ECB to become a printing press without such integration—for good reasons.

Business Standard, New Delhi, 24 November 2011.

33

Waiting for the ECB and 'Big Bertha'

The first of the International Monetary Fund (IMF) articles of agreement provides for temporary liquidity support to its membership for stabilising a country's external payments. There is no provision for providing such support to stabilise a member's domestic debt. Why then is the IMF providing support to countries in the Euro zone, whose problems are ostensibly fiscal?

While a country can of course choose to renege on both its external and domestic debt, a country need never be hostage to the markets for funding its domestic debt because of the unlimited central bank backstop, including the printing press, through which it can inflate its way out. This may trigger domestic macroeconomic instability, but monetary and fiscal policies will not spill over externally, unless there is a large external demand for its domestic currency.

The central bank backstop however cannot insulate a country against unsustainable external imbalances, as it cannot print its way out to finance deficits denominated in reserve currencies. When a country loses market access to fund external liabilities, it may need to turn to the IMF, the external lender of last resort, which provides liquidity support to countries as they adjust their external payments position towards the sustainable.

The distinction between external and domestic debt is of little relevance, however, in the case of the four freely convertible international reserve currencies (the US dollar, sterling, the euro and the yen) because their domestic currencies are also international reserve currencies with a large external demand that enables them to run large external and domestic deficits—both of which are denominated in the same currency—with apparent impunity. Thus,

Japan's high fiscal deficits and debt, and America's large twin deficits have not had a commensurate impact on their borrowing costs or the values of their currencies.

In short, reserve-issuing countries have an additional policy lever in that they can use domestic monetary policy to finance external imbalances and also sustain higher levels of domestic debt. This lever has become increasingly potent on account of the proliferation in financial assets that now dwarf real economy flows. This is why these large economies, which account for over 50 per cent of global GDP (gross domestic product) at market exchange rates, do not turn to the IMF for liquidity support.

In recent years, large emerging markets that account for a substantial chunk of the remaining global GDP have accumulated huge international reserves. This self-insurance has made it unlikely that they would need to turn to the IMF for liquidity support in the foreseeable future.

The potential needs of the remaining countries are limited in size, as they account for a relatively small share of global GDP. This explains why the global firewall maintained by the IMF for combating crises was relatively small, at about $250 billion, prior to the global financial crisis.

The IMF's resources have however been increased by almost five times over the last few years. This is primarily on account of the potential needs of the large Euro zone, which accounts for almost a fifth of the global economy.

As pointed out, reserve currency countries do not ordinarily need liquidity support from the IMF. However, if a reserve currency-issuing area is a monetary union of independent sovereign states, the situation can change dramatically.

If such a monetary union were to have a common central bank that provided unlimited liquidity backstop to sovereigns there would be no problem. The problem arises when each country has its own central bank which cannot issue its own currency, over which the European Central Bank (ECB) has a monopoly. In such a situation the domestic debt of the government takes on the characteristics of external debt. This is precisely what has happened in Euro zone countries, compelling them, *inter alia*, to turn to other Euro zone countries, the ECB and the IMF for providing liquidity support for domestic adjustment as their fiscal deficits and debt ballooned out of control and they lost market access to their own currency.

There is no provision in Euro zone treaties for member countries or the ECB to bail out individual countries; they are expected to maintain the fiscal discipline necessary to enjoy continued market access to finance deficits. However, as the deficits and debt of some peripheral countries spun out of control, and they lost market access, member countries were compelled to bail them out through a hastily devised temporary European Financial Stability Fund (EFSF), later expanded into the permanent European Stability Mechanism (ESM). The ECB was also constrained to lend to European banks to enable them to buy troubled sovereign bonds, assuming the role of the central bank backstop through its one-time Long Term Refinancing Operations (LTROs) to prevent a break-up of the Euro zone. More controversially, the IMF has played a supplementary role by providing additional funds.

The recent increase in the European and IMF firewalls and the LTRO helped stabilise sovereign bond markets in the euro periphery. Markets are however turning nervous once again, pushing up the yields on Spanish and Italian sovereign bonds. Markets fear that these two large economies, with a cumulative public debt of about \$3.5 trillion, are too big for the ESM and IMF to bail-out through their recently enhanced aggregate 'big bazooka' firewall of about \$2 trillion. There is likely to be little appetite for continually increasing the size of this global firewall. The credibility of the bazooka is also in question because it may be difficult to meet the usual IMF conditionalities on the one hand—while most of the Euro zone firewall is a pie in the sky that would need to be raised from markets precisely when they are revolting.

If peripheral sovereign yields continue to widen, the ECB may be compelled to repeatedly intervene to maintain integrity of the European Monetary Union and thereby become the *de facto* central bank backstop. The markets recognise that the ESM and IMF firewalls are mere field artillery, and the real 'big bazooka'—the Big Bertha so to speak, with the unlimited capacity to fund sovereigns—is the ECB. The big question is whether, in the likely absence of commensurate economic growth and willingness of member countries to share the losses, much of the liabilities assumed by the ECB in the process would eventually have to be inflated away, as in the case of all unsustainable domestic debt, or whether the external demand for the euro would help cushion most of the losses.

Business Standard, New Delhi, 6 May 2012.

34

Global Financial Crisis on its Sixth Birthday

The credit freeze associated with the global financial crisis is usually traced to the collapse of Lehman Brothers in September 2008. Many observers hold that but for the monumental failure to bail it out, the crisis may never have occurred. Be it as it may, the New Year marks the sixth year since tremors from the sub-prime segment in the US housing market were first felt in financial markets. These came to a head in August 2007 with a crisis of confidence in the interbank market reflected in a sharp widening in TED (difference between interest rates on 3 months US treasury bonds and 3 months Euro dollar LIBOR) and OIS (overnight indexed swaps) spreads, widely acknowledged as a measure of health of the banking system.

The crisis of structured finance was apparent by early 2008, but not yet of financial intermediation itself. Economic growth was still strong. There were lingering doubts whether the so-called sub-prime crisis would significantly impact the real economy. Sub-prime was only a small segment of the US housing sector in a putatively deep financial market.

Ben Bernanke, Chairman of the US Federal Reserve (Fed), who presciently took preventive action to ward off deflation by aggressively lowering interest rates even as the European Central Bank (ECB) was still fighting inflation, told the US Congress in August 2007 that toxic assets were in the region of only $150 billion.

The collapse of Lehman Brothers in September 2008 put paid to all optimism. The collapse of western financial intermediation fell like a sledgehammer on the global economy, pushing it into recession and a synchronised downturn.

During several quarters following the collapse of Lehman Brothers, it appeared from charts on industrial output, trade and asset prices put out periodically by Barry Eichengreen on the *vox.eu* website that the global economy was headed for a second Great Depression. What pulled the global economy back from the brink?

In hindsight, it appears that there were three major saviours, famously coordinated by a resurgent G20. First, Helicopter Ben, the eminent historian of the Great Depression, by happenstance at the helm of the US Fed, neutralised the rapid deleveraging and fall in the velocity of money circulation through aggressive quantitative easing to prevent deflation that was a defining feature of the Great Depression.

Second, the long shadow cast on macroeconomic policy by Lord Maynard Keynes countervailed the sharp contraction of private demand through an aggressive expansion of public demand. This stalled a freefall in national income that was the second defining feature of the Great Depression.

Third, Jim O'Neill of Goldman Sachs had given advance notice of the rebalancing that was rapidly increasing the share of large emerging markets in the global economy. During the Great Depression, the colonies were so dependent on demand in western economies that they were sucked into recession. Although their growth suffered on the margin this time round, they continued to grow relatively strongly and remained solid nodes of stability in the global economy.

These causes were only proximate as most observers pointed to deeper ultimate causes. First, mounting global imbalances and the associated savings glut put downward pressure on interest rates, veered monetary policy off the tried and trusted Taylor rule, and incentivised leverage by falling returns to capital that inflated asset bubbles.

Second, financial deregulation facilitated regulatory arbitrage that pushed financial activity to lightly regulated shadows. Unlike during the Great Depression, financial panic did not emanate from conventional deposit-based banking but from a shadow banking system linked to deposit banking through off-balance sheet vehicles.

Observers also pointed to a third ultimate cause, namely the moral hazards of government policy that lowered credit standards to promote inclusive house ownership.

This potent brew was fortified by a fourth toxin. Some Euro zone governments exploited a birth defect in the European Monetary Union to overextend their balance sheets. Markets failed to distinguish between countries with weak and strong balance sheets even though there were explicit provisions against bail-outs in the Maastricht Treaty on one hand, and no central bank backstops on the other. Markets assumed—and they may well be proved right—that stronger countries would eventually bail-out weaker ones.

Underlying the Euro crisis was an increase in both private debt (reminiscent of the US housing bubble, such as in Spain and Ireland) and public debt (as in Greece, and partly Portugal). Unlike Greece, both Spain and Ireland went into the crisis with low and declining public debt/GDP (gross domestic product) ratios. These ratios deteriorated rapidly on account of the need to bail-out (private) banks. The fiscal burden was greater because unlike the US, European banks dwarfed the GDP of individual European sovereigns. As governments scrambled to bail out their financial systems, while simultaneously trying to stimulate their economies against a backdrop of falling revenues, the crisis of public finance became more generalised. Both private and public balance sheets came under greater market scrutiny.

Although public balance sheets in advanced countries outside the Euro zone are also overstretched, a combination of central bank backstops and weak private demand is presently keeping their borrowing costs low. There is growing realisation however that ageing societies with falling growth and generous social contracts will find it more difficult than in the past to grow their way out of high levels of public debt. The Euro crisis has only anticipated a generalised structural crisis in public finance in advanced economies. This is a problem that even the US needs to speedily address, and also developing countries like India that are designing social contracts. Europe illustrates how politically difficult it is to renegotiate such contracts once they are in place.

The recovery of 2010 was short lived and asymmetric. To what extent can this be attributed to differences in policy response? The recovery is more robust in the US, which has also had the most aggressive and sustained policy stimulus. In retrospect, ECB's monetary policy response has been no less dramatic, although it was slower off the blocks. On balance, while non-conventional monetary policy may have prevented deflation, it has also led to a liquidity trap that has emasculated monetary policy and financial intermediation on both sides of the Atlantic. The experience of the Japanese who invented quantitative easing in the 1990s was no better. This is constraining the US to increasingly rely on a policy tool—fiscal policy—discredited by its political overtones.

The Euro zone has lapsed into a double dip recession. The US recovery remains tepid and uncertain. It could plausibly be argued that the asymmetric recovery is on account of design flaws that deprive Euro zone countries of policy tools, such as exchange rate and fiscal space. The International Monetary Fund (IMF) has recently estimated that fiscal multipliers are unusually large because of weak private demand and liquidity trap. We are still far from the endgame.

Historical experience shows that recovery from balance sheet recessions is long and painful. Since high debt was the original sin, it is arguable whether transfer of debt from private to public and tepid growth is a more sustainable combination than accelerated deleveraging and painful adjustment upfront. Hazards associated with withdrawal of policy life support on the revival of private demand dangle overhead like the Damocles Sword. High levels of public debt and monetary expansion could quickly translate into unsustainable debt dynamics through rising interest rates, and inflationary outcomes through acceleration of the money multiplier. The jury is still out on whether continued stimulus or greater austerity can better drive a sustainable recovery, and whether advanced western economies can avoid a return to financial repression.

The Economic Times, New Delhi, 21 January 2013.

35

The Crisis in Global Governance

The roots of globalization as it is commonly understood can be traced to the great age of European Enlightenment and discovery, beginning with vast improvements in maritime and military technology from the second half of the last millennium.

In its second stage, globalization accelerated with the Industrial Revolution in the 19th century that facilitated faster mobility on a mass scale inconceivable with animal and wind traction. It also opened up a big technological gap between the west and the rest—the great divergence—that saw uprooting of the great civilisations and mighty agrarian empires in Asia and the Americas. Globalization through colonial integration accentuated age-old intra-European rivalries and culminated in the 20th century with the first global wars.

A globalising world needs global institutions of governance. The first such institution was arguably the Papacy, but it was soon undermined first by the Spanish Emperor, and then by the Henrican Reformation in England.

The Concert of Europe was the second attempt at global governance, spawned in the early 19th century in the wake of the Napoleonic Wars, to maintain peace in Europe through a balance of power. After maintaining peace for several decades, the Concert broke down towards end of the 19th century on account of inability of the old European powers to accommodate the rise of a new great power, namely Germany united by Bismarck. Germany was integrated into global governance only after two catastrophic world wars.

The Concert of Europe notwithstanding, global governance in the 19th century was dominated by England, the pre-eminent industrial and global hegemon instrumental in defeating Napoleon. Likewise, the institutions of global governance in the post-war period, with the (mostly European) G7 at their epicentre, are dominated by the

United States (US) that replaced Great Britain as the new global power instrumental in defeating the axis powers in both the world wars.

In the post-war period, it became increasingly clear that participation in global governance depended on economic size, in turn a combination of demographic size and level of industrialisation. This is what made Germany, Canada and Japan automatic members of the G7. But the G7 shared other attributes as well. They all had high per capita incomes, were open economies and societies, and technologically dynamic. At the core of the G7 Charter of 1975 was the notion of 'shared beliefs and responsibilities'.

Only the US currently combines large demographic size with high per capita income. The EU/Eurozone, which incorporates a number of smaller high income countries, matches it, but does not always work as a coherent political entity.

The third stage of globalization beginning from 1970s started reversing the Great Divergence, a process accelerated by hyper growth in big emerging powers like China and India. These are middle-income countries whose aggregate GDP (gross domestic product) now matches those of G7 countries (other than the US) because of their demographic size. They may also rival the US in aggregate GDP in the near future. Other big developing countries, such as Brazil, Indonesia and Nigeria, might also catch up. The question that arises is how would these emerging economic powers be integrated into institutions of global governance?

The G7, like the Concert, is a nimble, informal institution dominated by summits where leaders sit across the table and discuss and thrash out major issues. Formal, treaty-based inclusive institutions of global governance, that formulate rules of global engagement, such as the UN, WTO, IMF, WB, UNFCCC, BIS, FSB etc., are post-war phenomena that meet at ministerial level. They are slow moving bureaucratic silos, devoted to a single object.

Despite their inclusive membership, formal institutions of global governance are all dominated by the G7, through special bodies (such as the security council) or through their shareholding structures. There is reluctance on the part of the existing powers to downsize and cede shares to the rising powers. They perhaps have the confidence to do so on account of their stranglehold on the international monetary system and of technological innovation that has driven globalization all along, now ring-fenced by a stringent intellectual property rights regime. These institutions are consequently losing their legitimacy, as the rising powers are increasingly unwilling to abide by rules effectively set by G7 countries.

This has created a crisis in global governance, with formal treaty-based institutions becoming dysfunctional and less influential, which is reflected in stalemates in multilateral international trade and climate change negotiations on one hand, and the rise of plurilateral arrangements on the other.

Where do we go from here, and can history be a guide?

First, the experience with Germany in the late 19th and early 20th centuries is a warning from history regarding the perils ahead if rising powers are not accommodated within institutions of global governance.

Second, the G7 recently reached out to co-opt major developing countries, especially the BRICS (Brazil, Russia, India, China and South Africa), into the informal global economic governance structure through the Heiligendamm process and more recently by upgrading the G20 to summit level.

Third, formal institutions need to be aligned to the informal governance structure, even though the G20 needs to encompass non-economic issues as well. Any asymmetry in this regard would make the G20 dysfunctional and irrelevant as the emerging powers might lose interest and form their own parallel institutions instead of taking greater responsibility for global outcomes through the G20. In its present form, the G20 works as a coalition of pressure groups such as the G7, BRICS and MIKTA (Mexico, Indonesia, Korea, Turkey and Australia). Only the G7 has a sense of shared responsibility. The BRICS still believe in 'common but differentiated responsibilities' that puts the onus on G7 for equitable and optimal global outcomes.

Fourth, the fragmentation of global governance has already begun through Chinese initiatives on multilateralisation of the Chiang Mai Initiative, the Asian Infrastructure Investment Bank, and the New Silk Road; BRICS initiatives on the New Development Bank and the

Contingent Reserve Arrangement; and the US initiatives on the Trans-Pacific and Transatlantic Trade and Investment Partnerships.

Fifth, post-war institutions of global governance have been dominated by powers that believed in open markets and open societies. The new powers believe in keeping international markets open, as these determine their economic rise, but few are open societies. Civil society in G7 countries on the other hand increasingly sees itself as a victim of globalization, rather than as its first beneficiary. What does all this augur for the shape of global governance in future?

IV

The Coordinated Policy Response

Rise and Decline of the G20

And if a house be divided against itself, that house cannot stand.

The Gospel according to St. Mark, 3:25

36

Global Financial Crisis and Economic Policy

The macroeconomic response to the recent crisis is tempered by lessons learnt from the Great Depression, and the use of policy tools following the shift from the gold standard to the fixed exchange rate Bretton Woods System and finally to the free-float fiat money system. This has enabled central banks and governments to by and large eschew the cardinal sins, such as contractionary monetary and fiscal policies, and the kind of extreme protectionism embodied in the infamous Smoot-Hawley tariffs of the 1930s, that culminated in the Great Depression. It would be well to consider what is at stake. The economic and social disruption caused by the Great Depression facilitated the rise of fascism in Europe and culminated in war. While President Roosevelt's New Deal partly helped, fiscal stimulus was counterbalanced by concerns over mounting deficits. It was the destructive fiscal stimulus provided by World War II—the war economy—that finally put growth back on track.

Theoretically, Keynesian demand management policies should not be overly inflationary, since fiscal expansion merely substitutes for the contraction in private demand. In practice, governments tried to push the envelope and over-stimulate the economy, and central banks, no longer constrained by the gold standard, accommodated the expansion through issue of fiat currency (monetising the deficit), thereby making fiscal policies inflationary. The *reductio ad absurdum* was reached in the 1970s, following the oil price hike, when fiscal policies failed to adjust appropriately, leading to hyper-inflation even as growth remained below trend ('stagflation'), destabilising the widely acclaimed Phillips curve trade-off between growth and inflation.

Milton Friedman and the Chicago School sounded the death knell of Keynesian economics by placing monetary policy at the heart of macroeconomic policy. It was Paul Volcker's monetarism that finally slew the dragon of hyper-inflation. Over time, monetary policy tools have become rule-bound. The US Federal Reserve (Fed) has by and large followed the Taylor Rule, adjusting short-term interest rates to attain targeted inflation and trend growth.

There are, however, limits to the use of rule-based monetary policy, since interest rates cannot dip below zero. These limits are breached as inflation rates drop and the output gap grows, and there is little demand for money even when the central bank discount rates are zero-bound. This is the liquidity trap, into which Japan fell in the 1990s, and arguably the US in the wake of the recent global financial crisis. Ben Bernanke, current chairman of the US Fed and a historian of the Great Depression, postulated that in these circumstances central banks are constrained to resort to unconventional monetary policy, expanding money supply not only through its discount window, but also through purchase of government (quantitative easing) and/or private (credit easing) assets, giving him the epithet of 'Helicopter Ben,' as this is tantamount to dropping money by helicopter.

In a true liquidity trap, however, neither conventional nor unconventional monetary policy works, as monetary policy transmission channels break down altogether. In these circumstances, macroeconomic policy is constrained to fall back on fiscal policy, as in Japan since the 1990s and in the US and much of the developed world currently, to pull the economy out of crisis.

Accelerated globalization has also queered the pitch for both monetary and fiscal policies, since their national scope is blunted by cross-border spillovers through financial and trading channels. Alan Greenspan, erstwhile Chairman of the US Fed, famously remarked that the Fed was losing control of long-term interest rates. To a great extent, this surge in cross-border flows is associated with exchange rate interventions on an epic scale, in what has come to be called 'Bretton Woods II,' and consequential build-up of global imbalances. Global integration makes monetary policy impact the price of domestic asset markets much more than traded goods and services that comprise consumer price indices targeted by central banks. Thus, loose monetary policy in the US in the run-up to the crisis led to asset price inflation, even as consumer prices remained stable. Fiscal policies also leak abroad and are less effective in stimulating domestic demand.

It is difficult at this point in time, with little benefit of hindsight, to determine whether we are passing through yet another financial crisis that has punctuated economic history from time to time, or that globalising forces have forced a historic tipping point that will change macroeconomic policy in fundamental ways.

Firstly, the severity of the recent financial crisis is at least in part due to the fact that macroeconomic policy did not adjust to globalization. Recognising this blunting of macroeconomic policy tools, the G20 has been co-ordinating policies of systemically important economies, so as to make them more effective.

Secondly, the crisis has underscored the limits of monetary policy, and endowed fiscal policy with the new-found halo of macroeconomic tool of last resort. If aggressive fiscal policy can put the economy back on the path to sustainable growth quickly enough, it can be practically self-funded through the rise in revenue. Conventional wisdom on the efficacy of fiscal policy is however discouraging, for it has worked only where it was timely, temporary and targeted. Political economy considerations make such a happy confluence challenging. A protracted recession moreover queers the pitch for fiscal policy through a rapid and unsustainable rise in public debt, leading to a 'Domar' debt trap. In such an event, governments may have no alternative but to inflate their way out.

Japan was able to fund persistent deficits that has seen public debt rise to twice its GDP, since public dis-saving was offset by private savings through large current account surpluses. This would not have been possible in a globally synchronised downturn, such as what prevails presently. US deficits, on the other hand, have access to the glut in overseas savings as issuer of the global reserve currency. Other countries follow the unique Japanese and US models at their own peril.

Thirdly, although the origin of modern central banking—certainly of the US Federal system—was primarily in response to financial panics and instability in the opening decades of the 20th century, this has over the years been overlaid by the imperative to stabilise growth.

The recent global financial crisis has however drawn attention back to the original mandate of central banks. Consequently, while remaining the first line of defence in stabilising growth, monetary policy is likely to move from simple consumer inflation targeting to also explicitly target asset prices, thereby ensuring financial stability. Since short-term interest rates may be too blunt an instrument for targeting asset prices, additional instruments may be necessary. Arguably, monetary policy could have two separate targets and instruments: targeting liquidity through short-term interest rates and targeting financial instability induced by hyper-leverage through regulation.

Business Standard, New Delhi, 28 February 2010.

37

Seoul-searching in G20

The proximate trigger for the trans-Atlantic financial crisis lay in the US sub-prime housing market. Most analysts, however, trace the ultimate origins of the crisis to the interrelated phenomena of weaknesses in financial regulation and monetary policy in advanced markets on one hand, and to the build-up of global imbalances on an epic scale on the other.

The most concerted response to the global financial crisis, that may have averted a second Great Depression, came from the G20, which has since assumed the mantle of the premier multilateral forum for economic cooperation. Eminently successful in crisis situations, going forward, the challenge before the G20 lies in proving its efficacy in addressing structural issues in non-crisis situations.

The "Framework for Strong, Sustainable and Balanced Growth," agreed upon by G20 leaders at their fourth Summit in Toronto in July 2010, needs to be perceived against such a backdrop. Groups of advanced and emerging surplus and deficit countries committed to appropriate baskets of policy actions to reduce imbalances and raise potential growth. Since country circumstances within the same group can vary, they also agreed that at their fifth Summit in Seoul in November 2010, they would commit to country-specific policies to further refine the framework.

The assumption in the framework exercise is that future risks to the global economy would be considerably mitigated if countries moved towards external balance. Since much of the demand behind high global growth in the period preceding the crisis came from leveraged consumption in advanced deficit countries, it is also assumed that as such countries move towards greater external balance and clean up their financial systems, global growth could decline permanently, unless structural policies, such as those recommended by the Organisation for Economic Co-operation and Development (OECD) in its "Going for Growth" framework, are implemented to raise the growth potential of all, but particularly advanced economies.

Despite this ambitious exercise, the International Monetary Fund (IMF) expects global imbalances to widen further rather than wane. Moreover, there needs to be a single storyline that is consistent with imbalances, growth, development, climate change, demographic transition and fiscal consolidation—all of which are being debated directly or indirectly within the G20.

Implicit in the framework is the assumption that growth and development should primarily be based on domestic savings. However, according to traditional development economics, developing countries should run current account deficits (CADs)to top up domestic savings with external savings for boosting investment. The size of the deficit should, of course, be prudent and sustainable, or contained at levels that can reasonably be expected to be funded over the medium to long term. There could be liquidity crises from time to time, deriving from financial shocks and consequential sudden stops, but the IMF exists to provide liquidity backstop.

The problem arose because the equation was reversed, and developing countries started running huge current account surpluses and developed countries similarly large deficits. This led to a 'savings glut' that lowered the cost of capital, fuelling excessive consumption *via* a leveraged asset price boom in developed countries through financial innovation in a lightly regulated financial system.

If this analysis is correct, should the IMF and the G20 shift their focus from imbalances *per se* to their structure and direction? While the American and Chinese imbalances appear anomalous, it is not clear why the surpluses of Germany and Japan are a major problem. As developed countries, they should run surpluses to smoothen global developmental imbalances by generating savings for investment in developing countries. Of course, if developed countries end up exporting low-technology consumer goods, they could stifle growth in developing countries. But this is patently not the case, as both Germany and Japan increasingly specialise in high-technology/ productivity products and capital goods.

From the viewpoint of climate change too, the wisdom of advising some developed countries with high per capita incomes to further increase consumption, while at the same time inducing them to agree to stiff and binding emission cuts to create environmental space for developing countries to grow, seems contradictory.

Traditional development economics overlooked the growth dynamics of ageing. As the share of the working population shrinks, savings in developed economies can be expected to decline, although structural reforms, such as raising the age of retirement and liberal immigration policies, can stagger this process. Nevertheless, one would expect developed economies to eventually move from external surpluses to deficits, which would need to be funded through current account surpluses of either younger, newly emerged countries and/or middle income developing economies, like China.

Since America is not an advanced ageing economy, its huge deficits are anomalous. They are sustained at their present levels only through the reserve currency status of the US dollar. Being a low middle income developing country, Chinese surpluses are also anomalous and sustainable only on account of American deficits which they mirror.

To the extent American household consumption might decline through deleveraging and repair of household balance sheets, Chinese surpluses should shrink. However, the increase in US government deficits has countervailed the rise in US private savings. But such expansion cannot be sustained indefinitely, and the G20 countries have consequently separately agreed on a road map of fiscal consolidation. The moot question is: Will staggered US fiscal consolidation result in the long-awaited disorderly unwinding of global imbalances and collapse of the dollar? It is intriguing that the IMF had long anticipated a financial crisis through a disorderly unwinding of global imbalances and collapse of the dollar fuelled by private deficits. The global crisis, however, further strengthened the safe haven status of the global reserve currency. There are now even fewer signs of public deficit-fuelled imbalances weakening the global reserve currency.

It is only when public deficits in advanced countries shrink significantly can we expect global imbalances to start unwinding. This unwinding can be expected to adversely affect global trend growth

—the so-called 'New Normal'—unless difficult structural changes are effected to sustain growth in advanced deficit countries and boost domestic demand in emerging surplus countries. Such changes are politically challenging and take time to take effect. Even so, capital may continue to flow uphill and, therefore, the financial system needs to be strengthened to prevent past excesses.

Business Standard, New Delhi, 25 September 2010.

38

Infrastructure and Global Rebalancing

The imperative of global demand rebalancing requires domestic demand in emerging market economies (EMEs) to grow faster, and structural reforms to be implemented in both developed and developing countries, if the world is to return to pre-crisis levels of growth.

In this context, the Indian Prime Minister's suggestion at the Seoul G20 Summit that global imbalances could be leveraged to address developmental imbalances, including *inter alia* bridging the infrastructure deficit in developing countries, was widely welcomed.

There has been large, but uneven, investment in infrastructure in developing countries. However, the big gap with advanced countries, especially in urban infrastructure, needs to be quickly bridged. Over the next few decades, more people would move into urban areas in developing countries than the number residing in cities presently. By any measure, the financing requirements for urban infrastructure are mind-boggling. Several trillion dollars of investment is needed for orderly and environmental friendly urbanisation.

Cross-border infrastructure—broadly defined to include wholly nationally owned infrastructure with cross-border connectivity to contiguous countries—is also particularly deficient mainly due to the difficulties of burden-sharing in international cooperation and the problem of political risk. Since intra-regional trade (especially in Asia) is growing faster than the total world trade, greater cross-border connectivity is needed, particularly in South Asia, which is the least integrated region in the world.

The absorptive capacity of several developing countries, including those in Africa, which have been growing at much faster rates than before, has increased of late. Large infrastructure investments will increase national income and also make higher developing country growth rates more sustainable. This would also help converge national per capita incomes and help bridge the development gap.

Infrastructure development typically requires huge public investment. While the fiscal position of EMEs is now generally better than those of advanced countries, national budgets would nevertheless need to be substantially augmented to meet the huge demands for infrastructure.

There is a basic difference between public investment in infrastructure and most other kinds of public expenditure. The latter tends to deprive the private sector of resources that could be invested to boost growth, except during economic downturns, while public investment in infrastructure actually 'crowds in' more private investment by increasing investment opportunities and returns. It frequently involves building ahead of demand on account of its multiplier, productivity and crowding-in effects. Public borrowing for infrastructure is consequently eminently justified as it will pay for itself through higher growth and revenues.

The challenge is to direct the large savings available in the global economy, which were in the recent past directed towards unsustainable leveraged consumption in developed countries, towards infrastructure, especially urban and cross-border infrastructure, in developing countries.

However, historical experience and current trends suggest that infrastructure investment is a big challenge in the best of circumstances.

With many an advanced economy facing recession, their national budgets are in disarray and foreign aid is likely to shrink in real terms.

Since most of these excess global savings are generated in developing countries themselves, rebalancing also requires an 'enabling environment' for investment so that these savings are spent on infrastructure and not exported, especially since most accumulated savings in the EMEs remain with central banks rather than with governments.

To direct savings towards developing country infrastructure, public expenditure patterns must shift from subsidies to allocating more taxpayer funds for infrastructure investment.

Secondly, more private savings need to be attracted to infrastructure through public-private partnerships. This would entail a more enabling investment environment, especially greater political support for user charges to facilitate cost recovery, and development and deepening of financial markets including long-term finance.

Thirdly, it must be recognised that the bulk of such investments would have to be publicly funded or guaranteed, as has been the case in the past. Private investment is likely to be limited to some sectors such as telecom, transport and power. Therefore, residual, unabsorbed, private savings would need to be redirected to government debt for investment directly or indirectly in infrastructure. What level of public debt is sustainable? While this depends on potential growth and interest rates, the Domar debt sustainability equation indicates that given higher levels of growth, the public debt bearing capacity of developing countries is higher than that of the developed countries.

Fourthly, while a Greenfield international investment fund is a possibility, this would be akin to existing multilateral development banks (MDBs).

MDBs have a wealth of experience and expertise in the area of infrastructure financing to channelise global surpluses productively into financing infrastructure in the developing countries. They can mop up the global savings glut and redirect the resources to infrastructure investment, thereby shifting the utilisation of these savings from leveraged consumption to leveraged investment. This will require massive recapitalisation of MDBs, currently being resisted in certain quarters. Only a small proportion of this, however, needs to be paid up; the balance could be in the form of callable capital against which MDBs could borrow from governments and international markets, giving returns slightly higher than US Treasury Bonds.

The advantage of MDB intermediation is that this would address political and repayment risks, since governments would generally be more willing to lend to and counter guarantee MDBs than individual countries. MDBs need not pass on such large funds as project finance as this would require huge expansion of MDB staff and capacity. The same objective could be achieved through national budget programme support.

The Economic Times, New Delhi, 31 January 2011.

39

The Unfinished Business of Global Rebalancing

The G20 has won critical acclaim for coordinating an aggressive global macroeconomic policy response to the global financial crisis and averting a second Great Depression. It has since turned its attention to addressing unresolved medium- to long-term structural problems in the global economy. It is currently debating and guiding the outcomes on a wide range of important global issues. However, most of the original work is being done elsewhere, such as financial sector reform within the Financial Stability Board (FSB) and Basle system, World Bank and International Monetary Fund (IMF) reforms within the international financial institutions system, international trade within the World Trade Organisation (WTO), climate change and finance within the United Nations Framework Convention on Climate Change (UNFCCC) and anti-corruption within the United Nations Convention against Corruption (UNCAC). The Framework for Strong, Sustainable and Balanced Growth, on the other hand, is a signature initiative of the G20 where the original work is being done by the latter itself.

The issue of global rebalancing is arguably the most high profile unfinished business currently before the G20. Its credibility in addressing long-standing structural problems in the global economy arguably hinges on the success of this exercise. Global imbalances are nothing new.

They were a prominent feature of the economic landscape both preceding and following the Great Depression. According to the 'Triffin Paradox,' the issuer of the global reserve currency must necessarily have substantial external imbalances to provide global liquidity; developing countries are expected to run current account deficits (CADs) financed by surpluses of developed countries to top up domestic savings to optimise investment; as developed societies age, their savings rate can be expected to decline and consequently their current account balance may turn negative and need to be financed by capital inflows; economies with higher productivity or with large natural resources are also likely to run large surpluses.

Economic literature suggests that under a floating exchange rate regime the market penalises, and hence corrects, large CADs. However, this does not hold good for current account surpluses, as pointed out by Keynes several years ago. Nevertheless, in the absence of intervention in currency markets, the current account surplus should automatically adjust and move towards balance through an appreciation of the real exchange rate.

Floating exchange rates have however not worked to correct external imbalances for a number of reasons. Firstly, some East Asian countries, most notably China, have followed a neo-mercantilist policy of export-led growth. They have intervened in currency markets to prevent their currency from appreciating against the global reserve currency—the US dollar—despite mounting current account surpluses.

Secondly, the other major countries running big current account surpluses, namely Japan and Germany, have floating exchange rates. Japan's surplus however derives from its investment income as its trade is more or less balanced. Germany has sustained a huge current account surplus despite a floating currency because the Euro currency area has suppressed the exchange rate equilibrating mechanism. This has allowed countries with higher productivity, such as Germany, to run big surpluses, and low-income countries to run big deficits, even though the Euro area as a whole is externally balanced. Such internal imbalances have nevertheless spilled over into global financial markets. Since peripheral Euro countries have accessed global financial safety nets (IMF resources), and adversely impacted global sovereign debt markets, these imbalances cannot be treated as simply internal to the Euro area.

Thirdly, the market does not penalise the US, the major deficit country, because its domestic currency is also the global reserve currency. There is a global demand for US dollars that extends far beyond the demand for financing US CADs. The IMF has long been warning about a disorderly unwinding of global imbalances through a collapse of the dollar. However, the safe-haven status of the dollar has prevented it from depreciating in tandem with growing US external deficits. Indeed, the US dollar has become the bellwether currency, signalling the appetite for risk-taking in the global economy. Risk-aversion results in safe-haven flows and strengthening of the dollar, and *vice versa*.

Fourthly, large cross-border capital flows prevent exchange rates from responding to fundamentals even under a floating currency regime. Thus, exchange rates of countries such as India and Brazil are under upward pressure despite current account deficits, on account of large capital inflows far exceeding levels required to balance the current account.

The chief concern regarding large persistent imbalances at the present juncture is the continuing deleveraging, demand retrenchment and consequential increase in private savings in Organisation for Economic Co-operation and Development (OECD) countries. This makes it difficult to return to pre-crisis levels of growth in the absence of global demand rebalancing between developed and developing countries. The G20 framework exercise seeks agreement on indicators that would identify imbalances, as well as policy instruments that would essentially get surplus countries and the global reserve currency issuing deficit country to adjust their imbalances. It is hoped that this would put global growth back on a high growth trajectory on a sustainable basis.

Broadly speaking, there are two types of policy interventions to address large imbalances. The first is trade-based, where the entire burden of adjustment is borne by the exchange rate. The second approach focuses on the savings-investment behaviour that drives imbalances. Such behaviour can be influenced through monetary, fiscal and other structural policies, although it is generally considered to be sticky and much less amenable to policy action. Exchange rate adjustment, on the other hand, can be done through market intervention. An eclectic approach based on both approaches could be considered.

While monetary, fiscal and structural policy instruments can be used by all countries, in countries with fixed exchange rates and non-fully convertible currencies, exchange rate policy constitutes an additional critical policy lever. Recent experience with the use of fiscal and monetary policies during the global financial crisis indicates that their aggressive use can have adverse fiscal and liquidity consequences as well. The G20 would therefore need to be mindful of the possible spillover effects of policy guidelines and actions so as to correct large imbalances.

Business Standard, New Delhi, 13 February 2011.

40

It's a Long Road from Keynes to Cannes

The co-ordinated macroeconomic policy response of the G20 is widely credited with having saved the global economy from a second Great Depression. Considering that this was no ordinary cyclical recession, the almost V-shaped recovery was certainly impressive, even if tepid, especially if we keep in mind what Rogoff and Reinhart and also the International Monetary Fund (IMF) had to say about the long and painful trajectory of recovery from recessions originating in the financial and real estate sectors in the past.

In its recent *World Economic Outlook* of September 2011, appropriately entitled, *Slowing Growth, Growing Risks*, the IMF has however painted a grim picture of the current state of the global economy and financial system. These have once again entered a dangerous phase, recalling the pre-Lehman Brothers scenario. Not only is global growth weakening significantly, but financial markets, that had never quite recovered since the crisis of 2008-09, have become even more risk-averse, widely anticipating a default of Greek sovereign debt and contagion spreading to sovereigns, and banks that hold their debt, that are too big to bail-out. At the Summit at Cannes, therefore, G20 leaders were expected to co-ordinate another global rescue, perhaps even another round of short-term stimulus, while ensuring that long-term consolidation remains on track.

The current situation therefore raises the overwhelming question as to whether the G20 declared victory too early, and indeed whether the widely acclaimed co-ordinated policy response, with its focus on aggressive short-term fiscal and monetary stimulus, was appropriate.

We need to address the question as to why this V-shaped recovery was tepid in advanced countries, and why the output loss has still not been made good fully. The recovery has all along been based on extraordinary macroeconomic life support, and haunted by fears of a second dip recession.

The fact of the matter is that even as the attention of the G20 turned from short-term macroeconomic management to long-term external demand rebalancing and fiscal consolidation, the rebalancing of internal demand from the public sector to the private, which alone can make recovery sustainable, never took place. This is continuing to strain the balance sheets of both sovereigns and central banks in advanced countries. The current situation, therefore, is not entirely attributable to the Euro zone crisis.

The western recovery stands in sharp contrast to the relatively robust recovery, at least till very recently, in emerging market economies (EMEs), which used the same macroeconomic policy tools to stimulate their economies. The differential output response to the same set of policies is remarkable and needs to be explained, especially since policy transmission channels in EMEs are believed to be weaker.

The likely explanation underlying this differential response is that the two recessions were structurally different—a balance sheet recession in the west with its growth model based on leveraged consumption riding asset booms broken, leading to a permanent decline in disposable incomes, and a cyclical downturn in EMEs on account of a temporary crash in external demand. In hindsight at least, it appears that the co-ordinated policy response should have been calibrated to accommodate this basic difference: short-term macroeconomic stimulus in EMEs and adjustment in advanced economies. This adjustment to repair growth drivers could well have entailed some fiscal expansion—but to repair household balance sheets to rebuild consumer confidence rather than simply trying to substitute for the decline in private demand by shifting leverage from private to the public sector.

Short-term macroeconomic policies can stimulate the economy back to growth only when the decline in private demand is cyclical. It cannot do so where there has been a permanent loss in income. Tepid growth can of course be ensured through public expenditure, but fiscal multipliers are notoriously weak and tend to decline over time. If stimulus is sustained over an extended period, the resultant rise in public debt would need to be brought down subsequently by the robust growth that usually follows deep recessions.

One would have thought that policy makers had learnt the right lessons from the oil price shock of the 1970s, which administered a lasting negative shock to final disposable income in oil importing countries. However, besotted with the new-found macroeconomic policy flexibility, enabled by the emergence of fiat money (as the world had recently gone off the gold standard) and inspired by the Keynesian revolution in economic thought, western economies tried to stimulate their way out of the problem. The result was stagflation, until Paul Volcker came along and forced painful adjustment on America by raising—rather than lowering—interest rates.

Extended macroeconomic stimulus has now damaged sovereign balance sheets to the point that they are being forced to adjust by markets losing confidence in the ability of policy makers to repair them through prudent (non-inflationary) means. This has made internal rebalancing even more challenging according to the 'rational expectations' school of thought. The underlying fear is that the medium- to long-term growth prospects of advanced economies, particularly those in Europe, are nowhere near as good as they were in the post-war period, when they were not only young, but growing even younger, riding on the post-war baby boom.

Be that as it may, there is widespread scepticism about the ability of these economies to grow their way out of high levels of debt as they had done in the post-war period. Consumers and investors may therefore be pricing in future tax increases or inflation in their calculus and therefore becoming even more risk-averse through 'Ricardian Equivalence.'

The intellectual battle lines at Cannes would therefore be drawn between those subscribing to Keynes and those subscribing to rational market expectations, or Hayek in short. Where the market has already started imposing penalties, there may be little choice. However, countries with reserve currencies that attract safe haven flows still have a choice. The Nobel Committee, at least, has made it clear on which side it stands by awarding this year's Nobel Prize in economics to Thomas Sargent, a doyen of the rational expectations school.

Business Standard, New Delhi, 30 October 2011 .

41

Flawed Signals from Cannes

The sixth G20 Summit was held at Cannes (3-4 November 2011) in difficult circumstances. The tepid global recovery was grinding to a halt, and there was renewed instability in financial markets emanating from sovereign debt concerns, especially, but not exclusively, in the Euro zone periphery.

Just prior to the Summit I had written that, in these circumstances, the Cannes Summit might be compared to the 'trillion dollar' London Summit ("It's a long road from Keynes to Cannes", *Business Standard*, 30 October 2011). Also, since policy makers went into the summit with empty pockets and depleted policy instruments, unlike London, the intellectual battle over policy would be between the Keynesian and rational expectations schools.

A quick glance at the Cannes Declaration would reveal that despite the leaders inability to put any numbers on the table, Keynes won hands down.

The market's response to the outcome at Cannes was not kind: several Euro zone sovereign bonds going into free fall ever since, as the contagion spreads rapidly from the periphery of the Euro zone to the core and beyond. This has dented the image of the G20 as the premier multilateral forum for international policy co-operation and crisis management. Why should this have been the case? Is it possible that the market deconstructed the Cannes Communiqué as outlined in the stylised subtext below:

> We have reached agreement on a number of ongoing G20 issues. However, we don't have a fix on the two big 'crisis' issues of the Euro zone and faltering private demand. Even though the Euro zone problem is of systemic importance, and will affect us all, it is too big for us to handle. It is for the Europeans to find a solution. We can help by further

enhancing IMF's resources, but are not in a position to commit anything.

At London we agreed to collectively commit one trillion dollars to international organizations, and to using fiscal and monetary policies to the hilt, to deal with the greatest threat to the global economy since the Great Depression. At Cannes, where we face a similar situation, we are not in a position to commit more resources to international organizations, but instead commit to country specific short-term and long-term actions to address concerns regarding growth and sustainability. These commitments are enshrined in our Cannes Action Plan, the piece de resistance of our Communiqué, which is an aggregation of existing national budgets and plans.

We remain committed to fiscal consolidation, but now is not the time (recall St. Augustine's medium to long-term commitment to chastity), because there can be no fiscal consolidation in the absence of growth. Through our Action Plan we will continue with short-term macroeconomic stimulus, despite the spiking debt/GDP ratios that markets are concerned about, as long as growth is below our expectations (which may be unrealistic, based as they are on unsustainable pre-crisis levels), and until we are disciplined by markets (Greece, Portugal, Ireland, Italy, etc), at which point we shall turn to non-commercial sources (countries with deep pockets such as Germany, China, oil-rich countries, the IMF) so that we can carry on at least till the next elections. However, if market pressures continue to remain overwhelming, we are prepared to adjust sharply straightaway, even if demand does not bounce back (Europe). Wherever possible, and to the extent possible, in such cases we will shift the burden of stimulus to central banks, even though we are unsure that monetary policy transmissions are working well. We will continue with quantitative easing (QE) to support/replace fiscal policy, especially since inflation is not an issue and our findings show that QE does not spillover to inflate commodity prices and EMEs. Inflation in the latter is a supply side issue that they need to address themselves.

We are very concerned about persistently high levels of employment. Therefore, while conventional wisdom suggests that greater flexibility in labor markets stimulates

> investment, our growth strategy will be employment led and not the other way around. We also encourage all countries to put in place the social protection schemes that we can no longer afford.

This stylised subtext suggests that markets may have felt that the G20 is fixated on short-term growth that pleases electorates (the Keynesian world view that in the long-term we are famously dead is at heart a very political statement) while they were focused on medium to long-term sustainability of public finances. This paradox, which lies at the heart of capitalist democracies is more apparent than real. This is because if markets do not step up to the plate, the burden eventually falls on the taxpayer who is also the elector.

What alternative messages could markets and investors have been looking for from Cannes from a rational expectations perspective?

First, they could have been expecting some introspection regarding the aggressive Keynesian response at London to what was, in essence, not a cyclical but a balance-sheet recession, especially since it does not seem to have worked as expected.

Second, they may have hoped for more pointed recognition that public debt in advanced countries is already too high given a realistic outlook for long-term growth, factoring in the long-lasting downward pressure on growth from balance-sheet recessions, ageing and uncertainty over the pace of global demand rebalancing. They might have expected a candid acknowledgement that more leverage cannot resolve a problem of excessive leverage, and that shifting leverage from private to public and finally to central bank balance sheets, was unlikely to reassure financial markets. This would have meant that there was no getting away from short-term adjustment (especially since the long-term is an aggregation of short-terms) and pain (structural reforms to improve efficiency and competitiveness) that would put growth and public finances on a sustainable footing going forward, even if this came at the cost of sacrificing some short-term growth. The bottom line is: an acknowledgement that there is life beyond the present and that the long-term matters.

Third, while assurance was no doubt needed that social safety nets would be in place to cushion persistently high levels of unemployment, they may have expected a clearer message on the interplay between growth and jobs that could have made rebalancing from public to private demand, and consequently fiscal consolidation, easier.

Fourth, on the Euro zone, markets may have expected an acknowledgement that there was a structural flaw—monetary union without a banking and fiscal union—that needed to be fixed quickly.

Business Standard, New Delhi, 10 December 2011.

42

G20 and a New Political Economy of Globalization

Macroeconomic policy cooperation within the group of 20, or G20, has evolved through at least five distinct stages since the first summit in Washington DC held over three years ago.

The first two summits at Washington DC and London marked the first stage of policy co-operation, culminating in the trillion-dollar London Summit. G20 leaders resolved to do whatever was necessary to stall the slide in the global economy through an aggressive, coordinated macroeconomic response to the financial crisis.

It is pertinent, however, that no country-specific commitments were asked for, and none were given. The policy response was also fairly undifferentiated across countries.

The G20 deliberations fed into domestic policy, with each country doing what it considered appropriate. Although there were no country-specific commitments, this policy co-ordination was, nevertheless, a spectacular success, even though questions are now being asked whether the recipe itself was fully appropriate. A second Great Depression and deflation have been avoided, but growth remains below trend.

At the third G20 Summit at Pittsburgh, it seemed that the coordinated response had pulled the global economy back from the brink of a second Great Depression. The G20 now turned its attention to what it felt were long-term structural problems impeding a return to strong, sustainable and balanced growth, going forward. The G20 Framework, or Mutual Assessment Process (MAP), was conceived at Pittsburgh while preparing to exit from the aggressive and co-ordinated stimulus.

The second stage of policy co-operation at the fourth summit at Toronto (2010) was differentiated across countries because of market reactions, a two-speed recovery and the need to rebalance global demand for strong, sustainable and balanced growth. Consequently, unlike the first stage, the G20 arrived at different policy prescriptions for different groups of countries: advanced deficit, advanced surplus, developing surplus, developing deficit and resource-rich economies.

Perhaps because it was quite clear to what group each G20 country belonged—once again there were no country-specific commitments—apart from some general fiscal commitments given by advanced economies to reassure financial markets, since the G20 seemed mindful of the potential divisiveness of 'naming and shaming.'

The third stage was at the fifth summit at Seoul, where there was a realisation that there was little forward movement in the desired direction. The possibility of country-specific commitments was seriously considered for the first time. A consensus was, therefore, arrived at to develop indicators on the basis of which country-specific commitments could be worked out and therefore, made more acceptable.

The fourth stage of policy co-operation was at the last G20 summit at Cannes, in the form of the Cannes Action Plan, which contains country-specific commitments. However, problems regarding measurement and timelines persist and are still unresolved, especially since these commitments were made at a time when a cloud was hanging over the global recovery, and this cloud appears even darker now.

An attempt was, therefore, made to distinguish between short-term and long-term policy commitments. Also, commitments were 'country-led' in the best G20 tradition, and mostly what the countries had committed as part of their own domestic policies in the public domain. The G20 debate is, nevertheless, clearly weighing on the trajectory of domestic policies.

These four stages indicate that the movement has been clearly forward and within a fairly short period of time. Therefore, as the G20 moves towards its fifth stage of macroeconomic policy co-ordination at the seventh summit in Los Cabos, Mexico, in June 2012, of assessing country commitments and holding them accountable, caution is warranted in placing unrealistic expectations on the budding G20 process going forward.

First, domestic policies respond to changing circumstances. If the compulsions of short-term and long-term policies point in different directions, how can these be harmonised, especially since the long-term is a stringing together of the short-terms. For instance, prospects for the global economy have deteriorated considerably since commitments for fiscal consolidation were given at Toronto. How can commitments and assessments accommodate the need for such dynamic policy shifts?

In the deliberations leading up to the Toronto Summit, there were differences of opinion over whether fiscal commitments should be date-specific or benchmarked to the pace of recovery. This issue remains as relevant as ever.

Second, a huge divide now appears to have opened up between what electorates and markets expect from governments. Both electorates and markets are in revolt. Electorates are voting against severe austerity in country after country in Europe, unseating governments. While sovereigns should not allow themselves to be held hostage by the markets, they ignore markets at their own peril, as the taxpayer has to foot the bill of market revolt upfront.

They already started footing the bill through negative real deposit rates. A sharp rise in public debt always follows deep crises and recessions, but this time round, markets do not seem too sanguine regarding the prospects for long-term growth necessary to bring down debt ratios going forward in countries where public debt has risen appreciably, and are, therefore, demanding higher returns. As a result, policy makers need to reassure markets how debt dynamics would be managed by persuasively clarifying or creating the engines of future growth.

Third, how can the G20 nudge countries' policies in mutually agreed directions and hold sovereigns accountable for commitments given, especially since these are not legally binding, and in the absence of any enforcement mechanism?

The sovereignty of internal policies of nation states has been well recognised at least since the Treaty of Westphalia that is almost three and a half centuries old.

Counterbalancing these three negatives is the fourth, which is a clear positive for global cooperation going forward. It is becoming increasingly clear that the success of domestic policy actions in a fast-integrating world with growing policy and market spillovers is linked to global outcomes. Domestic growth and business cycles are becoming more and more globally aligned.

If rebalancing does not take place, growth will decline across the globe; but if rebalancing is uncoordinated, the outcomes could be even worse. Policy co-operation is, therefore, potentially win-win, since economic integration has moved far ahead of political integration.

While this is most clearly manifest in the case of the Euro zone and the European Union (EU), to a great extent, the challenges ahead facing the G20 are similar. In this sense, the G20 is a brave new experiment pushing the boundaries of globalization to harvest this co-operative dividend.

The issues are, no doubt, complex, double-edged and avant-garde. Perhaps this is why economists seem to be wringing their hands in despair, and policy makers are having to turn elsewhere for sage advice, such as St Augustine for the short-term ("Lord make me chaste, but not yet"), or *Alice in Wonderland* for the long-term ("Jam yesterday and jam tomorrow, but never jam today") and even to Aesop's Fables such as *The Ant and the Grasshopper* (to understand the dynamics of global imbalances) and *The Fox who Lost its Tail* (building a consensus on stimulus).

While economists have long been trying to adapt their tools to open economies, arguably what we now need is a new political economy of globalization.

The Economic Times, New Delhi, 21 May 2012 .

43

New Lows at Los Cabos?

When the leaders of the Group of 20 countries, or G20, meet at their seventh summit in Los Cabos, Mexico, on 18 June, they might be struck by the sobering thought that imminent threats confronting the global economy are, to all intents and purposes, the same they confronted at their last summit in Cannes, France, in November last year. If anything, these old challenges have become even more daunting.

The optimists would argue that this merely reflects the political compulsions of the current G20 presidency, on account of which two summits had to be held in quick succession. The pessimists would argue that this reflects poorly on the outcomes of the Cannes summit, which, despite a much-vaunted co-operative spirit and bonhomie, failed to adequately address these threats.

It is universally acknowledged that the Cannes summit agenda was hijacked by the gathering storm in the Euro zone, specifically the Greek question. The summit failed to address the problem squarely. As a result, the contagion spread beyond the solitary PIG (Portugal, Ireland and Greece, all of whom had lost sovereign market access before Cannes) to the bigger Euro zone economies of Spain, Italy, even France. Their sovereign bond spreads started spinning out of control within weeks of the summit. It was the European Central Bank (ECB) that rescued the Euro zone, with the salvos (long-term refinancing operations) of 'Big Bertha' battering sovereign bond markets into submission. Now that Big Bertha has fallen silent, sovereign bond markets are again in revolt, with the spreads of Spain breaching the dreaded six per cent barrier and Italian yields in hot pursuit (Surprisingly, French yields have drifted south following the leadership change there.) Leaders would now have to confront a much worse situation in the Euro zone at Los Cabos, with governments quietly planning for the exit of Greece, or even a catastrophic break-up of the monetary union. The Euro zone once again threatens to hijack the G20 agenda at Los Cabos.

The second threat facing leaders at Cannes was the dilemma of having to choose between austerity (market-induced fiscal consolidation) and growth (fiscal expansion to bridge the output gap). It tried to resolve the dilemma by making a (false?) dichotomy between the short-run (stimulate) and long-run (consolidate) continuum. By messaging that those who had the fiscal space should stimulate, and those who did not should consolidate, it sent out the rather perverse message that countries should continue to stimulate their economies till they are disciplined by markets, at which point they would need to consolidate irrespective of the output gap. While the flight to quality—sovereign bonds—seems to have created an illusion of fiscal space in a number of advanced countries to enable them to continue to stimulate, or stagger their consolidation, leaders seem to have left the recovery in the Euro zone hostage to markets. The dilemma that will confront the leaders at Los Cabos will be even more acute, as electorates have joined issue with markets, voting against austerity by unseating governments wherever elections have been held. They would be expected to devise a coordinated workable strategy to revive flagging global growth with markets and electorates revolting in different directions.

The third threat facing leaders at Cannes was the faltering global recovery and the persistence of high levels of unemployment, particularly youth unemployment. The Cannes Action Plan was subtitled "Growth and Jobs" because unemployment had become a political hot potato, with the concerns over growth, global imbalances and exchange rates stemming primarily from this. If the sleight of hand in the employment data is discounted to take stock of discouraged workers who have abandoned their job search, and thereby by definition not being unemployed any more, the employment scenario has only worsened in most parts of the developed world since Cannes. Growth and jobs will, therefore, once again be near the top of the Los Cabos agenda, especially with near-term economic data from the US, the UK, the Euro zone, and even major emerging markets like China, Brazil and India pointing towards another synchronised downturn.

The fourth threat to the global economy apparent at Cannes was the volatility and buoyancy in oil markets which were out of step with the depressed state of global demand and confidence, and which threatened to derail the recovery in emerging markets. This threat not only remains as strong as it was at Cannes, but is possibly graver on account of a new threat of a supply shock emanating from sanctions against Iran.

So what has changed materially since Cannes? First, Spanish, Italian and French sovereign bond yields rose after the Cannes summit, but are now rising prior to the summit. Second, while there is now greater confidence that the current account surplus of the country accounting for the biggest global imbalance, namely China, may have shrunk permanently, this is countervailed by the realisation that the biggest source of global imbalances has now shifted to the oil exporting countries (mainly Organisation for Economic Co-operation and Development [OECD] countries, Norway and Russia). The G20 would need to devise a new strategy to deal with this new imbalance. Third, with electorates revolting against austerity, the credibility of G20 commitments will be closely scrutinised by markets.

Fourth, the Los Cabos summit would also need to address three important sensitivities. First, Germany is unlikely to take kindly to the G20 meddling with what it considers to be an internal matter of the Euro zone, thereby undermining the G20's new halo as the principal forum for global economic co-operation. Second, Mexico's overarching focus on 'green growth' is in the cross hairs of its American neighbour, Brazil, which feels that this would undermine their Rio+20 summit to be held immediately after the G20 summit. Third, China is peeved with the G20 for not giving it due credit for its rebalancing efforts.

Such daunting challenges and sensitivities call for global leadership and statesmanship of a high order, of the kind displayed by the US and the UK (recall Gordon Brown and the trillion-dollar London summit) in the immediate aftermath of the global financial crisis. This appears unlikely at this juncture as the big three of the G20, namely the US, Germany and China, face elections and/or the prospects of a leadership change within a year of the Los Cabos summit.

While the medium-term agenda of the G20 is progressing satisfactorily, the outcome of the Los Cabos summit is likely to be assessed on its ability to effectively address these four big imminent threats. With an apparent crisis of leadership, nobody is holding their breath at what the outcome from the seventh G20 summit would be. The expectations from Los Cabos now appear to be so low that the summit can only surprise on the upside, not on the downside.

Business Standard, New Delhi, 9 June 2012.

44

The Surprises of Los Cabos

The seventh G20 summit was held at Los Cabos on 18 and 19 June. On the eve of the summit, I had written in the newspaper ("New Lows at Los Cabos?", *Business Standard*, 9 June 2012) that expectations were so low that the G20 leaders could only surprise on the upside. I had also said that while the medium-term agenda of the G20 was progressing satisfactorily, the outcome of the Los Cabos summit was likely to be assessed on its ability to effectively deal with (a) German sensitivities on the Euro zone, Brazilian sensitivities on the Rio+20 Summit and Chinese sensitivities on the exchange rate; and (b) four big imminent threats to the global economy that were not satisfactorily addressed at the sixth G20 (Cannes) summit—instability in the Euro zone, faltering growth, demand rebalancing and the threat of disruption of oil supplies.

How Did Things Pan Out?

The Los Cabos Leaders' Declaration consists of 86 paragraphs, with statements on all ongoing G20 agenda items such as financial regulatory reform, financial inclusion, employment, social protection, trade, food security, commodity price volatility, development, green growth, the fight against corruption, etc. However, it is what the Declaration had to say on the Euro zone and on reviving growth, in the first 19 paragraphs, that expectedly determined the outcome of the summit.

German sensitivities on the Euro zone were handled well. The extent to which Germany was forthcoming on Euro zone issues at Los Cabos was surprising. The G20 has for long talked about global rebalancing. But the Los Cabos Action Plan is the first G20 document that acknowledges the need for internal rebalancing in the Euro zone. Also, while no specific commitments were given, pointers to the banking union, severance of the negative 'feedback loop between sovereigns and banks' and measures to support growth agreed at the European Union (EU) summit 10 days later are all there in the Los Cabos Leaders' Declaration and Action Plan.

It is true that nothing definitive was stated about fiscal union, the issue of common 'Eurobonds' and conversion of the European Central Bank (ECB) into a regular central bank that can insulate sovereign bonds from market revolt. But this was primarily because there is no consensus amongst European leaders themselves on these issues. G20 commitments, it must be remembered, are country-led. Failure to address these fatal flaws in the Euro zone's design is also a major failing of the recent European summit, and tantamount to kicking the can further down the road yet again. Having discovered these major weaknesses, markets can be expected to revolt again from time to time. Seeking the comfort of a bottomless Coke that only fiscal union and a central bank can provide, markets see instead Dear Henry's leaky bucket.

Chancellor Merkel's statement that the Euro zone is in a race against markets might well prove prophetic, eventually pushing the Euro zone kicking and screaming into a fiscal union to prevent a catastrophic break-up—and sooner rather than later. Even a banking union might appear shaky to markets unless it is underwritten by harmonised and enforceable euro-wide tax-and-spend policies. Be it as it may, since the major outcomes of the European summit were all anticipated in the Los Cabos Leaders' Declaration and Action Plan, on the Euro zone issue, at least, the Los Cabos Summit surprised on the upside.

Despite the imperative of focusing more on growth and jobs, and providing global leadership on the trade-off between austerity and growth, neither the Leaders' Declaration nor the Los Cabos Action Plan went one whit beyond Cannes: continue to stimulate if you have the fiscal space, and consolidate if you do not. Arguably the only new thinking on growth was the inclusion of the suggestion of the Indian prime minister that infrastructure investment has a role to play in the global recovery.

It is intriguing that while the Los Cabos Leaders' Declaration exhorts countries with fiscal space to continue with stimulus, the linkage between fiscal space and stimulus that featured prominently in the Cannes Action Plan has been dropped in the Los Cabos Action Plan. This is perhaps because the general government debt-to-GDP (gross domestic product) ratios of the countries committing to further discretionary measures have deteriorated beyond the prudential 60 per cent (International Monetary Fund [IMF] Fiscal Monitor) and even 90 per cent (Reinhart and Rogoff). The borrowing costs of these countries are no doubt low currently because of the flight to quality, but market confidence can be fickle. This severance between fiscal space and stimulus allowed the US, which was not included in the group of countries with fiscal space at Cannes and now faces a 'fiscal cliff' deriving from the double whammy of automatic federal expenditure cuts and expiry of tax cuts, to now commit to continuing stimulus.

With the sharp decline in the Chinese current account surplus, and muddying of the 'rebalancing' argument by the new narrative on trade that highlights the growing importance of processing trade—and has the effect of sharply reducing China's bilateral trade surpluses—there was little option but to accommodate Chinese sensitivities on its exchange rate policy. Little attention was however given to the policy implications of the shift in the structure of global imbalances in the direction of oil-exporting countries.

With oil prices dipping below the three-figure mark, the issue of high oil prices and disruption of supplies was to all intents and purposes off the table at Los Cabos, even though the latter threat remains. The Mexicans also considerably watered down their 'green growth' initiative to accommodate the concerns of Brazil and other emerging markets, including India.

To sum up, while the seventh G20 Summit at Los Cabos went according to script in most respects, it nevertheless had something significant to say on the Euro zone. It could, therefore, be said that it has indeed surprised on the upside.

Business Standard, New Delhi, 1 July 2012.

45

Building BRICS without Straw

BRICS was an acronym for Brazil, Russia, India and China, later expanded to include South Africa. It was originally invented by Goldman Sachs, an investment bank, some years ago, to underscore the investment possibilities in four big, fast-growing emerging markets whose share in the global economy was expected to increase sharply over the next few decades. Following the recent global economic and financial turmoil, with major developed economies likely to grow slowly for an extended period, the share of BRICS in the global economy is expected to grow even faster than originally projected. Already, these countries account for over 25 per cent of the world's land area and GDP (gross domestic product) at purchasing power parity (PPP), and over 40 per cent of the population.

It is important to bear in mind that BRICS did not originate through an endogenously driven geopolitical impulse. Despite being large economies, and consequently members of the exclusive G20 club, there are major strategic and structural differences between BRICS which prevent them from acting effectively as a bloc, unlike the G7, for instance. Strategic and structural differences are so stark that it is difficult to say what exactly such disparate economies have in common.

While they are spread over three continents, the strategic relationships between China and India, and China and Russia, are complicated by the fact that they are neighbours, with competing geopolitical interests. Is Russia a developing economy? China stands out amongst the BRICS as being overly dependent on external demand for growth, while India runs a large current account deficit (CAD). China and India are commodity consumers, while Brazil, Russia and South Africa are commodity exporters. China's undervalued currency hurts other BRICS, while India's relatively high agricultural tariffs are an issue with Brazil, which is a competing agricultural power.

Chinese and Indian trend growth far exceeds those of other BRICS, as a result of which the Asian BRICS are pulling away from the others. Since foreign savings can play only a marginal role in increasing investment in large economies, this growth differential is largely explained by higher savings in China and India. India imports foreign savings in addition, while China exports domestic savings. Low savings and investment in Brazil, Russia and South Africa are more akin to the slower growing advanced economies or low income countries. Russia even manages to export capital despite low saving rates.

BRICS nevertheless have a certain congruence of international political and economic purpose in that they represent the aspirations of previously dis-empowered nations seeking to grow and protect their development space. While co-operation in some forums like the World Trade Organisation (WTO) and the UN Security Council has proved difficult, they have cooperated on climate change within the United Nations Framework Convention on Climate Change (UNFCCC), and in the reform of institutions of global economic governance, such as the Bretton Woods institutions and the Financial Stability Board, through the G20. Growing intra-BRICS trade and investment activity is leading to growing business and academic co-operation in civil society.

To be effective, an economic and geopolitical grouping must be credibly balanced to establish trust. In the G7, Europe is a counter to the US; in the G20, the US, China and Germany (representing Europe) are more or less on equal footing. In sharp contradistinction, China is the thousand pound gorilla in the BRICS club, accounting for about half of their GDP.

It is self-evident that competing interests would need to be harmonised for BRICS to act in a co-ordinated and effective manner, and that China would need to play a leading role. There is, however, a perception that much of the recent gains by BRICS within the G20 have been cornered by China, with increasing talk of a G2. It has also gained the most from the quota shift in the Bretton Woods institutions, and has strategic leverage independent of other BRICS in multilateral forums through which it can always cut a deal on its own strength.

The economic and geopolitical frictions within BRICS are apparent in developing a harmonised perspective on two recent high profile initiatives, namely setting up a new development bank, and pooling reserves for a BRICS financial safety net. These BRICS initiatives would redirect the global savings glut, much of which emanates from the BRICS itself, amongst them to rebalance global demand and help stabilise a teetering global economy.

Such redirecting has traditionally been the role of the Bretton Wood twins—the World Bank and the International Monetary Fund (IMF). However, neither their governance structure nor their resources have adjusted to the tectonic shifts in the global economy occasioned by the rise of BRICS, making them irrelevant for the big emerging markets. The collective financial safety net (foreign currency reserves) of BRICS exceeds that of even the augmented IMF by a factor of 4, while the long stagnant resources of the World Bank are now too puny for their developmental needs.

While there is congruence of purpose amongst BRICS for these initiatives, economic and geopolitical differences diverge sharply. India, which took the initiative for a BRICS-led new development bank, needs large resources to bridge its domestic infrastructure deficit. Brazil, on the other hand, is more likely to see the bank play a supporting role for trade and investment overseas. Unlike India, which has relied on financial markets, China and Brazil have successfully used financial repression to leverage large amounts of savings at low cost and channel them into infrastructure through state directed investment vehicles. From a Chinese perspective, the bank is better used as a secure channel for its risky investments in resource-rich developing countries, particularly in Africa. While South Africa has large internal developmental needs of its own, its geopolitical objectives coincide with those of China as it seeks to enhance its sphere of influence in its backyard.

While Brazil took the initiative for bilateral swaps and reserve pooling amongst BRICS, it is in the economic interests of all BRICS to shelter behind China's huge stock of foreign currency reserves on account of the volatility inherent in capital flows to developing countries. For China, it makes eminent sense to use the BRICS forum to counter the exorbitant privilege of the US dollar, of which it has been the most articulate critic in recent times.

Divergent economic interests of BRICS can be harmonised through negotiated mandates for these new institutions. Accommodating the gorilla in a harmonised governance structure would be much more challenging. The gorilla could, of course, be cut to size, but because it brings vast resources to the table, an equitable governance structure would come at the cost of size. These new institutions would then suffer the same infirmities of the existing Bretton Woods. There are ways of getting around this by associating key developed countries on an equal footing. This would also improve the credit rating of the new institution.

The challenges of being optimistic about the recent co-operative initiatives of BRICS are matched only by the undeniable benefits enatailed by such economic co-operation. In a post-crisis world buffeted by financial instability and weak growth in major advanced economies, BRICS have a historic opportunity to enhance their position in global institutions of governance, and to be a stabilising force through demand rebalancing so as to weather global economic and financial turbulence. The benefits of co-operation are therefore immense for BRICS as well as for the global economy, but the challenges en route are daunting.

The Financial Express, New Delhi, 1 April 2013.

46

EMEs at St Petersburg

Petering Out

The eighth G20 summit will take place in St Petersburg, Russia, on 5-6 September 2013, in an interesting and unfamiliar environment. This is the first summit where International Monetary Fund's (IMF's) near-term data to be presented to leaders are likely to show growth strengthening in the US and Japan, and recovery in the UK and the Euro zone, while the prospects for growth in the emerging market economies (EMEs) might be shown as further weakening. What impact would such a scenario have on the deliberations and the final summit declaration from an EME perspective?

Macroeconomic stabilisation, growth and jobs—which dominated the first two G20 summits at Washington DC and London, respectively—returned to occupy centre stage in the last two summits at Cannes and Los Cabos in the wake of the Euro zone crisis and fears of a double dip.

These concerns remain paramount despite some improvement in the near-term data. Labour participation rates have not recovered from their crisis lows, and there are concerns about the quality of job creation. Trend growth may have also moved lower because of some permanent loss of demand. According to IMF's WEO July update, advanced economies are expected to grow at just 1.2 per cent in 2013. Even if this is revised slightly upwards by the time of the summit, they are growing at only about half the pre-boom (1993-2002: see table) rate.

Growth in developing countries, on the other hand, is now at around the pre-boom average. The boom in global growth after 2004 was basically an EMDE (emerging market and developing economy) phenomenon, as a result of which their growth differential with advanced economies almost quadrupled over the 1993-2002 average.

They also weathered the first phase of the global financial crisis remarkably well.

This recovery has, however, tended to stall after 2011, with the growth differential lower than what it was in any year in the post-2002 (boom) period. Growth concerns have magnified over the past few months by market expectations of imminent rollback of the abundant global liquidity arising out of non-conventional monetary policies in advanced economies, pressuring the financing of their current account deficits (CADs) and their currencies.

The case of India, which has all along been the second-fastest growing G20 economy, perhaps best illustrates this down slide. Its near-term quarterly growth has fallen below 5 per cent, and the rupee is falling to new lows. The situation in several other EMEs is similar.

Would these developments diminish the voice and impact of EMEs at the summit? The choice of the G20 forum as the new premier forum for international economic co-operation, taking over the baton from the G7, was largely on account of the prolonged economic boom in EMEs that accelerated the income convergence between advanced economies and EMEs. There is now a danger that G7 countries, who have been dragging their feet all along on the issue, may be less willing to concede ground or to listen to the BRICS on matters raised by them on issues such as IMF governance reform and the new quota formula, especially since they have not got what they wanted on issues such as trade and climate change. While all the usual motherhood statements are likely to be repeated in the summit document, G20 camp followers would as usual need to delve deep into nuanced phrases and constructive ambiguities that are a masquerade for deep divisions within the forum.

It may be recalled that the G20 turned to addressing structural issues such as global imbalances (Pittsburgh), public debt management (Toronto), and development (Seoul) even before the global recovery had stabilised. The G20 also branched out into a number of contentious areas with little relevance for the recovery.

It is not entirely clear how some of these items got into the G20 agenda even as it was engaged in fire fighting. The most plausible explanation is that, following up on the Heiligendamm process, this was an attempt by G7 countries to engage systemically important emerging markets directly across the table to close contentious negotiations stuck in larger multilateral fora like the IMF (exchange rate policies), the WTO (Doha Round), the UNFCCC (climate change), the United Nations Convention against Corruption (UNCAC) (anti-corruption) and the International Labour Organization (ILO) (labour laws). Some sort of grand bargain was probably envisaged, giving a greater share to EMEs in the governance of multilateral bodies such as the IMF, World Bank and the Financial Stability Forum. The timing of some of these interventions, such as green growth, stronger social protection, and now 'Base Erosion and Profit Shifting,' is certainly strange as they can queer the pitch for boosting private investment and confidence—charging 'animal spirits'—that is necessary for a sustainable recovery.

Be it as it may, while it is difficult to get any item off the international agenda once it is on the table, there are two new issues on the G20 agenda in St Petersburg on which EMEs need to take a considered stand, since they stand to be hugely affected by both. The first issue relates to non-conventional monetary policies adopted by advanced economies, and the management of their public debt. The second issue relates to international tax matters. What stand they could take on these issues will be considered in the second part of this article. The extent to which they can influence the summit outcomes at this stage is, of course, another matter.

The Financial Express, New Delhi, 22 August 2013.

47

EMEs at St Petersburg

Emerging Issues

There are likely to be two issues of vital interest from an emerging market perspective at the eighth G20 summit to be held in St Petersburg, Russia, on 5-6 September 2013. They need to somehow ensure that their interests are protected at a time when faltering growth is undermining their voice within the G20.

The first issue relates to non-conventional monetary policies adopted by advanced economies, and the management of their public debt. It may be recalled that the initial reaction of emerging market Economics (EMEs), and particularly of the BRICS (Brazil, Russia, India, China and South Africa), to quantitative easing (QE) was on the whole, negative. This was reflected in G20 summit declarations. China was critical because it devalued the dollar, and therefore the value of its large holding of US Treasuries and government sponsored enterprises (GSE) (mortgage) holdings. As a commodity exporter, Brazil stood to gain from the rise in commodity prices. Its objection was to the appreciation of the Real on account of the sharp increase in capital flows. Guido Mantega, the Finance Minister of Brazil, famously coined the term 'currency wars' before imposing capital controls as a result. India was most affected by commodity price inflation. However, on account of the need to finance its large current account deficit (CAD), its views on capital inflows were muted.

The EMEs' reaction to QE3, especially following the Bank of Japan's decision to purchase \$75 billion treasury bonds each month (over and above the US Federal Reserve's [Fed's] monthly purchase of \$85 billion), is however subdued. Brazil, Turkey, Indonesia, South Africa and India experienced sharp depreciation as CAD increased and capital inflows declined. Brazil started rolling back capital controls, and India is in line to ease them, to attract more foreign capital. The recent rise in US treasury bond yields has sharply reduced capital flows to EMEs and aggravated the problem. If just the talk of QE rollback has triggered tremors in EMEs, the situation could worsen to crisis proportions when it actually starts. It is, however, difficult for EMEs to take a position against this rollback in view of their earlier opposition to QE.

Monetary policy the world over responds to the domestic business cycle. The case of the US Fed is, however, singular in that its policies also shape cross-border capital flows by virtue of the dollar being the effective global reserve currency. This constrains the monetary stance of other countries in ways that may be inappropriate for their own business cycles. In 2007-08, when the Fed turned on the liquidity tap, EMEs, who recovered relatively quickly from the crisis, hesitated to tighten monetary policy for the fear of attracting more capital inflows. India's currency appreciated despite a widening CAD. Now when growth is weakening, EMEs hesitate to loosen monetary policy because of capital outflows. Reserve build-up in EMEs is as much a defensive response to US monetary policy as the pursuit of export-led growth.

It is for this reason that EMEs argued for greater policy flexibility in dealing with cross-border capital flows in the run-up to the Cannes G20 summit. India has imposed some outbound capital controls, and also raised customs tariffs on a number of items as part of a slew of measures to lower the CAD. While these increases are within its WTO-bound limits, India should be prepared for some adverse attention at the summit in view of the 'trade standstill' agreed to earlier by the G20 countries. It could underscore the curbs' temporary nature, while leveraging them to make a case for an orderly tapering of QE that keeps in mind its international ramifications. While it is not clear how this conundrum can and should be addressed, the focus of the G20 Framework Working Group, of which India is a co-chair, needs to shift from global demand rebalancing to this issue.

Closely related to QE is the issue of public debt management in advanced economies. Two separate themes seem to have got mixed up in recent G20 deliberations on debt management, namely the long-standing problem of external debt management in developing countries, and public debt management in advanced economies which is an emerging post-crisis concern. Unsustainable external debt, irrespective of whether it is private or sovereign, in developing economies can lead to market revolt, collapse of the domestic currency, and a balance of payments (BoP) crisis. High fiscal deficits, and the build-up of domestic public debt as a lagged consequence, on the other hand, can have inflationary outcomes, but market revolt and financing of fiscal deficits are never an issue because of the central bank backstop.

A few notable exceptions apart, such as Japan and Italy, excessive public debt was mostly seen as a developing-country problem. While the position regarding external debt has not changed, in recent years the equation with respect to public debt has vastly changed. As advanced countries aged, and trend growth slowed, their public debt/GDP (gross domestic product) ratios started to rise, while the ratios in EMEs tended to decline as growth rates picked up. This fiscal divergence has been accelerated by the need for protracted fiscal stimulus, and falling revenues, in advanced economies as a result of negative and low growth over the last half decade.

The problem with the G20 fiscal commitments agreed by the advanced economies at Toronto is that they were 'date' rather than 'condition' dependent. While there is no doubt that fiscal deficits and debt need to be brought within prudent limits, advanced economies will continue to grapple with the 'growth-austerity' dilemma as long as private demand remains weak. The Toronto fiscal commitments, therefore, need to be calibrated with the pace of recovery, i.e., cyclically adjusted, which may mean revisiting the agreed timelines for debt/GDP targets. The targets themselves may need to be revisited in due course as the ageing process and associated fiscal demands, and lower trend growth and attendant revenue declines can be expected to continue. Fiscal projections for the advanced countries, even by some reputed bodies like the Bank of International Settlements (BIS), look quite alarming.

Since the domestic debt of advanced countries is denominated in international reserve currencies, their future borrowing requirements can have huge spillovers on EMEs who need to attract capital flows to finance trade and investment. This is why the talk of withdrawal of

QE, through which central banks purchase sovereign debt, is currently destabilising EMEs. Accelerated fiscal adjustment in advanced economies may reduce the pressure on EME currencies, but given the extent this has a negative impact on growth in advanced economies, their own faltering recovery would be at greater risk. The asymmetric impact of fiscal management in advanced economies through the trade and financial channels is another conundrum that EMEs would need to sort out.

The second 'new' issue on which EMEs are required to take a stand relates to international tax matters. In the past, India has enthusiastically backed the Global Forum-Organisation for Economic Co-operation and Development (OECD) initiative on automatic exchange of tax-related information because of domestic concerns about large amounts parked by Indian nationals in tax havens abroad. The issue of 'base erosion and profit shifting' (BEPS) is however altogether different, and one on which EMEs need to tread carefully, study the full implications and consult with other BRICS leaders who will meet on the sidelines of the summit.

The need for higher taxes to reduce fiscal imbalances in OECD countries has gone hand in hand with loss of competitiveness and migration of production and, increasingly, services as they become more tradable, to EMEs. Attractive tax rates have also played a part. Much of this migration is facilitated through transnational corporations (TNCs) from OECD countries. This shift in economic activity has raised growth in EMEs, and along with economic activity and growth has come higher tax revenues. It is natural for OECD countries to eye a share in this revenue stream generated by their own corporates overseas.

A recent editorial in the US edition of *The Wall Street Journal*, dated 23 July 2013, cited data indicating that there has not been any long-term decline in corporate tax revenue across OECD countries, as this has fluctuated between 2 and 3 per cent of GDP depending on the business cycle. If this is indeed the case, the rationale for this OECD and G7 initiative, which is now sought to be endorsed by the G20, may well be to strengthen their fiscal position at the cost of EMEs.

Be that as it may, the timing of this initiative could be self-defeating in a broken global economy low on investment confidence. When growth and animal spirits are low, and governments want private investment to take over the load from public expenditure for a sustainable recovery, an international initiative to tighten or aggressively target tax avoidance, especially when corporate tax receipts have not dipped out of proportion to the fall in growth, can only make the recovery more difficult. Of the two 'rebalancings' identified by the G20 itself for a sustainable recovery, global demand rebalancing is clearly in evidence, but a question mark still hangs over the second, namely from public to private. Perhaps the G20 leaders need to listen more attentively to what the B20 (Business 20) leaders tell them in St Petersburg in this regard before they contemplate new measures that may queer the pitch for the global recovery.

The Financial Express, New Delhi, 22 August 2013.

48

St Petersburg G20 Summit

Unintended Consequences

The eighth G20 Summit declaration issued from St Petersburg, Russia, on 6 September, is another massive 27-page document that incorporates and builds on much, if not all, of what was said in previous summits, mostly reiterating motherhood statements and constructive ambiguities concealing sharp internal differences that we have come to expect from the G20, while adding its own distinctive 'St Petersburg' veneer.

So what is distinctive about the St Petersburg Summit Declaration for which it will be remembered by G20 historians?

The first G20 summit in Washington is remembered for what it was—the first G20 summit, where leaders of systemically important countries resolved to co-ordinate macroeconomic policies to counteract the global financial crisis, and where they first diagnosed its deeper, underlying causes, namely financial deregulation and mounting global imbalances.

The second 'London' Summit remains Gordon Brown's summit where leaders, staring down the barrel of a gun, resolved to do whatever it takes to avoid a second Great Depression, and also put together a 'trillion dollar' package to insulate developing countries from its worst effects.

At the third 'Pittsburgh' Summit, with green shoots of recovery clearly visible, leaders famously shot the gun with their infamous "It worked" fifth paragraph, declared that the G20 had replaced the G7 as the premier multilateral forum for international economic co-operation, agreed greater voting power for emerging market and developing economies (EMDEs) in the International Monetary Fund (IMF) and the World Bank, and turned their attention to addressing long-standing structural constraints in the global economy with the launch of the G20's signature "Framework for strong, sustainable and balanced growth."

With the beginnings of market revolt against mounting public debt, the natural corollary of crisis management, at their fourth 'Toronto' Summit, leaders first underscored the need for targeted fiscal consolidation.

The fifth 'Seoul' Summit is best remembered for injecting 'development' into the G20 agenda, apart from the pitched battle between the US and China on the exchange rate issue.

With global economic prospects worsening sharply again in the wake of the Euro zone crisis, the sixth Cannes and seventh Los Cabos summits, following close on the heels of the other, will be remembered for the policy dilemma that pitched austerity against growth.

The first big new issue on the St Petersburg agenda of interest to emerging markets and economies (EMEs) was the devastating impact of exit from unconventional monetary policies that is leading to a sudden stop of capital flows foreboding a currency and external payments crisis.

The second issue was 'base erosion and profit shifting' (BEPS), a G7 initiative to counter tax avoidance by their own transnational corporations. The summit however seems to have been hijacked by what happened on the sidelines—the crisis in Syria—especially since concerns regarding the economy were muted on account of the apparent recovery in the US, UK, Japan and even Europe. This was the first summit where the forward-looking prospects of EMEs were actually worse than those of Organisation for Economic Co-operation and Development (OECD) countries, although the decline is not of crisis proportions to date.

Be it as it may, EMEs' diminishing prospects seem to have muted their voice and influence at the summit. The speech of the Indian Prime Minister stood out amongst his EME counterparts in voicing concern over the absence of G20 co-ordination on monetary policies in general, and the disorderly unwinding of unconventional policies in particular.

Equally eloquent was his silence on the issue of BEPS, indicating that EMEs are still some way from thinking through its implications on their own tax base. While the St Petersburg (framework) action plan was the first that clearly spelt out the monetary policy stance of the four reserve currency area central banks, the St Petersburg Accountability Assessment bared the sharply differing perspectives of advanced and emerging market economies. The final summit declaration underscored that monetary policies respond to domestic conditions while underplaying cross-border spillovers, and also endorsed the G7 BEPS initiative.

Did EMEs gain anything substantive from the summit? This is not the first time that a G20 summit agenda, meticulously negotiated by Sherpas, finance deputies and working groups over a full year, has been overtaken by events and hijacked by the flavour of the month. The Euro zone crisis had hijacked the agenda at Cannes. But this is the first G20 summit not dominated by economic issues. Is this an indication of how the G20 is likely to shape up in future as the global economy recovers—an opportunity for leaders of systemically important countries to directly exchange views on sidelines of the Summit on the most pressing strategic international issue of the day? The main action was of course on the sidelines, and not reflected in the Summit document. But this could change in future summits, given that leaders are not bound by pre-set rules.

If things were indeed to turn out that way, EMEs perhaps need to worry less about the short-term unintended consequences of 'tapering' and quietly celebrate the long-term unintended gains from the Syrian crisis at St Petersburg. At their Pittsburgh Summit, leaders anointed the G20 as the premier multilateral forum for international co-operation. The G7/G8 however remained the pre-eminent forum for non-economic issues. If this were to change, and a consensus amongst systemically important countries worked out in G20 summits rather than in a fractious and indecisive United Nations Security Council (UNSC), where they are anyway under-represented, this could mark a major victory for EMEs at the expense of the G7/G8.

This would merely reflect the tectonic shift occurring in the global economy in the new millennium. While the rise of EMEs' share in the global economy measured in purchasing power parity (PPP) has longed been written about, what is even more striking is the doubling of their share over the last 13 years when measured at market exchange rates, which matters more to OECD countries since this measure is more relevant for international trade and hence for their own growth prospects (see Table 49.1). Indeed, their share has increased from around 30 per cent since the first G20 summit in 2008 to 40 per cent currently. All forward looking growth projections indicate that this rapid shift would continue, the current downturn notwithstanding. As Paul Kennedy underscored several years ago, geo-political advances are invariably preceded by economic rise.

Table 49.1

Share in Global GDP

(in %)

	At Market Exchange Rates		*At PPP*	
	AD Economies	*EMDEs*	*AD Economies*	*EMDEs*
1990	79.9	20.1	69.3	30.7
2000	79.7	20.3	62.8	37.2
2008	68.7	31.3	54.5	45.5
2013	60.7	39.3	49.1	50.9

Notes: PPP: purchasing power parity; AD Economies: Advanced economies; EMDEs: Emerging market and developing economies.

Source: WEO April 2013, International Monetary Fund.

Business Standard, New Delhi, 11 September 2013.

49

Rebooting the G20 Framework

As we approach the ninth G20 Summit at Brisbane, Australia, in mid-November 2014, the global economy continues its excruciatingly slow and painful recovery from the worst global financial and economic crisis (GFEC) since the Great Depression. It is perhaps an opportune time to revisit the signature contribution of the G20—the forward-looking 'Framework for Strong, Sustainable and Balanced Growth.'

Conceived and launched at a time it was felt that the global economy was firmly set on the path to robust recovery, the initial focus of the G20 Framework was to target large, unsustainable global imbalances that were perceived as one of the ultimate causes of the crisis. As the strong recovery of 2010 petered out, the G20 turned its attention to the 'strong' leg of the framework trinity that has more of a short- to medium-term focus. This is where matters currently stand, as the recovery remains tepid.

The current downturn in emerging markets (EMs) is cyclical, largely deriving from lower growth in advanced market economies (AMEs). The business cycle in AMEs, on the other hand, faces structural headwinds to growth in motion prior to the GFEC. These headwinds arise from a failure of economies to adjust to the disruptive and asymmetric effects of ageing, technology, globalization and anthropogenic climate change. These headwinds however also create new opportunities that can not only help mitigate their impact, but also generate new engines of growth.

The G20 Framework currently assumes that global GDP (gross domestic product) can be increased two per cent above current projections over the next five years, and future risks to the global economy considerably mitigated, if countries implement growth enhancing reforms and move towards external balance.

This may be an eminently sensible framework over the short to medium term. Over the longer term, however, the IMF and the G20 needs to equally underscore the sustainable panel of the triptych by shifting their focus from imbalances *per se* to their structure and direction in such a manner that the Framework has a single storyline consistent with the headwinds and opportunities inherent in demographic transition, globalization, technology and climate change. All of these are being debated directly or indirectly within various forums of the G20. The long term, after all, passes through the short and medium terms. The means cannot be very different from ultimate objectives.

Ageing vastly changes the structure of the workforce resulting in shrinking workers and burgeoning old age dependents that lowers trend growth and can result in fiscal stress. This however also creates new income generating opportunities in poorer, younger societies.

Technological change and globalization have combined to vastly improve efficiency and productivity that have a deflationary impact on consumer prices globally. While 'enforced globalization,' or free trade, during the colonial era widened income disparities between advanced economies and developing ones, the current post-nationalist phase of globalization has created opportunities for narrowing these income differences. In a globally integrated labour market, returns to labour have fallen, as high income AMEs become uncompetitive in labour-intensive manufacturing that is shifting to EMs.

The global economy, that grew very slowly right up to the 18th century, accelerated at an unprecedented rate over the last three centuries following the spread of the Industrial Revolution. This is resulting in anthropogenic climate change that threatens human existence if mitigating steps are not undertaken. This requires capping the overall rate of increase in human consumption. The most equitable way of doing so is by dampening consumption growth in countries with high per capita incomes that have contributed to most of the existing stock of greenhouse gases (GHGs), in order to compensate for the inevitable increase in emissions from developing countries to the point that per capita incomes converge—a process already underway.

Adaptation and mitigation of climate change however are also spawning new 'green' technologies that can be new engines of growth in advanced economies that retain their technological edge.

Accelerated globalization has exacerbated anomalous global imbalances, with EMs running current account surpluses and exporting rather than importing savings. This is what enabled AEs to grow robustly during the 'Great Moderation' through leveraged consumption despite stagnant wages. This model has arguably broken down with financial re-regulation, leading to a decline in growth in both AMEs and EMs.

EMs need structural reforms to rebalance their economies towards domestic demand as their primary engine of growth for a return to high growth. This will also enable them to avoid the middle-income trap. Advanced, ageing economies need structural reforms to become more competitive with EMs in the international market for labour. This twin rebalancing would further narrow per capita disparities between AMEs and EEs (emerging economics)— where EMs save less and consume more, and AEs save as well as invest more.

The Framework assumes that growth and development in a globalised world should primarily be based on domestic savings. Developing countries however need to run current account deficits (CADs) to top up domestic savings with external savings to boost investment and growth. The size of the deficit should, of course, be prudent and sustainable so that it can be funded by the market over the medium- to long-term, and reasonably secured against sudden stops. The counterpart of EM deficits is AME surpluses that can accelerate global income convergence. (Resource-rich countries are in a class of their own, as they are likely to run current account surpluses irrespective of whether they are developing or developed.)

The American and Chinese imbalances appear incongruous according to the above storyline, while the surpluses of Germany and Japan do not. As developed countries, they should run surpluses to smoothen global developmental imbalances by generating savings for investment in developing countries, and also to limit consumption growth. Of course, if developed countries end up exporting low-technology consumer goods, they could stifle growth in the developing countries. But this is patently not the case, as both Germany and Japan increasingly specialise in high-technology products and capital goods.

To conclude, the G20 Framework needs a rebooted thematically and temporally consistent storyline that ties together the forces of globalization, technology, demographic transition and climate change for strong, sustainable and balanced growth of the global economy going forward.

Business Standard, New Delhi, 24 July 2014.

50

The Great Stagnation and the G20

Since 2010, annual growth in both Advanced Economies (AEs) and Emerging Markets and Developing Economies (EMDEs) has fallen serially. It is far from clear whether it has bottomed out as International Money Fund's (IMF) current projections, notorious for subsequent downward revisions, for 2014 indicate. In 2013, AEs grew at less than 50 per cent of the 15 year average up to 2007. EMDEs grew at 4.6 per cent, or at around the 10 year pre-boom average of 1994-2003. It is important to remember that the sustainability of even this tepid recovery is untested, based as it is on extraordinary fiscal and especially monetary life support.

All major economic zones of the global economy are struggling. What seems like a robust revival in one quarter quickly yields to gloom in the next. Abenomics is struggling in Japan as the crucial third arrow of promised bold structural reforms has still to fire; the Eurozone is struggling as major economic and financial fault lines deriving from an unstable monetary union have been bared by markets; the US and China, the relatively strong nodes of the global economy, need major structural changes to rebalance their economies, externally and domestically—US needs to save more and become more competitive, and China needs to expand domestic demand—for a sustainable recovery; the serial growth decline in EMEs has still to bottom out, even as the 'Fedexit' and interest rate 'pivot' hang like the proverbial sword of Damocles overhead.

The economic boom of 2004-07 preceding the global financial crisis was mostly an EMDE phenomenon. They grew at an average of 7.9 per cent, pushing up global growth upward of 5 per cent compared to the 1994-2003 average of 3.5 per cent in what came to be described as the 'Great Moderation'. AEs continued to grow just below 3 per cent during this entire period. This boom was unsustainable as it was not driven by investment and income growth in AEs but by leveraged consumption, as both real wages and jobs growth remained stagnant. This consumption growth was facilitated by easy monetary policies, financialisation and outsourced production to EMDEs where large productivity shifts were taking place. This put downward pressures on consumer prices, led to mounting external imbalances and a savings glut as consumption growth in EMDEs did not rise commensurately.

This model of growth collapsed with the global financial crisis. The contours of new engines of growth are still unclear. Meanwhile, several of the infirmities of the Great Moderation have not only resurfaced but may have actually intensified.

First, the global savings glut has been compounded after the crisis by extra-accommodative monetary policies which, as before, are fuelling asset rather than investment booms.

Second, with asset prices unusually buoyant considering the depressed state of the economy, the disconnect between asset and consumer prices is now compounded by the disconnect between economic growth and financial markets.

Third, stagnant real wages and jobless growth, in particular falling labor participation rates, continue to depress consumer demand in advanced economies. The resultant growing inequality has only been compounded by ultra-easy monetary policy that rewards asset owners over savers.

Fourth, fiscal headwinds emanating from demographic transition prior to the crisis have only picked up speed with lower growth and the strong fiscal response to combat the crisis.

Fifth, high levels of leverage in the economy have not unwound, as the accelerated build up in public debt has countervailed private sector deleveraging.

Sixth, it is not clear that regulatory reform has made financial markets less risky, as Basel III retains pro-cyclicality through retention of the mark-to-market mechanism, and as shadow-banking, the source of financial instability in the global financial crisis, has rebounded at the expense of the more tightly regulated component.

Seventh, structural flaws in the European Monetary Union that were always latent have now been uncovered by markets that can now be expected to revolt periodically, keeping the union in a constant state of instability.

Eighth, the external demand rebalancing problem is now been compounded by the need for internal rebalancing of economies from public to private demand.

The common theme running through all these impediments to growth in major economic zones is the need for far reaching structural reforms. Thus far policy makers have mostly let macro-economic policies, especially monetary, do the heavy lifting. But macro-economic policies can only fix cyclical downturns and not structural impediments to growth. The G20, which famously co-ordinated the rescue from the global financial crisis, is now attempting to coordinate and nudge countries to carry through difficult structural reforms to drive up global growth. This Brisbane Action Plan is expected to be the centrepiece of the Leaders' Declaration at the forthcoming 9th G20 Summit in mid-November 2014. But such reforms are ultimately dependent on domestic political appetite, rather than on non-binding commitments in plurilateral fora. The appetite for deep-seated land, labour and product market reforms seems to be by and large weak currently, as democracies will try everything else first, and lower growth alone may not spur them into animated action. Therefore, until a dynamic new engine of growth emerges, the global economy, including emerging markets may well be headed for a 'Great Stagnation' in sharp contrast to the recent Great Moderation.

Mint, New Delhi, September 26, 2014.

PART TWO

Thematic

V

Bail-out and Stimulus

Global Financial Crisis and Fiscal Policy

Please, sir, I want some more.

Oliver Twist, *Charles Dickens*

51

Fiscal Paradoxes

After initially falling more sharply than in the first 12 months of the Great Depression of 1929, global output, industrial production, equity markets and trade have picked up smartly. While the recovery in advanced countries is anaemic compared to that in previous recessions, and is relatively jobless, dynamic emerging market economies seem to be firing on all cylinders once more.

Although extraordinary fiscal and monetary policies adopted by G20 countries are widely credited with having averted a second Great Depression, the global economy appears to be at an inflexion point. It is teetering between recovery in the real economy and renewed strains in financial markets, induced by a crisis brewing in the Eurozone that is threatening to boil over into the global economy. This disconnect between the real economy and financial markets is eerily familiar—it is a throwback to the confounding debate in the early stages of the global financial crisis. It was forgotten then—and is perhaps overlooked now—that the real economy lags behind developments in the financial sector. Financial markets eventually caught up with the real economy—and how! They could well do so again.

While large brick and mortar companies have been able to tap bond markets, the extent of recovery in financial markets is shallow. The banking sector started making profits through quantitative easing and taxpayer bailouts, but nevertheless it continues to deleverage, parking growing amounts of its own funds with the Federal Reserve (Fed); toxic mortgage-backed securities, which are a significant source of financial intermediation in recent years, never showed real signs of recovering their 'fair market value'; interbank borrowing spreads and US housing prices, after initial signs of recovery, are under renewed distress; delinquency rates for US residential and consumer loans have continued to rise and are at levels never seen since the US Fed started maintaining records from the mid-1980s, indicating that household balance sheets are still to recover.

The flip side of the unprecedented macroeconomic response to the global crisis is the unprecedented rise in fiscal deficits and public debt in advanced countries which has not been seen since the Second World War. The over-leveraging that lay at the heart of the global financial crisis is not going away, as public overleveraging is simply replacing private deleveraging.

In the past few weeks, fears regarding sustainability of sovereign debt have once again started to roil financial markets. Sovereign borrowing spreads are rising sharply in southern Europe; corporate borrowing costs are going up; capital flows to emerging markets are falling back; and safe haven flows are rising. The rescue package of €110 billion for Greece and the €750 billion financial backstop for the wider Euro zone have not quelled market fears about the health of the European banks and speculation that the crisis could spread, especially since deficits in some advanced countries outside the Euro zone are even higher.

As the German Chancellor Angela Merkel sagely observed, large deficits make governments cede control to markets since deficits need to be funded. If sovereign borrowing costs were to rise, servicing even the current debt levels would become more difficult. Markets also fear that this might constrain central banks to keep policy rates unnaturally low for an extended period of time, fuelling asset bubbles.

While an increase in public debt is the usual aftershock of deep recession and financial crises, structural deficits in several advanced countries were already rising even before the crisis on account of age-related expenditures. Moreover, the failure of transmission channels of monetary policy, the first line of macroeconomic response to downturns, placed a disproportionate burden on fiscal policy. There are now fears that cyclical deficits and anaemic growth could push countries into a debt trap unless longstanding social compacts are re-negotiated and structural reforms to raise growth are started quickly.

Governments can either grow their way out of high levels of public debt, as in the aftermath of the Second World War in advanced countries when the overall growth environment was good, and as India is currently doing, or inflate their way out, as in the 1970s following successive oil price shocks. Since long-term growth prospects in most advanced countries look shaky, market fears regarding future inflationary outcomes will not dissipate easily.

The International Monetary Fund (IMF) expects policy makers to navigate a narrow Goldilocks policy zone that is neither too early as to derail the recovery, nor too late as to provoke a market revolt. Emerging markets facing inflationary pressures should start exiting, which they are mostly doing, and advanced countries should 'stagger in' exit depending on fiscal and market pressures on individual countries. The US, the issuer of the global reserve currency with few market pressures on its borrowing programme, seems to echo the IMF view. Major European countries at the epicentre of the potential crisis are in favour of front-loading fiscal exit.

Yet while long-term fears are real, and some advanced economies may indeed be in a debt trap, some of the short-term fears are overblown. Even as sovereign borrowing spreads have risen in southern Europe, they have fallen in major advanced countries during the same period. Paradoxically, despite being insolvent, a number of advanced sovereigns do not have a liquidity problem. Collectively, sovereign borrowing costs and liquidity problems can worsen only if private demand is on track. Market fears regarding future inflation and sovereign default are countervailed by the current need to seek refuge in safe havens. Indeed, in such circumstances, rising sovereign borrowing costs is something to look forward to, akin to a canary in the goldmine signalling the revival of private demand and the time for fiscal exit.

This is where lies a second paradox, what Keynes described as the "paradox of thrift." Historical experience indicates that it is indeed possible to combine fiscal consolidation with growth, especially where there is greater reliance on expenditure control than on tax increases. Implementing structural reforms could also raise growth potential, making debt levels more sustainable and exercising a calming influence on markets. These medium-term issues are being addressed by the G20 through its ambitious Framework for Strong, Sustainable and Balanced Growth.

However, it is highly unlikely that it would be possible to have fiscal consolidation during a severe, synchronised economic downturn, more so since monetary policy transmission channels are still clogged. It is difficult to compress expenditure commensurate with the compression in revenue, especially since this has to partly substitute for the steep contraction in private consumption and investment. Even so, past experiences indicate that most of the fiscal deterioration in a downturn is through decline in revenue rather than through increase in automatic stabilisers or discretionary stimulus.

If there are cautionary lessons to be learnt from Greece, which has recently been penalised by markets for lack of fiscal credibility, there are also lessons to be learnt from Japan in the 1990s, and the US in 1937, where premature fiscal tightening resulted in both a deflationary spiral and an explosion of public debt. An undeniable virtue in normal times, fiscal chastity is of dubious value in deep recessions. Advanced countries could perhaps seek solace from the ancient Christian scholar, St. Augustine of Hippo, who famously beseeched the Lord to make him chaste, but not yet.

Business Standard, New Delhi, 1 July 2010.

52

New Roles for Fiscal Policy?

The recent financial and economic (crisis) has underscored the limits of monetary policy, and endowed fiscal policy, severely mauled several years ago by Milton Friedman and the Chicago School, with the new-found halo of macroeconomic tool of last resort. What is less prominently underscored, however, is that beyond restoring growth, the crisis has also defined entirely new spheres for fiscal policy, such as financial stability and correcting global imbalances. These new roles would make fiscal exit, already complicated by the confluence of rising (crisis related) cyclical and (ageing related) structural deficits, even harder. They also compound the difficulties of keeping public debt, including contingent liabilities in the form of effective public guarantees, within sustainable levels.

Some emerging markets had no doubt been using fiscal policy as part of their overall strategy to counter the destabilising impact of large capital inflows. Financial stability, however, has traditionally been addressed through regulation that ensured transparency, avoided conflicts of interest through firewalls, protected consumer and shareholder rights, ensured liquid and competitive markets, put limits on leverage, and mandated adequate capital buffers to avoid liquidity traps and provision for losses, etc. The recent crisis has now underscored how fragile and procyclical financial markets can be and, with several financial institutions being considered too systemically important to be allowed to fail, taxpayers' money and guarantees are likely to be used to bail-out what are essentially public utilities.

One way of addressing the issue is to break up financial institutions too large to fail, and raise capital buffers, including fee-based contributions by financial institutions to Federal Deposit Insurance Corporation (FDIC)-type insurance bodies that can resolve individual failures. The international consensus, at least in advanced economies, however, appears to be veering in the direction of taxing the financial sector to recover, and provide for future, public bailouts in the belief that, consequential moral hazards notwithstanding, these are eventually unavoidable. The underlying belief is that it is neither desirable nor practicable to break up big financial institutions. The International Monetary Fund (IMF) has lent its considerable authority and influence to this viewpoint. These taxes may initially be a new source of revenue but have the potential of distorting markets, fuelling new public expenditures and subjecting taxpayers to greater risks in the long run.

Despite the fact that the global economy has rarely been balanced, and current account imbalances reflect developmental, demographic and cultural asymmetries across nation states, the recent crisis has painted global imbalances as the fall guy whose disciplining is essential to reduce future risks to the global economy. Reducing global imbalances has become the subject of a raging debate amongst economists, in financial daily opinion pieces and within the G20.

Unfortunately, the debate has focused excessively on economies with the biggest current account imbalances and the role of pegged exchange rates. Simplistic solutions like tweaking the dollar-yen exchange rate under the Plaza Accord did little to reduce Japan's current account balance. Neither did the appreciation of the Chinese yuan post-2005 diminish that of China. Since a disproportionate share of China's exports involves processing of imported goods, Chinese exports are likely to be less affected by currency appreciation that would only make imports cheaper. Moreover, in the absence of other adjustments, the US may simply end up importing similar but costlier goods from other countries that are less competitive and productive than China, but more than the US. Even countries with floating exchange rates, such as Germany and Japan, have significant external imbalances, and there are imbalances even within the Euro zone. Indeed, given the vast differences in productivity between Germany on one hand and Southern Europe on the other, an appreciation of the euro could actually worsen current account imbalances of the latter.

External imbalances simply mirror domestic savings and investment imbalances, and can ultimately be adjusted only through changes in domestic consumption and investment patterns. While public policy can influence both, consumption patterns are largely cultural and behavioural in nature, whereas investment responds more to economic opportunities and policies. Thus, the loose monetary policy in the noughties in the US fuelled an asset-based consumption boom, while similarly low real interest rates fuelled an investment boom in China. US households are increasing their savings to repair their asset price-inflated balance sheets, but this is being partly offset by rising public sector government dis-savings as the government tries to compensate for the fall in private demand to stimulate growth, and takes on the liabilities of the over-leveraged financial sector. While changes in monetary policy may be required to prevent a relapse into overconsumption through future asset price booms, short-term interest rates may be too blunt a policy instrument for this, as there is likely to be collateral damage to investment and growth. Over the medium to long-term, beyond reducing government's own deficit, fiscal policy may be required to dampen private consumption, as the current US debate on the introduction of a new value added tax indicates.

Then again in surplus countries, either government expenditures would need to rise, or taxes lowered, to increase consumption. The jury, however, is still out debating whether such policy changes would induce the behavioural changes necessary to reduce savings and enhance consumption, especially since these would need to counter the logic of demographic transition and cultural preferences. Japan's burgeoning fiscal deficits have not resolved external imbalances. Would putting extra money in the hands of a Swabian housewife induce her to spend more or save more? Would increased government expenditure on social security nets in China induce Chinese households to collectively spend more of their current income even as dependency and poverty ratios fall? If fiscal adjustments simultaneously enhance fiscal deficits, as is likely although theoretically not necessary, there would be the additional pitfall of *Ricardian equivalence* as consumers may simply save more to offset higher taxes in future.

Ironically, despite being discredited for contributing to economic crises in the recent past, and question marks on its efficacy, since monetary policy has also been found wanting, the recent crisis has not only crowned fiscal policy as the macroeconomic policy tool of last resort, but is also resurrecting it for new functions to address financial stability and global imbalances. This could bring fiscal policy under increasing pressure not only in deficit countries, where it is already an issue, but also in surplus countries, where it is presently not an issue. While the tool itself may be robust, policy makers would need to use the tool adroitly, especially since there could be conflicting objectives at the best of times. Moreover, experience indicates that fiscal policy tends to get emasculated by the political minefield it has to necessarily navigate. Going forward, this does not bode well for either inflation or interest rates.

Business Standard, New Delhi, 27 April 2010.

53

Growth Now, Need for Austerity Next

It is not only India that had a disastrous fourth quarter in calendar year 2012. All major advanced economies—the US, the UK, Japan and the larger Euro zone, including Germany, Italy, Spain and France—registered negative growth. Moreover, the peripheral economies of the Euro zone have been in steep recession for some time. And the strong recovery in emerging markets seems to be stalling. It is, therefore, a little surprising that the communiqué of G20 finance ministers and central bank governors issued from Moscow on 16 February 2013 should rather complacently talk about a reduction in near-term tail risks, and focus more on medium- to long-term challenges.

It is possible that the G20 finance ministers took a deliberate decision not to spook markets. However, the markets can also be spooked if they feel that policy makers are not on top of the situation. It is, therefore, likely that too much has been read into the increase in asset prices and the reduction in sovereign borrowing spreads in the Euro zone periphery.

Indeed, if we consider the Dow Jones Industrial Average (DJIA) as a proxy for the financial markets, it has been improving almost continuously since it reached its nadir following the collapse of Lehman Brothers. The DJIA is now pushing 14,000—the peak during the Great Moderation, prior to the global financial crisis. Trading volumes, however, are much lower compared to the Great Moderation, and the buoyancy is not account of the increase in exposure of the financial markets to the real economy, but of policy actions by central banks.

These policy actions have repeatedly injected record levels of liquidity that has fed asset prices but with little impact on the real economy, since normal transmission channels of monetary policy remain dysfunctional on account of continued deleveraging by households and banks. US personal savings, which hovered between 1.5 and 2.5 per cent of the domestic personal income in 2005-2007 were still at a high 4.7 per cent in the fourth quarter of 2012. The abnormally large deposits that banks have parked with the US Federal Reserve (Fed) since 2008—a measure of risk aversion by banks on the one hand and a lack of demand on the other—remain at their crisis highs. Central banks now seem to be fuelling the kind of asset price inflation that is attributed to shadow banks in the run-up to the global financial crisis. The most recent rally since November 2012 is not a response to current growth trends, but on the expectation that central banks will continue to keep their taps open in response to the dismal fourth quarter growth numbers.

It may be recalled that the boom in asset prices during the lead up to the global financial crisis was accompanied by an economic boom—not because rising wages were increasing demand but because financial innovation and weak regulation translated the asset boom into a consumption boom through the wealth effect and leverage. Central banks in advanced countries are now waiting for this wealth effect to kick in to lift economic growth. The G20 has given carte blanche to central banks, although the fourth quarter figures indicate that this is still not happening, and despite cross-border policy spillovers ('currency wars'). So, what needs to be done if Godot does not turn up?

The G20 communiqué perhaps has the right prescription for growth: fall back on fiscal policy, despite the dramatic increase in fiscal deficits and public debt. The tension between the need for austerity over the medium-term and the need for growth over the short-term is reflected in the latest communiqué, as it indeed has been ever since the fourth G20 summit at Toronto in June 2010. The Russian presidency's initiative to seek technical advice from international organisations on dealing with the alarming overhang of public debt is timely. The case for Keynesian stimulus in a situation of weak private demand, low inflation, tight sovereign borrowing spreads and dysfunctional monetary policy is also impeccable. The recovery has been the most robust, relatively speaking, in the US and China—the two countries that have had the most aggressive and sustained fiscal stimulus. The International Monetary Fund (IMF) has also recently revised potential fiscal multipliers for advanced economies.

But fiscal multipliers do not seem to have attained their potential, since fiscal policy seems to be hamstrung by Ricardian equivalence (the US) and premature austerity (Europe). The recovery has been tepid and unsustainable since the rebalancing from public demand to private is not taking place. A Japan-like situation is developing, in which a dose of fiscal stimulus lifts the GDP (gross domestic product) slightly for a while (the most recent spurt in Japanese growth was in the wake of the post-Tsunumi stimulus), then falls back again, even as public debt continues to rise alarmingly. Japan at least has a huge domestic demand for government bonds, supplemented on the margin by the original quantitative easing factory—the Bank of Japan. US government bonds are dependent on both external demand and the US Fed.

The recent G20 focus on infrastructure investment—that the Indian Prime Minister has underscored in all recent G20 summits—as a mechanism for reviving growth and creating jobs appears to be spot on, although it is perhaps too sanguine about private investment taking the lead. A change in the fiscal mix in advanced countries from consumption to investment could create the kind of demand that crowds in private investment, and increase fiscal multipliers by countering Ricardian equivalence, as jobs are created directly, giving the sense of permanent increase in income and generating the confidence to spend.

The G20 has come a long way from viewing infrastructure investment as a developing country issue to be handled in their Development Working Group, to recognition of the role it can play in reviving growth and creating jobs in developed countries by shifting it to their flagship Framework Working Group. The nitty-gritty is still to be fleshed out, even as G20 commissions yet another study on the subject by international organisations.

Business Standard, New Delhi, 22 February 2013.

54

Austerity and Growth

A Road Map

Advanced economies have been growing significantly below trend for several quarters despite aggressive policy support. There is a pressing need to find a solution to their slow growth and high unemployment. The short-term answer lies in increasing government expenditure, but medium-term considerations require that the fiscal deficit and debt should be brought under control. In fact, some will argue that even short-term considerations require reduction in the fiscal deficit, as markets might penalise governments by increasing borrowing costs. Interest rates have already risen sharply in peripheral Euro zone countries that do not have a central bank backstop. Their debt dynamics are already unsustainable as a result. However, even in those advanced economies that have the advantage of a central bank backstop, when private demand returns and interest rates normalise, debt dynamics could quickly look unsustainable given relatively low potential growth.

Growth in advanced countries is, however, not back on track, as they are growing at only about half the 1994-2003 (pre-boom) averages.

Since private demand continues to be weak and monetary policy ineffectual, the International Monetary Fund (IMF) has recently clarified that fiscal multipliers are larger than usual. Not only would fiscal contraction make matters worse, but low interest rates and inflation have created the fiscal space to continue with stimulus measures. There have, of course, been episodes of 'contractionary expansion' in the past, but this looks unlikely in a synchronised recession and fiscal tightening.

The G20 and IMF recipe for resolving this policy dilemma is that those countries that have fiscal space must stand ready to continue with fiscal stimulus, should conditions deteriorate. It is not clear what countries that do not have this space, mostly in the Euro zone periphery, should do in the circumstances. A comprehensive restructuring of the Euro zone, currently under negotiation, combining fiscal and banking integration, central bank backstops and mechanisms for fiscal transfers, is necessary in such cases.

It is also not clear how short-term and medium-term objectives should be harmonised. In real life, the short-term and the long-term are part of the same continuum. What policy makers, therefore, need is a road map with clear signals along the way that would enable them to move seamlessly from the short to the medium to the long term.

In particular, policy makers need to know when to start exiting from extraordinary policies currently in place. They should be open to the possibility that a return to former growth rates may not occur on account of a permanent loss in demand. Policy makers should, therefore, not be looking at growth, but at treasury yields and inflation. These could be the canaries in the goldmine signalling the revival of animal spirits and closing of the output gap. At that point monetary policy would need to take over the mantle of macroeconomic stabilisation from fiscal policy, finely balancing the need to anchor inflationary expectations on one hand by gradually normalising interest rates and unwinding unconventional monetary measures, while gradually inflating away high levels of public debt through some degree of financial repression on the other.

Operationally, macroeconomic policies may need to pass through four broad stages to balance conflicting short-term and long-term objectives. The first stage—the present—would consist of continued fiscal stimulus and easy monetary policies.

Rising yields on sovereign bonds and/or inflation would be the first signal of the return of private demand and stability in financial markets, and the narrowing of the output gap. In this second stage, the withdrawal of fiscal stimulus should be calibrated and gradual, so as not to choke off the incipient recovery. The mantle of stimulus would also be increasingly borne by monetary policy, which would remain easy, although unconventional methods such as quantitative and credit easing, which suppress market signals relating to government borrowing costs, would need to be phased out.

In the third stage, when the recovery is secure and robust, fiscal consolidation should be accorded top priority. During this phase, central banks may need to keep interest rates low not only to support the recovery, but also to assist in fiscal consolidation. Given the combination of high levels of public debt and low trend growth, there may be little option but to inflate part of the debt away by keeping real interest rates negative to stabilise debt.

The fourth stage would be when policy makers have the confidence that debt dynamics have stabilised. This would mark a normalisation of interest rates and return to conventional, rule-bound monetary policies, such as the Taylor Rule.

The rollback of central bank balance sheets would have to be deftly managed. Unconventional monetary policies have led to a sharp increase in the monetary base. As private demand picks up, large amounts parked by depository banks with central banks would go back in circulation as the money multiplier returns to more normal levels. This could be inflationary, unless the central bank shrinks its balance sheet and soaks up the excess money in circulation. The rollback of the balance sheet could be measured and calibrated in the third phase to keep real interest rates slightly negative, while anchoring inflationary expectations. Be it as it may, in view of the huge expansion in their balance sheets at a time of rock-bottom interest rates, unless deftly managed central banks may be constrained to book huge capital losses in the process. This burden would ultimately need to be passed on to the taxpayer through the budget.

The austerity-growth policy equation in developing countries is quite different. For example, in India, growth has slowed but inflation remains high. On the one hand, this is constraining the space for monetary policy. On other hand, the imperative for fiscal consolidation is greater and immediate. This is not on account of possible market revolt—despite high deficits debt/GDP (gross domestic product) ratios have scarcely changed—but to avoid crowding out of private demand and reducing interest payments as a proportion of revenue.

Business Standard, New Delhi, 7 January 2013.

55

How Risk-free is Domestic Sovereign Debt?

The resurgence of the Euro zone sovereign debt crisis in Cyprus, and the proposed 'bail-in' of bondholders, has once again raised some fundamental questions regarding sovereign debt, long considered the risk-free benchmark over which all other debt is priced at a spread.

Until the Latin American debt crisis of the 1980s, the widely held view, famously articulated by Walter Wriston, head of Citibank, was that sovereigns could not go bankrupt. They could, and did, wilfully default on their debt, but nominal default could be avoided by central banks printing money. Several governments, including advanced countries, have inflated their way out of high levels of debt right through history, and may well do so again in the wake-up of the recent build-up of public debt to unsustainable levels.

Widespread public debt defaults during the Latin American debt crisis put paid to this belief. These defaults were hardly wilful. Latin American governments did not have the capacity to repay debt that was not denominated in their own currencies. Governments, indeed whole countries, could and did go bankrupt insofar as external debt was concerned because their central banks could not print the reserve currencies in which this debt is denominated.

The Latin American debt crisis, however, merely qualified the general belief regarding the 'non-bankruptibility' of governments by excluding the external debt component from conventional wisdom. This gave rise to a whole new industry focusing on external debt management.

This belief has now been further eroded in the wake of a full-blown sovereign debt crisis in the Euro zone. Peripheral countries are bankrupt not because of their inability to service or repay foreign debt, but on account of debt denominated in their own currency, the euro. This raises some interesting new issues regarding the sustainability of domestic public debt.

In a federation, where both the centre and states have independent or separate fiscal powers, these issues are better appreciated through the lens of the famous Mundell-Fleming 'impossible trinity.' According to this trilemma, it is possible to have only two of the following three: a fixed exchange rate, monetary independence and free capital flows.

A country may adopt any constellation of the impossible trinity. The US, the UK, Euro zone and Japan—the reserve currency areas—have monetary independence, free capital flows and a floating exchange rate. India's 'managed float' closely resembles these countries. China, on the other hand, has chosen a fixed exchange rate, monetary policy independence and capital controls.

At the sub-national level, however, be it a federation or monetary union, the equation is always the same no matter what constellation is adopted at the federal level: a fixed exchange rate, capital mobility within the federation/monetary union, and monetary dependence.

Monetary dependence not only means that sub-national entities cannot use monetary policy for macroeconomic stabilisation (which they of course cannot), but also that their debt does not have a central bank monetary backstop. Their fiscal policy can consequently be hostage to market forces, as in the Euro zone presently, where peripheral sovereign borrowing spreads have risen sharply. In sharp contrast, sovereign spreads are at historic lows in other reserve currency areas, including in the economically stronger Euro zone countries and where debt/GDP (gross domestic product) ratios are higher, on account of the general flight to safety in financial markets and generous quantitative easing by central banks.

Federations have found a way out of the trilemma by substituting federal fiscal backstops for central bank backstops, thus insulating sub-nationals from market revolt. The moral hazard inherent in such fiscal backstops is addressed through the imposition of hard budget constraints on sub-national entities.

Thus, American states are constitutionally barred from running budget deficits. While Indian states can run fiscal deficits, Article 293 of the Indian Constitution severely restricts the borrowing powers of sub-national entities by requiring prior permission of the federal authority. In China, much of the sovereign borrowing is done by sub-national authorities and state-controlled banks. The current market view, however, is that these are backstopped by the federal government. Should the federal government signal that they are not, a Euro zone type debt crisis could erupt in future.

This federal fiscal backstop and transfer mechanism is what enables sub-national governments to borrow at rates similar to those of the federal government, with the market mostly overlooking differences in sub-national balance sheets and productivity. Thus, debt stressed Indian and American states, such as Kerala and California, are able to borrow at more or less the same rates as the federal government and other states with better balance sheets.

This is exactly what happened in the Euro zone following the monetary union. The market treated the Euro zone like a fiscal federation, despite the fact that there was only a fiscal compact (the Maastricht Treaty) and not a hard budget constraint, and no fiscal or monetary mechanism for bailouts. As a result, peripheral countries with weak finances and banking systems and lower productivity—the PIIGS—were able to borrow at rates similar to countries with far stronger economies and public finances through capital inflows from other countries within the Euro zone that ran current account surpluses.

The global financial crisis laid bare this fatal flaw in the design of the Euro zone. The market discovered that there was neither a monetary nor fiscal backstop for the constituent countries. The adhoc fiscal stops put in place, like the European Stability Mechanism, were too small to bail out the larger Euro zone countries like Spain and Italy that were in trouble with bond markets. Peripheral Euro zone countries, with large fiscal and current account deficits (CAD) (that made them dependent on external capital flows), consequently became hostage to market forces, with borrowing spreads diverging sharply as capital fled to safer havens within the Euro zone.

The outright monetary transactions announced by the European Central Bank (ECB) calmed markets by holding out the hope that Euro zone sovereign debt now had a conditional central bank monetary backstop, leading to a sharp fall in bond yields. However, this belief could well be belied in future if the conditions are not met. After all, the proposed 'bail-in' of Cypriot bank debt is effectively a nominal default of sovereign debt as investors are expected to absorb the sharp fall in the face value of Greek government bonds in which their money was invested. This, however, has not affected market sentiment within the Euro zone because these investors are mostly 'outsiders' (Russians). If the Cyprus model becomes the template for resolving future sovereign debt troubles in the Euro zone, which it well might be, bond vigilantes can revisit their recent risk re-profiling of Euro zone sovereign debt.

The bottom line is that external debt as well as sovereign domestic debt in poorly designed monetary unions is not free from the risk of nominal default. However, in federations and unitary states, public debt denominated in the domestic currency will always remain the risk-free benchmark.

Business Standard, New Delhi, 10 June 2013.

56

Rogoff and Reinhart

How Much Debt is Cool Enough?

In a vastly influential paper "Growth in a Time of Debt," based on a data set from 44 countries and spanning two centuries, economists Kenneth Rogoff and Carmen Reinhart (R&R) arrived at crisp conclusions that shaped the growth-austerity public policy debate in advanced economies.

They argued that while the relationship between government debt and real GDP (gross domestic product) growth was weak for debt-GDP ratios below a threshold of per cent of GDP, when debt-GDP exceeded 90 per cent median growth fell by 1 per cent, and average growth considerably more.

Economists pointed to errors in the spreadsheet used by R&R, which generated an animated debate. R&R admitted the error, corrected their spreadsheets and concluded that the error merely moderated their numbers without substantially weakening the underlying argument.

They also clarified, first, austerity was not the only policy prescription for high debt that emerged from their study. Second, it was never their argument that the correlation implied that the line of causation led from high debt to low growth, as it could also be the other way round. Three Core Issues When dust settles on the storm in the teacup, there remain three issues relating to public debt sustainability that have not been addressed in the debate: first, the role of high levels of debt *versus* the current fiscal balance in determining the sustainable level of debt; second, the ahistoricity implicit in the arguments; and third, a disregard for the geopolitics of debt.

First, the sustainable level of debt depends both on the level of debt as well as the structural government balance, in relation to the underlying growth dynamic of an economy. Debt may shoot up dramatically on account of high cyclical deficits caused by war, financial crises, etc.

However, as long as primary balance is attained subsequently, a country can live with high levels of debt through growth. High levels of debt nevertheless matter because large interest pay-outs make it more difficult to achieve a primary balance.

Second, R&R's averages are derived from an era where trend growth in advanced economies was higher, and their structural deficits lower, because societies were younger and less developed. They could consequently grow out of higher levels of debt compared with what is possible today.

These economies therefore have already started defaulting on public debt through financial repression engineered by central banks. Fast growing emerging markets, in contrast, can now sustain higher levels of debt compared with the past. Third, the US can sustain higher levels of public debt on account of the privilege that generates a bottomless global appetite for the dollar as premier reserve currency.

Some European countries face market revolt at lower debt levels. Japan is an outlier in this regard on account of unusually high domestic private savings. Fast growing emerging economies, for the same reason, cannot sustain high levels of external debt. R&R arrived at lower thresholds of external debt for developing (non-reserve issuing currency) countries.

When we put all the pieces together, we are left with the great macroeconomic conundrum of the day in advanced economies: slowing growth is associated with rising debt; expansionary fiscal consolidation is not possible because demand has collapsed. Therefore, as long as inflation remains low, there may be no option to running large deficits and increasing debt to revive growth.

The Economic Times, New Delhi, 17 May 2013.

57

Resurgence and Limitations of Keynesianism

The dominance of Keynesian economics in the post Second World War period is largely credited to the widely-held belief that it was expansionary fiscal policy that was effective in countering the Great Depression of the 1930s. The case for Keynesian stimulus is straightforward, following directly from the National Income identity (Y = C+I+G+Net Exports) and the investment-income multiplier. An expansion of government consumption and investment merely substitutes for the contraction in private demand to restore the economy to trend growth and full employment through the multiplier process. When domestic demand destruction is combined with external demand shock, and monetary policy is also ineffective, theoretically there is no alternative to fiscal expansion to restore growth over the short-term. It is relevant to note that Keynes made no distinction between government consumption and government investment, as far as impact is concerned.

Fiscal policy, however, soon became a political minefield, easy to navigate while in expansionary mode, but difficult to exit following the recovery. Fortified by the Phillips curve that postulated a trade-off between inflation and growth, and difficulties in estimating potential growth, governments kept pushing the fiscal envelope to increase growth even when fiscal stimulus was not necessary, and even when it was contra-indicated. Fiscal policy therefore had an inherent inflationary bias that tended to crowd out private demand. This ultimately culminated in the 'stagflation' of the 1970s, with the widely acclaimed Phillips curve breaking down.

Milton Friedman sounded what appeared at that time to be the death knell of Keynesian economics by placing monetary policy at the heart of macroeconomic stabilisation. He identified inflation as basically a monetary phenomenon. While strict monetarism was never followed, Paul Volcker's dogged and aggressive monetary tightening finally tamed hyper-inflation. Inflation rates have been well anchored ever since in advanced economies. Over time, monetary policy tools were streamlined and became more rule-bound, with several central banks following variants of the 'Taylor Rule.'

The dominance of monetary policy was assisted, on one hand, by the decline in the role of public sector in the economy, and the deepening and sophistication of financial markets through which monetary policy is transmitted. It therefore emerged as a powerful, and arguably more easily manageable, alternative tool to stabilise the economy. Discretionary fiscal policy fell into disrepute, although fiscal policy continued to play a role through 'automatic stabilisers,' such as unemployment benefits, that kicked in as economic activity fell below trend, and were automatically phased out as growth recovered, keeping the structural balance stable.

Given the sharp contraction in economic activity in the wake of the global financial crisis of 2007-08, both monetary and discretionary fiscal policy were used in what was an unprecedented aggressive and globally coordinated policy response under the aegis of the G20. As the crisis deepened and lingered, and conventional monetary policy rapidly reached its lower zero-bound limits, unconventional monetary policies, such as quantitative easing (outright purchase of long-term government bonds and private assets) quickly followed.

The effectiveness of unconventional monetary policies during the Great Recession is controversial. There is a broad consensus that the liquidity pumped in by central banks was effective in countering the deflationary spiral that characterised the Great Depression in the US. Beyond this, opinion is divided as the current recovery from recession is the worst on record in the post-war period. Monetary policy seems stuck in a liquidity trap, with the liquidity pumped in by central banks being washed back through a sharp and unprecedented increase in bank reserves parked with them. The excess liquidity is also creating asset bubbles and spilling overseas, with both asset prices and emerging market exchange rates responding to signals from the US monetary policy rather than to economic fundamentals.

The current revival of Keynesianism is underpinned by the realisation that while both monetary and fiscal policy have a role to play in macroeconomic stabilisation, discretionary fiscal stimulus remains a powerful macroeconomic policy tool in certain circumstances. We need to understand what policy is optimal in different circumstances.

While each growth crisis has its own defining features, and are often hybrid in nature, for the purpose of analytical clarity, one could perhaps classify growth crises into three different types as follows:

(a) If the decline in growth is because of demand (domestic or external, or both) slackening over the business cycle—usually associated with spare capacity and inflation falling below target—this could be termed a *Type A* growth crisis.

(b) If the decline in growth is because of a supply shock (such as oil price increase, monsoon failure or 'sudden stops')—usually associated with rising inflation and falling real growth—this could be termed a *Type B* growth crisis.

(c) If the decline in growth is because of a collapse in both demand and supply caused by financial crises and associated deleveraging and deflationary tendencies—this could be termed a *Type C* growth crisis. This is the kind of protracted crisis that advanced economies are currently experiencing.

In Type A crisis, conventional easy monetary policy along with a small dose of 'automatic' fiscal stimulus over a relatively short period should ordinarily be adequate to revive growth, as the decline in private demand is cyclical. The attendant increase in public debt on account of the decline in revenue (because of lower growth) and stimulus would be relatively modest, and the economy should be in a position to grow out of this subsequently.

In Type B crisis, Keynesian fiscal stimulus will only aggravate the crisis—as in the stagflationary 1970s—as trend growth may shift downward permanently if the supply shock is permanent. Since there is no decline in private demand, macroeconomic stimulus is not warranted. Indeed, monetary tightening may be warranted to keep a lid on inflation, although this would do little to address the underlying supply shock which lies at the root of the crisis. If the supply shock cannot be neutralised through administrative actions, a combination of adjusting to the decline in growth over the short-term and structural reforms over the medium term to raise growth potential (including addressing specific supply shocks) is the optimal strategy. Such a strategy is however politically challenging, as there would be pressure for fiscal and monetary expansion to counteract the decline in growth.

In Type C crisis, the need for stimulus is manifest on account of the decline in private demand. Since monetary policy transmission channels are likely to be impaired by deleveraging, and constrained by zero-bound interest rates, the burden of stimulus falls disproportionately on fiscal policy. Fiscal multipliers in such circumstances are therefore potentially higher than usual, and even more so if the collapse in demand is global. Fiscal multipliers however can still be hobbled by Ricardian equivalence and deleveraging. Tax cuts and direct transfers could be used to pay down debt, or saved in anticipation of future tax increases, rather than consumed. The optimum fiscal strategy in such circumstances would be to, first, accelerate the deleveraging, and second, design a fiscal mix that relies minimally on broken transmission channels. This could involve direct government expenditure in areas such as investment in infrastructure which has both demand and supply side features, and can crowd in private investment.

There are three caveats to the stylised argument above. The first caveat is that if the underlying crisis is national or regional, the recovery could be accelerated by external demand, and therefore extended stimulus may not be necessary. This is what happened in the aftermath of the East Asian crisis. However, if the financial crisis is global, such as the present one, a period of extended fiscal stimulus may be necessary until such time private demand returns, leading to a dramatic rise in public debt over a relatively short period.

The second caveat is that if trend growth is permanently impaired there is danger of 'over-stimulation.' Hence inflation—both consumer and asset prices—rather than the growth rate, should be the signal for policy makers to exit stimulative policies. Many observers are now of the view that the US Federal Reserve (Fed) should have tightened policy much earlier, in 2003 and 2004, when asset prices were exploding, even though core consumer price inflation remained within its target of 2 per cent. Likewise, in his testimony before the US Congress on 22 May 2013, while giving the first indications of 'tapering' to markets, Ben Bernanke cited financial stability as a concern even though employment, inflation and GDP (gross domestic product) growth were all below target.

The third caveat is that the dramatic increase in public debt, the lagged effect of a protracted period of high budget deficits and falling revenues on account of low growth, would need to be addressed and an answer found.

The historical record indicates that growth crises caused by financial crises can be protracted. Financing large fiscal deficits over an extended period is therefore an issue, and depends on a number of factors. Keynes never elaborated how the additional government expenditure is to be financed. Financing deficits through money creation and through borrowing from the public have clearly different effects. Excessive money creation can stoke inflation while pure borrowing can push up interest rates.

The 'flight to quality' creates some fiscal space during financial crises as it enables governments to finance larger deficits than usual without an adverse fall out on borrowing costs. Where government deficits are countervailed by large private surpluses, as in the case of Japan, it is even possible to run up public debt in excess of 200 per cent of GDP without apparent macroeconomic instability such as inflation or high borrowing costs. This fiscal space is limited by the quantum of private surpluses available, beyond which government's borrowing costs would begin to rise. However, where there is a large external demand for domestic debt—as in the case of the US—it may be possible to finance large deficits over extended periods even in the absence of private sector surpluses.

Beyond private and external sources of demand for public debt stands the central bank, the lender of last resort. In the current era of fiat money, they can theoretically finance any level of budget deficit to meet their nominal interest rate target, which is exactly what quantitative easing is doing. They are constrained only by prudential self-restraint as uncontrolled money creation can destabilise their macroeconomic objective of price stability and full employment, which is precisely what occurred in the stagflationary 1970s. Indeed, in such circumstances, to a great extent the divide between fiscal and monetary policy collapses as monetary policy becomes simply an extension of fiscal policy, as it enables the government to finance large deficits without tax increases while keeping borrowing costs low.

Where the initial public debt is high, and private sector surpluses and external appetite are exhausted, large budget deficits sustained over long periods can lead to market revolt without the central bank backstop. This is precisely what happened in the European Monetary Union, where the ECB is not mandated to support sovereign bonds of individual countries, and where some peripheral countries had run up large amounts of public debt. Following the market revolt, peripheral sovereign bond yields in the Euro zone stabilised only after ECB's announcement of its programme of outright purchase of peripheral sovereign bonds without limit in pursuit of its financial stability mandate, which is the equivalent of a central bank backstop.

From the above, it would be clear that the ability of a country to run large budget deficits over an extended period in a recessionary period would vary from country to country. The flip side of this is that the deeper a country's pocket in a recessionary environment, and the bigger and longer deficits it runs relative to its underlying growth potential, the more difficult it might be to exit these policies when the economy shows signs of recovery without creating macroeconomic instabilities that might derail the recovery itself.

This is the problem that both Japan and the US face today: the former has a huge public debt, while the latter's central bank has a swollen balance sheet. It is difficult to see how these can be unwound without renegotiating social compacts or a destabilising phase of financial repression. Indeed, all countries will need a map for the short- and medium-term. Unless there is a convincing programme of medium-term fiscal consolidation, market revolt in the short-term can become severe.

The current Type C crisis in advanced economies has spilled over into the emerging market and developing economies (EMDEs) through trade and investment channels, leading to a Type A crisis, and in some cases a Type B crisis. Macroeconomic policies in these economies should therefore be very different from those in advanced economies. The focus in those countries should be not so much on stimulus as on addressing the underlying supply shocks and structural reforms, including investment in infrastructure through a change in the fiscal policy mix.

Financial Express, 23 October 2013.

VI

Helicopter Ben

Global Financial Crisis and Monetary Policy

58

Cowry Shells to Helicopter Ben

Exchange of goods and services through trade and markets existed since the dawn of human civilisation. Beginning with barter, exchange systems inexorably gravitated towards money that is universally traded in exchange for any good or service.

While the earliest forms of money, or currency, were fashioned from, or comprised, scarce and coveted items such as cowry shells, settled civilisations gravitated towards first minting their currencies in, and later pegging them to, precious metals.

Barring brief and intermittent suspensions, the world's major economies were on the gold standard until as recently as the 1970s. The gold standard severely limited the scope of macroeconomic policies in stabilising growth as money could not be created by fiat.

Fiscal expansion took place either through crowding out private demand, through higher taxes or debt (i.e., deferred taxes), or through war and plunder. Sovereigns were also tempted to try innovative means to balance their budgets, debasing the currency or issuing more currency than the amount of precious metal in stock—like the US under the post-war Bretton Woods system—being the most popular.

Such innovations were subject to Gresham's Law, by which bad money drove good money out of circulation, as market participants hoarded the underlying precious metal and offloaded the debased currency. The world finally went off the gold standard in the early 1970s when it emerged that the US was minting dollars far in excess of its stock of gold.

Monetary policy under the gold standard was limited to interest rate adjustments that could impact the velocity of money in circulation but not its quantum. Money supply was endogenous due to movement in gold at fixed exchange rates in response to trade surplus or deficit.

Since the use of monetary policy is contingent on developed financial markets that can transmit short-term interest rates to the wider economy, its utility as a macroeconomic policy tool is a relatively recent phenomenon. The efficacy of transmission mechanisms continues to be an issue in most emerging markets even today, constraining them from effectively using short-term interest rates and to rely, in addition, on monetary aggregates, like the statutory liquidity ratio and the credit reserve ratio, in the case of Reserve Bank of India (RBI).

Sudden expansion in the supply of precious metals, such as following the Spanish conquests of Latin America, or the gold rush in the second half of the 19th century in the US, could lead to price inflation. On the whole, however, the gold standard ensured remarkable price stability. There was limited scope for seigniorage to compensate for the increase in the supply of goods and services in the economy, as money creation was dependent on increase in the supply of precious metals. Indeed, it could be argued that the gold standard had an inbuilt bias towards deflation, just as the move away from the gold standard has an inbuilt bias towards inflation.

Modern macroeconomic policies to stabilise growth, consisting of the familiar mix of monetary and fiscal policies, are generally traced to the aftermath of the Great Depression of the 1930s. Milton Friedman argued that the Great Depression could have been averted had the Federal Reserve lowered, rather than increased, interest rates in the face of deflation. It was compelled to do so to protect the value of the dollar as speculators demanded gold for currency. However, it was the Keynesian solution of using expansionary fiscal policy to counteract the precipitous fall in private demand that finally pulled the US out of the depression.

Fiscal policy, however, is more susceptible to political considerations than monetary policy. Governments were tempted to flog fiscal policy too hard, constraining central banks to accommodate such expansion far beyond the expansion in economic activity. Milton Friedman and the Chicago School sounded the death knell of Keynesian economics by placing monetary policy at the heart of macroeconomic policy. Over time, monetary policy tools were refined and streamlined and became more rule-bound. The US Federal Reserve (Fed) has by and large followed the Taylor Rule, adjusting short-term interest rates to attain targeted inflation and trend growth and rates. Some central banks moved to pure inflation targeting.

There are, however, limits to the use of monetary policy since interest rates cannot dip below zero to stimulate the demand for money. This is the liquidity trap, into which Japan fell in the 1990s, and arguably the US in the wake of the recent global financial crisis. Ben Bernanke, current chairman of the US Fed and a historian of the Great Depression, postulated that in these circumstances central banks should expand money supply not only through the discount window, but also through purchase of government (quantitative easing; QE) and/or private (credit easing; CE) assets, giving him the epithet of 'Helicopter Ben,' as this is tantamount to dropping money by helicopter.

In a true liquidity trap, however, neither conventional nor unconventional monetary policy works, as monetary policy transmission channels break down altogether. In these circumstances macroeconomic policy is constrained to fall back on fiscal policy, as in Japan since the 1990s, and in the US and much of the developed world currently, to pull the economy out of crisis.

Conventional wisdom on the efficacy of fiscal policy is, however, mixed. According to the International Monetary Fund (IMF), past experience on the use of fiscal policies indicates that they have been by and large ineffectual in developing countries, and even in developed countries. They have worked only where they have been timely, temporary and targeted. Political economy considerations make such a happy confluence challenging at best, and in case of a protracted downturn sovereigns may once again be constrained to eventually inflate their way out of a debt trap like in the 1970s in the wake of the oil price shock.

The Economic Times, New Delhi, 30 March 2010.

59

Quantitative Easing and the Great Recession

Did US Federal Reserve's (Fed) aggressive monetary policy, and in particular quantitative easy (QE) and credit easing (CE), pull its economy from the brink of a second Great Depression?

The Great Depression of the 1930s was caused by a simultaneous contraction in credit and money supply. Deleveraging reduces the velocity of money. According to Fisher's equation ($M*V = P*Q$), at any given money supply, a reduction in the velocity of money would lead to either a decline in nominal prices (deflation) or output, or both. Hence increasing money supply should stabilise GDP (gross domestic product).

Central banks have little control over credit markets. But they can certainly influence money supply. Could better use of monetary policy have prevented the Great Depression of the 1930s? Yes, say two celebrated historians of the Great Depression, one of whom is none other than Ben Bernanke, current chairman of the US Fed and the other is of course Milton Friedman. During the Great Depression, the US Fed was constrained by the gold standard in driving up money supply to counteract deleveraging. Rather fortuitously, one of these economists was at the helm of the US Fed just as the world stood on the brink of a second Great Depression in 2007-08.

This time round the US Fed was ahead of the curve. It started monetary easing even when policy makers elsewhere were still combating inflation. Deflation was perceived as the greater danger that lurked just beyond the inflationary horizon. As the threat of deflation crystallised with the credit freeze, US monetary policy became aggressively zero bound. The Bank of England and the European Central Bank (ECB) followed in its wake as the Great Recession unfolded.

The limits of monetary policy were tested in the 1990s during the banking crisis in Japan when interest rates became zero-bound following repeated cuts. The Bank of Japan continued to pump liquidity by buying government treasury bonds in what came to be known as QE. Central banks had long been accommodating fiscal policy through purchase of treasury bonds. However, used as a purely monetary policy tool following zero bound short-term interest rates was a Japanese innovation.

Quantitative easing could not stimulate the Japanese economy back to former levels of growth. There was, therefore, no proof that it was the way out of a liquidity trap. It could nevertheless be argued that Japanese trend growth itself was declining consequent on structural and demographic shifts.

This did not deter Ben Bernanke from testing his theories during the recent financial crisis. QE on the epic scale envisaged by Ben Bernanke virtually amounted to dropping money on the economy by the aerial route, and had earlier earned him the epithet 'Helicopter Ben.' The US Fed embarked on aggressive QE (purchase of treasury bonds) and CE (purchase of private securities) on a scale unmatched even by the Bank of Japan in the 1990s.

After retreating for six quarters, the US economy is back on the path of growth, albeit tepid and below trend, as is to be expected in the case of balance sheet recessions. Did aggressive monetary policy, and in particular QE and CE, pull the economy from the brink of a second Great Depression? This is, at present, a matter of conjecture, and a lively subject for future research. There are, however, at least three reasons to doubt its efficacy.

First and foremost, instead of expanding credit, much of the fiat money created by the Fed found its way back to the Fed through a sharp and continuing increase in the voluntary holdings of depository institutions. While one can quibble whether the problems lie more on the supply or demand side, this strongly suggests that QE is no way out of a liquidity trap. Instead of stimulating the domestic economy, the flood of liquidity is spilling into emerging markets and inflating asset and commodity prices. Neither has QE devalued the dollar to the extent that the US could export its way out of low growth and unemployment, perhaps because of its reserve currency status.

Second, while monetary policies might influence the investment behaviour of firms, the extent to which they influence consumption and savings by households is arguable. This behaviour is culturally specific and very sticky. The predilection of US households to borrow, and of the Swabian housewife to save, is legendary. Investment behaviour is ultimately dependent on the consumption patterns of households and overseas demand that drive animal spirits. The response of US households to their damaged balance sheets is to sharply increase savings, which have risen from a low of 1.5-2.5 per cent of personal disposable income in 2004-2006 to almost six per cent at present. Since the post-war average is closer to 10 per cent, the savings rate could continue to rise consequent on balance sheet repair and regulatory tightening. Easy monetary policy is not inducing households to consume more.

Third, the rise in personal savings and fall in investment was countervailed by government dissavings that pushed up the budget deficit from 1.2 per cent of the GDP in 2007 to 8.9 per cent in 2010. This dramatic fiscal expansion, unparalleled in peace time, may be propping demand. It is, at present, difficult to separate the effects of monetary and fiscal policies in counteracting extreme recessionary conditions. Indeed, it is argued that the firewall between the two has broken down, and that the two have become virtually indistinguishable.

Monetary policy is currently crippled by the monetary trap deriving from the breakdown of transmission channels. Have central bankers now flogged monetary policy beyond limits, just as governments had earlier done with fiscal policy? And will this excess, like the fiscal excesses of the 1970s, eventually lead to inflationary outcomes? Would central banks be able to suck out the excess liquidity before it is too late? This could prove tricky if trend growth has indeed drifted lower, and the phenomenon of 'jobless growth' persists. Headline inflation in the US is rising, although core inflation continues to be low. Neither loose monetary policy before the crisis nor after the crisis could drive core inflation upwards, even as asset and commodity prices boomed. But this could simply be the tail-end of the 'good deflation' deriving from globalization, in particular the integration of China and India into the global economy. Why consumer price inflation is much higher in emerging market economies (EMEs) is another issue, but they are also growing at near trend and their inflation measurement is different.

Business Standard, New Delhi, 30 May 2011.

60

Ben Bernanke, the Great Innovator

There are several central bankers one could admire, especially those who held steadfast against widespread political opposition because the measures took time to take effect. Notable in this regard is of course Paul Volcker, who slew the dragon of inflation. In India, there were C. Rangarajan, who did much the same thing, and Y.V. Reddy who explicitly targeted asset prices when it was unfashionable, indeed heretical, to do so. And there is the self-effacing Ben Bernanke, with his bold innovations and perspicacity—even though the jury is still out on whether he is indeed fashioning the monetary tools of the 21st century.

Following the fiscal excesses of the 1970s, the mantle of stabilising growth fell increasingly on central bankers, as monetary policy conducted by independent central banks rather than politically charged fiscal policy became the first line of macroeconomic defence against economic downturns.

Ironically, as central bankers turned to inflation targeting, with short-term interest rates as their primary tool, the forces of globalization were relentlessly striking at the roots of both: the entry of large economies into the global market for labour unleashed deflationary forces that kept inflation low, making it less sensitive to domestic overheating.

Meanwhile, large-scale cross-border capital flows undermined central banks' ability to influence short-term rates, as Alan Greenspan presciently noted in what has come to be known as 'the Greenspan Conundrum.'

The consequential failure of monetary policy based on inflation and short-term policy rate targeting is widely blamed for inflating asset bubbles by keeping monetary policy unusually loose. Central bankers therefore must share the blame for the recent global financial crisis. As a member of the US Federal Reserve (Fed) Board, Ben Bernanke could be considered complicit with these policies.

As a historian of the Great Depression, Ben Bernanke was called upon to test his theories in real life when he took over as chairman of the Fed. The lessons he drew from the Great Depression probably explain why the American monetary authority's response to the sub-prime crisis was so different from that of the European Central Bank (ECB), which focused on the inflationary threat even as Bernanke saw potential deflation as the greater threat, on account of the deleveraging underway. He rapidly started lowering rates all the way down to the zero-bound. In retrospect, he made the right call, and other central banks followed suit.

Zero-bound interest rates did prevent deflation, but could not prevent recession. To address the latter, governments supplemented aggressive monetary easing with equally aggressive fiscal policy to counter both faltering private demand, and to support financial institutions that had become too systemically important to be allowed to fail. Fiscal policy, however, can be used only in short spurts, as protracted use can trigger market revolt, and it did. With both fiscal and conventional monetary space exhausted, it was time for Ben Bernanke to bite the bullet and put in practice a controversial theory he had propounded several years ago.

He had recognised the limits of conventional monetary policy, for interest rates cannot be pushed below zero. In such a scenario, he advocated a money-financed tax cut essentially equivalent to a 'helicopter drop' of money—or what is now popularly known as quantitative easing, or QE. Unlike a bond-financed tax-cut, which leads to tax increases down the line, a tax cut financed by money creation should theoretically not emasculate fiscal expansion through Ricardian Equivalence. Money creation would also have the impact of depreciating the currency, which he saw as another tool to combat deflation.

The US Fed under Bernanke was not, of course, the first central bank to deploy QE. Developing country central banks, like those of India, had long been accommodating loose fiscal policy by buying government bonds. This policy was phased out by C. Rangarajan in the 1990s as it impinged on the effectiveness of monetary policy, and hence on the independence of the central bank. Indeed, considering the bland experience of the Bank of Japan (BoJ) with QE, it was bold of Ben Bernanke to put it to test yet again.

However, he has used QE far more aggressively than the BoJ did, introducing innovations as he went along. QE became 'credit easing' (CE) when private assets were bought to stabilise financial markets. While central bankers typically intervene through short-term rates, QE was now also used to directly influence the upper end of the yield curve through 'operation twist,' since long-term rates could no longer be influenced by short-term rates that were already near zero.

Although QE has been able to keep the deadly downward deflationary spiral at bay by making up for the declining velocity of money caused by deleveraging; has had the effect of keeping sovereign borrowing rates low in the face of market revolt; and quickly cleaned up the balance sheets of stressed financial institutions through cheap funding, it has its critics and downsides.

First, much of the criticism has come from emerging markets, where there is a sense that the excess liquidity created is spilling into commodity markets, asset bubbles and inflation overseas. Second, QE has not depreciated the dollar, because of its reserve currency status. Third, it has obliterated the firewall between fiscal and monetary policies, with monetary policy increasingly becoming an extension of fiscal policy, thereby undermining independence of the central bank.

Fourth, whereas fiscal expansion leads to higher taxes down the line, the combination of zero-bound interest rates and QE is an immediate tax on savers, who in effect finance the stimulus. The tax on savings should induce people to consume and invest more and save less, but with impaired balance sheets they are possibly saving even more. It is therefore arguable to what extent QE is a way out of the liquidity trap, if it can revive animal spirits to kick off a virtuous cycle of demand and supply of credit to the real economy. Fifth, there are inflationary dangers ahead unless the QE is carefully unwound, calibrated to the recovery.

Nevertheless, Ben Bernanke has found an innovative answer and response to each new problem thrown at him so far, at a time when the recent past provided little guidance. It is too early to tell whether his remedies are the correct ones, whether they are working, and whether they will lay the basis of monetary policy in an age of deep global integration and fiat money. His place in monetary history is however secure, one way or the other.

Business Standard, New Delhi, 19 February 2012.

61

The Central Banker's *Brahmastra*

It has long been known that the limits of conventional monetary policy are reached when interest rates are lowered to the zero bound, inflation rates drop, the output gap grows, and there is still little demand for credit. This is the liquidity trap into which Japan fell in the 1990s, as did much of the developed world in the wake of the recent global financial crisis.

In such circumstances, central banks may be constrained to resort to unconventional monetary policy—expanding money supply not only through the discount window, but also through purchase of long-term government assets (quantitative easing or QE) and/or private assets (credit easing or CE). This can neutralise the sharp decline in the money multiplier owing to rapid deleveraging in a financial crisis. The liquidity injections are also expected to stimulate growth by stimulating both investment (by keeping the cost of credit cheap) and consumption (through the wealth effect of appreciating asset prices).

The signal triumph of QE and CE during the recent financial crisis was in having forestalled deflation. Milton Friedman advanced the theory, in his monumental *A Monetary History of the United States 1867-1960,* that it was the US Federal Reserve's (Fed) failure to pump in large amounts of liquidity to counter deleveraging, and the consequential decline in the money multiplier, that led to deflation and the Great Depression of the 1930s. On Friedman's 90th birthday in 2002, the current Chairman of the Fed—Ben Bernanke, another authority on the Great Depression and then a Fed governor—acknowledged that it was indeed the Fed that was responsible for the Great Depression.

Bernanke was perhaps less than fair to those at the helm of the Fed in the 1930s. The US was on the gold standard, and could not, therefore, print currency by fiat. The US went off the gold standard for a while in the 1930s, following which it was able to inject more liquidity into the financial system, and this helped to stabilise the financial system.

The post-War Bretton Woods system, however, restored the gold standard, which continued right up to President Nixon's announcement in 1971 that the value of the dollar would no longer be linked to gold but to, well, the dollar! QE is a monetary tool of the fiat currency era, since there is now no limit on how much currency can be created.

The first real-life experiment with QE was done by Japan following the financial crisis triggered by the collapse of the real estate boom in the 1990s. The Japanese experiment, however, could prevent neither deflation nor recession. Bernanke famously argued that this was because Japan's QE was far too timid. In hindsight, in the light of the much more aggressive QE by the Fed, and consequential better outcomes, this appears to be a valid argument.

This 'bond-financed tax cut' has, however, spectacularly failed in countering the liquidity trap. Most of the liquidity pumped into financial markets is simply coming back to the Fed as bank deposits —which are now at record levels, and still rising. Monetary policy transmission channels remain broken. The wealth effect of asset appreciation has not translated into consumption demand; low borrowing costs have failed to stimulate investment; the tax on savings has slowed deleveraging; spillovers have fuel fears of currency war and distorted commodity and gold prices.

So, would a 'money-financed tax cut,' where the central bank simply injects freshly minted money into the economy directly—say by mailing cheques to households or to the Treasury, instead of purchasing Treasury or private assets—work, as recently argued by Lord Adair Turner? This is the famous 'helicopter drop' (HD) of Friedman, advocated so strongly by Bernanke some time ago that he has been known as 'Helicopter Ben' ever since.

This is a fair question. In several respects, the outcomes of QE and HD are similar, but their differences are also crucial. First, there is a permanent increase in money supply, which is a downside. But excessive liquidity can always be mopped up by the central bank when the money multiplier normalises with the return of private demand through allocation of new treasury bonds directly to the central bank. Second, in this manner, the central bank can bypass the financial system, where transmission channels are broken, and provide liquidity directly to the end user.

In such a situation, the central bank would operate something like a cross between Santa Claus and a retail bank. Imagine this: Santa Claus dressed as a smart retail banker with a scholarly backpack, rather than in the familiar red and white garb with a sackful of toys slung over his shoulder; he is piloting a helicopter in choppy weather instead of being driven through freshly laid snow on a sleigh by Rudolph; and he is dropping bank cheques, instead of toy assets, down the chimney into the state treasury and/or stuffing peoples' Christmas stockings.

HD has never been attempted so far. Central bankers can go where none has gone before, the final monetary frontier. As such, HD is perhaps the final arrow in their monetary quiver—and strapped, as it happens, to the back of a person whose name is indelibly linked with this arrow.

Why has this arrow not been used so far, despite the very limited success with QE and CE? Instead, the burden of stimulus seems to have shifted back to long-discredited fiscal policy—by its very nature too political to be an effective and sustainable stabilisation tool. Is this possibly because of a lurking fear that HD could be akin to the *Brahmastra*—the proverbial double-edged weapon of last resort of Hindu mythology capable of extensive collateral damage? Too small a cheque might be saved by households. But too large a cheque could completely unanchor inflationary expectations. Or, worse, if the central bank, usually perceived as a conservative and stabilising institution, is now seen to be a technology incubator, it might drive the fear of God into households regarding the future of fiat currency itself, making them reach for you-know-what-more gold.

Business Standard, New Delhi, 2 April 2013.

62

Why IMF May be Wrong on 'Inflation Targeting'

The changing structure of the global economy is leading to rethinking on a number of long established macroeconomic relationships, particularly in the wake of the recent global financial and economic crisis. One of these is the relationship between inflation and the business cycle that has critical implications for the conduct of monetary policy by central banks.

There was a sharp decline in the consumer price index (CPI)-based inflation in both developed and developing countries over the last two decades. According to International Monetary Fund (IMF) data, it averaged under 7.0 per cent in developing countries between 2002 and 2010, as against 38.4 per cent between 1992 and 2001. In developed countries, it fell by about 20.0 per cent from 2.4 per cent to 1.9 per cent.

This decline coincided with monetary policies largely transiting to a regime of 'inflation targeting' across the globe. Central banks adopted variants of the Taylor rule of monetary policies that adjusted short-term interest rates to where current growth stood relative to potential growth, and current inflation relative to targeted inflation.

In its recent *World Economic Outlook* of April 2013, the IMF set the two developments alongside and drew a causal relationship between 'inflation targeting' and why the inflation dog has desisted from barking.

While independent central banks can be credited for initially anchoring inflationary expectations, the reality, however, is that inflation targeting also inflated the asset bubbles that were ultimate triggers of the recent global financial crisis.

The IMF has perhaps failed to give due credit to two major structural changes in the global economy that kept, and are keeping, inflation low, undermining the traditional role of consumer price inflation as a robust marker of business cycles.

First, there was the entry of two humongous developing countries, namely China and India, into the global labour market for goods and services, respectively. Between them, they account for about 40 per cent of the global population and virtually unlimited supply of cheap labour. Likewise, other populous low-income countries, such as Bangladesh, Vietnam and Indonesia, also entered the global labour market.

Second, there was an acceleration of globalising tendencies, with tariff walls coming down to nominal levels, rise of global production chains, services becoming more tradable through the use of IT (information technology), and large two-way capital flows. Goods and services exports as a proportion of the GDP (gross domestic product) rose from about 20 per cent between 1992 and 2001 to cross 30 per cent by 2007. Gross exports and imports rose even more sharply.

Consumer price inflation remained low even as the global economy grew at the unprecedented rate of over 5 per cent between 2004 and 2007. In a closed economy, such 'overheating' would have generated inflationary pressures. With increasing globalization, however, excess domestic demand was easily accommodated by cheap supply overseas.

Such spillages widen current account deficits (CADs). Ordinarily, a widening CAD leads to depreciation that narrows the current account gap. Depreciation also leads to inflationary pressures. However, systemically large CADs were in high-income reserve-issuing currencies countries. The current account surpluses of developing countries—facilitated and sustained by currency pegs that prevented their exchange rates from adjusting—were parked in these very countries. The reserve currencies, therefore, did not depreciate relative to their major surplus trading partners. Their consumers, thereby, gained from the deflationary forces triggered by productivity shifts in the big developing countries.

The deflationary impact on consumer prices was felt in both developed and developing countries. Although the fall was more dramatic, inflation nevertheless remained higher in developing countries since CADs exposed some of them to currency depreciation that raised the price of tradables. Currency depreciation, however, was frequently muted by large capital inflows.

The upshot of these structural changes in the global economy was the 'Great Moderation.' Economists now started talking about the end of business cycles, a new 'Goldilocks economy' of low inflation—high growth, and 'dark matter' that propped up the US dollar against mounting external deficits. Central banks were either deluded by the 'Great Moderation' into keeping interest rates low, leading to excessive leverage and liquidity and/or, as argued by Alan Greenspan, they lost control over long-term interest rates as large capital flows, amplified through the shadow banking system, neutralised their interventions at the short-end of the yield curve.

The liquidity overhang had to find some outlet, and it did so by raising the prices of assets, particularly financial assets and those physical assets such as housing, and commodities like oil, food and gold, that doubled up as financial assets. The consequential 'wealth effect' increased consumer demand despite stagnant and falling labour incomes.

Central banks were alive to the build-up of assets bubbles. Greenspan spoke of 'irrational exuberance.' However, these bubbles passed under their policy radar since they were focused on core consumer price inflation that discounted the price of volatile 'financial commodities' like oil. Their preference was for cleaning up afterwards, rather than calling asset bubbles and pricking them, lest they also pricked the business cycle in the process.

The subprime crisis in the US pricked the asset bubble, unleashing deflationary pressures through deleveraging, collapse of the money multiplier, and demand compression. Deflation was, however, averted by massive liquidity injections by central banks that are once again inflating asset bubbles, rather than stoking inflation to targeted levels. Likewise, current market speculation over 'tapering' of quantitative easing has dented asset prices.

Even if output in advanced economies were to get back to full potential, consumer price inflation may not rise commensurately because deflationary forces are still at work. Of course, the position could change if the world moves towards greater protectionism in response to high levels of unemployment in advanced economies. There is also a risk that central banks in advanced economies may keep interest rates below the inflation rate for an extended period to pay down public debt that has increased dramatically in the last few years as a result of crisis management.

If inflation is no longer a robust marker of business cycles, what other markers can take its place or at least supplement it? Since the anomaly of low inflation and high growth was induced by the wealth effect of inflating asset prices and growing leverage, these are automatic candidates. Both asset prices and leverage reflect the level of liquidity and demand in the economy. Central banks, therefore, need to keep their weather eye open to the credit cycle in addition to the business cycle. How, and whether, monetary policy rules, including the Taylor rule, change to accommodate new markers, or whether policy makers complacently persist with 'inflation targeting' following IMF's findings and continue to fuel asset bubbles, remains to be seen.

Business Standard, New Delhi, 24 June 2013.

63

What Ben Bernanke Didn't Say

On 10 July 2013, Ben Bernanke, Chairman of the US Federal Reserve (Fed) gave his Cambridge, Massachusetts, audience a brilliant *tour de force* of the evolution of US monetary policy over the past century, including his own views. His intimate knowledge and understanding of the Great Depression and creative use of monetary policy probably explains why this *tour de force* ended with the 'Great Recession' rather than with a second Great Depression. He also indicated that the Fed may be moving away from using the federal funds rate as the single signalling instrument to communicate the objectives and forecasts of its inflation and unemployment targets, thus giving it the constrained discretion to use different instruments at different times. His name will surely go down in history alongside, and arguably above, that of Milton Friedman in the shaping of US monetary policy.

The speech was nevertheless remarkable as much for the range of issues discussed as for what remained unsaid.

First, Mr Bernanke would be the first to admit that he was neither the first to suggest, nor to use, unconventional monetary policies. However, his successful use of the quantitative easing sledgehammer to counter the collapse of the money multiplier proved that his earlier criticism of the Bank of Japan's (BoJ) use of quantitative easing (QE) in the 1990s as being too timid to beat deflation was spot-on. Indeed, he had started addressing the deflationary threat through aggressive serial rate cuts even as other central banks were still battling inflation. This was a notable policy success during the Great Recession and a notable failure during the Great Depression. Yet QE could not prevent the Great Recession. The correlation between QE and GDP (gross domestic product) growth remains weak. Mr Bernanke did not discuss the limitations of monetary policy in countering the liquidity trap caused by deleveraging. Advanced economies have had to fall back on long discredited fiscal policy, with even the Fed batting for it to do more of the heavy lifting.

Second, he did not explain why he never felt compelled to use the helicopter drop that he had famously advocated for just such circumstances. A money-financed tax cut would surely not have had the destabilising impact of a bond-financed tax cut, as public debt would not have arisen alarmingly. Or has he already made the drop without us ever noticing? Supposing the Fed were to hold its treasury bond purchases to maturity, with all payments from the treasury transferred back as profits through book entries, QE would in retrospect be a helicopter drop of money. Any excessive liquidity would then be impounded through recalibration of reserve requirements rather than a roll-back of the balance sheet.

Third, Mr Bernanke underscored the US Fed's adherence to the Bagehot rule: of lending freely in a crisis at a penal interest rate. However, he did not explain whether the rate at which liquidity was made freely available had effectively large penalties or not. The same banks that had endangered the financial system and were bailed out by taxpayers are now making outsize profits despite continuing economic slack. Surely a penal rate would have ensured that some of these profits accrued to taxpayers who are, instead, being penalised in their capacity as savers.

Fourth, just as the Fed (before the Volcker era) was tolerant of high inflation because of the output gap during the Great Inflation, it was tolerant of above-trend output because of low consumer price inflation during the Great Moderation. In either case, it was deluded into keeping monetary policy too loose, unleashing stagflation and asset bubbles respectively. Mr Bernanke has however indicated that the Taylor Rule, with its equal focus on inflation and output, will continue to guide US Fed policy despite evidence of the flattening of the Phillips curve on account of deflationary pressures on consumer prices.

Fifth, while drawing attention to financial stability as the original mandate of the Fed, Ben Bernanke was silent on how monetary policy should deal with asset prices. This is particularly relevant for two reasons: first, because excessive liquidity during the Great Moderation was reflected not in consumer but asset-price inflation, and second, because his own easy monetary policy is contributing to new asset bubbles. He has of course indicated that this is work in progress. However, he could have clarified whether he still subscribes to the Alan Greenspan doctrine that central banks cannot, and should not, call asset bubbles and only clean up afterwards. Or whether he is now more open to taking a page out of emerging-market central banks that target financial stability more explicitly through new instruments?

Sixth, Mr Bernanke was silent on the global spillovers of US monetary policy owing to greater financial integration and growing dominance of the dollar as the international reserve currency. While monetary policy all over the world responds to the domestic business cycle, the case of the US Fed is singular in that its policies shape cross-border capital flows, thereby influencing the monetary stance of other countries in ways that may be inappropriate for their own business cycles. In 2007-08, when the Fed turned on the liquidity tap, emerging market economies (EMEs) that recovered relatively quickly from the crisis hesitated to tighten monetary policy for fear of attracting more capital inflows. India's currency appreciated despite a widening current account deficit (CAD). Now, when growth is collapsing, EMEs hesitate to loosen monetary policy because, whatever the Fed's real intention, the resultant monetary tightening is drawing capital out of them. The build-up of reserves in EMEs is as much a defensive response to US monetary policy as the pursuit of mercantilist policies by some EMEs.

These are no doubt all difficult and cutting-edge issues in the current global debate on monetary policy, with no ready answers. Central bankers are also reticent creatures. But Ben Bernanke is much more than a creative practitioner of his craft. He is one of the foremost academic authorities on unconventional monetary policy in general, and on the Great Depression in particular. His *tour de force* would have been fascinating, had he given us some more insights into his current thinking on these burning issues.

Business Standard, New Delhi, 5 August 2013.

64

When Rates Don't Matter

Financial deregulation is pilloried as the villain that ignited the global financial crisis. But John B. Taylor of Stanford has argued that one of the factors was loose monetary policy in the US and deviated from his celebrated rule. This appears to have been the case after the dot-com bust of 2000, as the Table 64.1 indicates. The potential GDP (gross domestic product) of the US is assumed to be 3.5 per cent, and the core inflation target as 2 per cent. All numbers are quarterly year-on-year (y-o-y) averages.

What were the factors underlying this deviation? There was a sharp decline in consumer inflation in both developed and developing countries over the last 20 years. The International Monetary Fund (IMF), in April 2013, concluded that 'inflation targeting' by central banks had been successful in anchoring inflationary expectations. An alternative explanation is that consumer price inflation ceased to be sensitive to the business cycle.

Instead of pushing up consumer prices, real wages and reducing unemployment—the classic symptoms of overheating—excessive liquidity inflated prices of assets like stocks, derivatives, housing and commodities like oil, food and gold.

These now doubled up as financial assets. Asset prices got delinked from the real economy, becoming more sensitive to financial liquidity than to sentiments surrounding growth prospects. The associated 'wealth effect' started driving growth, now based on leverage rather than income growth through higher investment and production.

The IMF failed to give due credit to two major structural changes in the global economy that kept, and are still keeping, consumer inflation low, undermining its role as a robust marker of business cycles.

First, the entry of China and India into the global market for goods and services at a time when large-scale productivity shifts were taking place in these countries.

Second, the acceleration of globalising tendencies, with falling tariffs, the rise of global production chains and services becoming more tradable through the use of IT (information technology). These productivity and efficiency gains had a deflationary impact on inflation as excess domestic demand was easily accommodated by cheap overseas supply.

Ordinarily, a widening current account deficit (CAD) leads to depreciation and inflationary pressures.

However, high-income countries issuing reserve currencies had systematically high CADs. The current account surpluses of developing countries were parked in these countries.

The reserve currencies, therefore, did not depreciate relative to their major surplus trading partners. Rising global imbalances, therefore, also played a role.

This new Goldilocks economy of low inflation, high growth and stable exchange rates deluded central banks into keeping interest rates unduly low by the yardsticks of the Taylor rule. Asset bubbles passed under their policy radar since they were focused on consumer price inflation.

Since this monetary policy framework remains unchanged, central banks are once again inflating asset bubbles, rather than stoking inflation and growth to targeted levels. The distortions from inflation targeting have been magnified in the post-crisis period.

While inflation targeting no longer works for advanced countries, it is still relevant for the developing countries. These countries also gained from deflationary forces on consumer prices, but commodity prices and exchange rate fluctuations led to periodic bouts of high inflation, though rarely in double digits as in the past. Food and fuel comprise a substantial chunk of the expenditure basket in developing economies. Therefore, core inflation seems much less relevant as a policy marker. Non-core inflation is less amenable to monetary policy actions.

Table 64.1

Dollar for Dollar

Period	*GDP Growth*	*Headline CPI Inflation*	*Core CPI Inflation*	*Dow Jones Industrial Average Inflation*	*Home Price Inflation*	*Deviation of the Effective Fed Fund Rate from the Taylor Rule**
1997Q1-2000Q3	4.6	2.3	2.3	18.9	6.4	0.50
2000Q4-2003Q2	1.6	2.4	2.3	-8.4	9.1	-0.97
2003Q3-2006Q4	3.3	2.9	2.0	9.3	11.3	-0.94
2007Q1-2008Q2	1.5	3.3	2.3	9.4	-7.8	-0.49
2008Q3-2009Q4	-2.4	0.9	1.9	-20.8	-13.3	-0.61
2010Q1-2013Q4	2.3	2.1	1.6	14.4	1.7	-2.60

Note: 1. Bureau of Labor Statistics, Department of Labor, US, *http://www.bisgov/cpi/.*

2. Bureau of Economic Analysis, US, *http://www.bea.gov.*

3. Economic Research, Federal Reserve Bank of St Louis, *http://research, Stloulsfed.org.*

4. Board of Governors Federal Reserve System, US, *http://www/federalreserve.gov.*

* Last quarter core inflation + 0.5 (last quarter GDP-potential GDP) + 0.5 (last quarter core inflation-2) + 2.

Source: Home Price Inflation calculated from National Composite Home Price Index for the US.

If inflation targeting in advanced countries is stymied by asset bubbles, in the developing countries, it is stymied by volatile capital flows, which is the spillover effect of loose monetary policy in advanced economies. Developing countries have found it impossible to use a single policy instrument, interest rates, to target both the economic cycle and the external financial cycle at the same time.

A policy instrument can be effective only if it has a single objective. Arguably, the policy interest rate is better suited to target domestic imbalances, while effective reserve management and targeting a neutral real effective exchange rate through market intervention is better suited to targeting external imbalances. This could free up the interest rate for inflation targeting.

Inflation targeting as currently conducted by central banks in both advanced economies and emerging markets has broken down and needs mending. The former need to tweak their monetary policy rules to take stock of asset prices and leverage. The latter need another policy instrument to target the external financial cycle so that the interest rate instrument is free to target inflation.

The Economic Times, New Delhi, 27 February 2014.

65

Inflation-control Dynamics

There have been two major watersheds in the evolution of monetary policy in the post-war period. The first watershed was reached with the realisation that on account of its overtly political nature, it was difficult to pursue countercyclical macroeconomic policy using the fiscal tool. Entry was easy but exit was not. There was also a realisation during the stagflationary 1970s that when the source of inflation lies in the volatile commodities sector, the Phillips curve breaks down and the central banks' chief monetary policy instrument gets blunted. The pole position in macroeconomic management was consequently taken by 'independent' central banks who started targeting core rather than headline inflation. The second watershed was reached when monetary policy setting by central banks became rule-bound rather than discretionary. The most widely used rule was the Taylor rule.

We may now be at a third watershed in the evolution of monetary policy.

Following the recent global financial crisis, John B. Taylor argued that a contributory factor was that US monetary policy was too loose as it deviated from his eponymous rule. What were the factors underlying this deviation? The story begins with the sharp decline in consumer price index (CPI)-based inflation in both developed and developing countries over the last two decades. According to International Monetary Fund (IMF) data, it averaged under 7.0 per cent in developing countries between 2002 and 2010, as against 38.4 per cent between 1992 and 2001. In developed countries, it fell by about 20 per cent, from 2.4 per cent to 1.9 per cent. On the basis of these data the IMF in its *World Economic Outlook* of April 2013 concluded that inflation targeting by central banks had been eminently successful.

Inflation targeting, however, was never an end in itself. It was the canary in the gold mine that central bankers watched to set the equilibrium interest rate at which incomes are optimally distributed between savings/investment and consumption so as to keep the economy growing at the production possibility frontier, or its potential growth rate.

If core consumer price inflation were however to lose its sensitivity to the business cycle, the targeted inflation would also cease to ensure macroeconomic stability. This is precisely what happened. Core inflation remained remarkably stable, despite sharp fluctuations in growth and periodic fluctuations in commodity prices. Savings declined, while investment and consumption increased, leading to an ever-widening US current account deficit (CAD). The Phillips curve became unstable all over again. The problem was much deeper than a simple deviation from the Taylor rule, as the connection between core CPI inflation and economic growth in the Taylor rule was predicated on a robust Phillips curve.

What was happening? And how was it that the US Federal Reserve (Fed) was able to keep interest rates low, although US savings were declining? The answer lies in increasing globalization.

First, there was the entry of two humongous developing Asian economies, China and India, into the global labour market for goods and services, at a time when rapid productivity shifts were taking place in these countries as large numbers of people moved out of low productivity agriculture. Between them, they account for about 40 per cent of the global population and virtually unlimited supply of cheap labour.

Other populous low-income Asian countries such as Bangladesh, Vietnam and Indonesia were never far behind. The attendant productivity and efficiency gains had a disinflationary impact on consumer prices, as excess domestic demand in advanced economies like the US was easily accommodated by cheap supply overseas without inflationary outcomes.

Second, such spillages widen CADs that ordinarily lead to currency depreciation and inflationary pressures. However, systemically large CADs were in high-income reserve-issuing currencies countries where the counterpart current account surpluses of developing countries were parked. The reserve currencies, therefore, did not depreciate relative to their major surplus trading partners, as the 'savings glut' in emerging markets exercised a downward pressure on global interest rates. Central banks were either deluded by the low core inflation into keeping interest rates unduly low, or as argued by Alan Greenspan, they lost control over long-term interest rates as large capital flows, amplified through an innovative shadow banking system, neutralised their interventions at the short-end of the yield curve. The liquidity overhang from loose monetary policy had to however, find some outlet, and it did so by raising the price of financial assets instead of consumer prices, with several physical assets such as housing, and commodities like oil, food and gold, crossing over to become financial assets. The consequential 'wealth effect' increased consumer demand despite stagnant labour incomes, while a misaligned policy rate fuelled a strong credit and liquidity bubble that enabled consumers in advanced economies gain from these disinflationary forces.

Thus, monetary policy focused on inflation targeting inflated asset bubbles even as core CPI remained stable. It is not as though central bankers were blind to asset bubbles. However, the dominant Keynesian paradigm was focused on short-term demand management of the business cycle that was challenged in its understanding of the dynamic of financial markets. It was impervious to longer-term financial cycles underscored by the Austrian School of Von Mises, Von Hayek *et al.*, where financial markets occupied centre stage.

An unreformed monetary policy framework is once again inflating asset bubbles, rather than stoking inflation to targeted levels. If anything, the distortions arising out of inflation targeting have been magnified in the post-crisis period, whether measured in terms of core inflation, asset inflation and deviation from the Taylor rule. Going forward, there is the added risk that central banks in the advanced economies may be constrained to keeping interest rates too low out of fear of triggering another financial crisis, and also to pay down public debt that has increased dramatically in the last few years as a result of crisis management.

If inflation is no longer a robust marker of business cycles, what other markers should supplement it? Since the anomaly of low inflation and high growth in advanced economies was induced by the wealth effect of inflating asset prices and growing leverage, these are automatic candidates. Monetary aggregates can also capture an emerging credit bubble, for instance, when growth in M3 is out of sync with nominal GDP growth through sharp increases in the money multiplier.

It could plausibly be argued that while inflation targeting no longer works for advanced countries, it is still relevant for developing countries where inflation remains an issue. With tightly regulated financial markets, and continued use of monetary aggregates, they have also been able to largely contain a destabilising interface between the financial and credit cycles. Indeed, John B. Taylor has argued that his eponymous rule is, *mutatis mutandis*, relevant for developing country central banks. There are, however, other factors emasculating inflation-targeting in emerging markets.

First, with food and fuel comprising a substantial chunk of the expenditure basket, core inflation seems much less relevant as a policy marker on one hand. On the other hand, non-core inflation is much less amenable to monetary policy actions. The latter may also be becoming volatile as commodities have become increasingly financialised through derivatives.

Second, volatile cross-border capital flows are now driving business cycles, including asset prices, in emerging markets, and simultaneously exerting disinflationary and inflationary pressures through exchange rate fluctuations. This constrains their central banks, following inflation-targeting, to tighten policy just when the external cycle turns and growth collapses, and *vice versa*. They have consequently found it impossible to use a single policy instrument, i.e. the short-term interest rate, to simultaneously target both the domestic growth-inflation cycle and the external financial cycle which is subject to the vagaries of monetary policies emanating from reserve currency issuing countries. Their inflation targeting keeps running up against the 'impossible trinity' or policy 'trilemma' as, according to the widely accepted Tinbergen rule, a policy instrument can be effective only if it has a single objective.

To recapitulate the central arguments, there have been two major watersheds in the conduct of macroeconomic policies in the post-war period. The first was the shift from fiscal policy to greater reliance on monetary policy to stabilise business cycles. The second was the adoption of rule-bound monetary policies such as the Taylor rule, which used core consumer price inflation as the canary in the goldmine to stabilise the business cycle at its production possibility frontier. In the wake of the global financial crisis, a third inflexion point in the conduct of macroeconomic policy may have been reached with inflation-targeting, as currently conducted by central banks in both advanced economies and emerging markets, breaking down. In advanced countries, it is stymied by asset and credit bubbles, and in developing countries by the nature of inflationary pressures and volatile capital flows. Repair of the macroeconomic framework in advanced economies would involve tweaking monetary policy rules to take stock of credit cycles in addition to the business cycle. Emerging markets need to find ways of targeting non-core inflation, and also a separate policy instrument to target the external financial cycle so that the interest rate instrument can be freed up for targeting the domestic growth-inflation cycle.

Financial Express, New Delhi, 16 May 2014.

VII
The Dollar and Emerging Markets
The International Monetary System Debate

"Watch Your Step!"

Los Angeles Times, November 14, 1925

Cartoonist: Edmund Gale

66

A Re-look at the Dollar as the International Reserve Currency?

The US dollar has been the world's reserve currency since as far back as most people can remember, and certainly since the breakdown of the gold standard and the Bretton Woods system. Its continuing resilience has long been an unexplained macroeconomic puzzle, as its relative value does not seem to respond to current account and fiscal deficits in the manner other currencies do.

A number of intrepid theories have been floated to explain its continuing strength, the most recent being that of Harvard economists Ricardo Hausmann and Federico Sturzenegger, who invoked the 'dark matter' analogy from quantum physics.

The fact of the matter is that in a globalised world the macroeconomic rules of the thumb applicable to other currencies do not apply to the reserve currency as the latter has a strategic and safe haven status that cannot be captured in financial models.

An important corollary of the dollar's reserve currency status is the blunting of macroeconomic policy tools of other nation states. *Ceteris paribus*, monetary tightening by the US Federal Reserve (Fed) results in a flight of capital to the US, and loose US fiscal policy devalues the international reserves of developing countries, and *vice versa*.

This unfair advantage devolving on the reserve currency has time and again led to calls for either competing reserve currencies or for replacing the dollar by a currency at arm's length from nation states, such as the Special Drawing Rights (SDRs) and even for a return to the gold standard.

The reserve currency status of the dollar has however only intensified in tandem with globalization. This was in ample evidence during the current global crisis that saw the dollar strengthen against all other currencies, and US treasury yields fall to historic lows, despite the US being the source of the financial crisis.

The reason for this has perhaps to do with the intrinsic nature of money itself. Exchange and trade, some of the oldest forms of human interface, gradually moved from barter to money since the latter is a convenient form of universal exchange and value. By the same logic, as economies integrate and become seamless, the reserve currency becomes the measure of universal international exchange and value.

In these circumstances, it is difficult to see how there can be more than one reserve currency in a rapidly integrating world. However, it is still possible that one reserve currency could be replaced by another, just as the pound sterling yielded to the dollar in the first half of the 20th century, given that the US economy became the biggest economy and trading nation.

The only currency area that comes even close to the US in size is the Euro area. Trend growth in the latter, however, is slower than the US and therefore, the relative size of the US economy is actually increasing with respect to the Euro area. The Chinese and Indian economies are growing much faster and rapidly bridging the gap with the US, but are still a small fraction of the latter at market exchange rates. China would moreover need to move away from mercantilism and float its currency.

The SDR is currently simply an accounting unit and not a payments currency. It could make a transition to becoming a currency, but for transactions to shift to SDRs would need somebody to act as a market maker on a monumental scale in order to negate the first mover advantage of the dollar, with all associated risks and costs. This appears unlikely. Reverting to the gold standard is not practicable since the governments and central banks would lose flexibility in use of monetary and fiscal policies to stabilise the economy.

It would moreover advantage countries rich in gold resources and would hence not be widely acceptable. The inescapable conclusion is that there is no alternative currency that can rival, let alone replace, the US dollar as the international reserve currency in the foreseeable future.

67

Revisiting Cross-border Capital Flows

Classical economics had made a strong case for the welfare effects of both free trade (based on the principle of comparative advantage) and free flow of capital (based on the assumption that capital would flow from low-return, capital-surplus countries to high-return, capital-deficit countries). Unsurprisingly, till recently, the International Monetary Fund (IMF's) policy advisory to developing countries was to gradually move to full convertibility on the capital account, with some caveats on pre-conditions and sequencing added in wake of the Latin American experience with capital flows.

This advisory was gradually abandoned, especially following the East Asian crisis. A broad consensus appeared to be emerging that limited capital controls in some form or the other would be imposed even by developed countries, especially in the area of foreign investment. While the argument in favour of free trade remains robust, with some notable exceptions, the current global financial crisis has, *inter alia*, reopened the debate on the welfare effects of capital flows and on a long-standing proposal to impose a 'Tobin tax' on cross-border capital flows.

Lessons from economic history should, however, caution us against knee-jerk reactions that impose restrictions on free markets, as there is usually a developmental price to be paid. The case of financial repression comes easily to mind. At the very least, we need to be certain whether the villain of the piece in the current crisis is regulation, imbalances, excessive leverage or capital flows. According to received wisdom, developing countries have a shortage of both savings and investment. Savings are low because per capita incomes are low. By definition, those below the poverty line have no savings whatsoever. Capital inflows from developed countries, where returns from capital are lower, are expected to partly plug these twin gaps.

The flipside of the savings-investment gap is the current account deficit (CAD), financed through a surplus on the capital account. A current account surplus is considered a bad thing for developing countries as this is tantamount to decapitalisation of the kind occurred in the aftermath of the debt crisis in Latin America.

Ideally, developing countries should run CADs at levels that can be reasonably expected to be funded through capital inflows on a sustainable basis. Generally speaking, higher the proportion of FDI (foreign direct investment) in total capital flows, the higher the sustainable level of CAD, since an excessive build-up of external debt exposes developing countries to ratings downgrade and/or sudden stops. By this yardstick, while portfolio flows are officially classified as debt, their macroeconomic impact is closer to short-term external debt. The significant difference between the two is that in the event of sudden stops, short-term borrowers incur exchange rate losses, while portfolio investors incur both exchange rate and capital losses.

Globalization of production chains and two-way volatile capital flows spawned a new export-led model of growth emanating in some east Asian countries, and especially China, that has punched conceptual holes into the two-gap model that was (implicitly) based primarily on domestic demand. It was essentially a closed economy model with capital flows as an autonomous external variable.

It now appears that developing countries may combine rapid growth with a surplus of savings over investment, despite low levels of per capita income, exporting the surplus savings by running current account surpluses. This is possible by relying on external demand in high-income countries as the engine of growth.

However, if the capital account were fully convertible and free, there would be an inherent tendency for the current account to move back towards balance through exchange rate adjustments. In these circumstances, the only way to sustain an export-led model of growth is to:

(a) maintain an open and fully convertible capital account in deficit countries, and a controlled capital account in surplus countries with central bank interventions to prevent exchange rate appreciation.

(b) use hard currency reserves built up through intervention in foreign currency markets in surplus countries to sustain consumption—household and/or government—in high income deficit countries.

Funding CADs primarily through debt (including portfolio flows) is potentially destabilising for both developed and developing countries on account of the risk of sudden stops and financial bubbles based on excessive leverage. The current global financial crisis would not have occurred had the US CAD been financed primarily through greenfield FDI rather than debt flows. In that event, the external imbalance would have been primarily on account of excess investment rather than excess consumption. If the major deficit country is also the issuer of the global reserve currency, destabilisation is likely to be through financial bubbles rather than sudden stops on account of the flight to quality.

In a sense, unrestricted cross-border capital flows are to the advantage of the country that mint the global reserve currency as they are supportive of its monetary and fiscal policies. But are they supportive of sustainable growth in developing countries? Quite apart from academic studies that have shown that there is no robust empirical link between growth and capital flows in developing countries, recent events have shown that capital flows other than greenfield FDI can be destabilising. Since cross-border capital flows respond to monetary and fiscal policies of the reserve currency issuing country, these are available in abundance when needed least (such as when monetary policy in the reserve currency country is loose and fiscal policy is tight, and there is a surge in capital flows into emerging markets to increase yields) and there is flow away from developing countries when capital is needed most (such as when monetary policy is tight and fiscal policy is loose with high treasury yields, leading to a flight to quality).

In these circumstances, what should be the stance towards capital flows by rapidly growing developing countries that do not consciously follow an export-led model of growth, and are neutral between production for domestic and export markets?

One, running CADs is a good thing as long as foreign savings are invested, since this can, *ceteris paribus,* raise rates of economic growth. Such deficits should be sustainable over the medium- to long-term.

Two, since FDI goes directly into investment, these should be encouraged without limits and restrictions, some strategic, brown-field areas excepted.

Three, external debt, especially the more volatile short-term component, needs to be limited to productive investment or variable capital to finance production. If external debt tends to imprudent levels, it should be further restricted to financing the foreign exchange component of investment and variable capital.

Four, portfolio flows need not be actively encouraged beyond what is necessary to fund the CAD. Such flows can be volatile, can inflate asset prices, lead to sudden, sharp appreciation of the currency, and queer the pitch for monetary policy. In these circumstances, central bank intervention to stabilise the exchange rate/smoothen the curve is eminently justified to protect the real economy from violent perturbations in financial markets. Consequential hard currency reserve build up may make management of monetary policy difficult, but can also protect the real economy in the event of sudden stops and also sustain higher CADs, and therefore higher growth over the medium-term.

In essence, while capital flows should be leveraged by developing countries to elevate and sustain growth, they also need to be prudently managed.

Business Standard Weekend, New Delhi, 17 October 2009.

68

The Rise and Decline of Fiat Money?

> Indeed the Idols I have loved so long
> Have done my credit in men's eye much wrong:
> Have drown'd my honour in a shallow cup,
> And sold my reputation for a song.

Read fiscal and monetary policies fashioned in the post-war period for Idols, and Omar Khayyam may well have been talking of latter day economic policy makers in his *Rubaiyat*. Although policy makers seemed blissfully unaware, the forces of globalization were straining and blunting the domestic macroeconomic policy framework honed in the post-war period.

In particular, the ageing of Western societies was straining the fiscal framework. The 'good deflation' triggered by the entry of China and India into the global market, rising cross-border capital flows arising out of Bretton Woods II, and financial innovation that gave rise to shadow banking were straining the monetary framework. Policy spillovers were also making the task of macroeconomic management enormously complicated.

The European Currency Union was an attempt to adjust to the forces of globalization. But it had one fatal flaw that was masked by the Great Moderation but became painfully apparent in the wake of the Great Recession. The latter has also further eroded the legitimacy of the international monetary system.

Macroeconomic policy and the international monetary system now seem to be at a historic tipping point, just as they were during the Great Depression. Reshaping them are the great challenges for the future. How might this be done? Does the past provide some guidance?

The Euro area's fragilities can theoretically—but not of course politically—be overcome by also returning to basics through an institutional re-unification of monetary and fiscal policies. How monetary and fiscal tools themselves need to be reshaped is less clear. Coordinated macroeconomic policies and structural reforms across borders are clearly part of this reshaping. However, except in crises, the G20 has still to figure out a way of how to go about this expeditiously and effectively. The benefits of policy coordination are nevertheless manifest. Apart from policy spill overs in an increasingly integrating global economy, it is apparent that even the unstable status quo is perhaps better than an un-coordinated rebalancing of the global economy. A rise in savings in one part of the global economy in the absence of a rise in consumption in some other part would lead to lower growth in the aggregate.

Could the World Trade Organization (WTO) serve as a model for arriving at a global agreement, or consensus, on the use of macroeconomic policy tools? Welfare gains from trade are symmetric, since most countries have at least some comparative advantage. However, gains from macroeconomic policies may be asymmetric, on account of the inherent advantages accruing to the issuer of the global reserve currency. An agreement on macroeconomic policy coordination within the G20 is, therefore, closely linked to the overhaul of the reserve currency system.

This looks unlikely at this stage. There is no good reason for the reserve currency issuer to give up its enormous advantage in the matter of financing internal and external deficits at low costs. No other currency appears to have the market depth or intrinsic strength to take over the mantle of an alternative reserve currency from the dollar. The euro in its current form suffers from obvious structural weaknesses. The much-touted Special Drawing Rights (SDR) does not have the essential requirements of a currency.

The reserve currency itself might change in future with shifting geo-political and economic fortunes, just as it transitioned from the pound sterling to the US dollar in the inter-war period. However, a shift to a more legitimate multi-currency system would be against the tide of history, which is moving towards greater universalisation and integration through trade and investment. The rise of money itself as a form of universal exchange on the back of barter was a manifestation of the universalising trend inherent in markets. A globalised world has space for just one reserve currency. The problem of the reserve currency advantage, attendant moral hazards and legitimacy issues will not go away. So where do we go from here?

Both fiscal and monetary policies have been debased within just 40 years of the end of the gold standard. Consider the 1970s and the current spike in public debt, or the Greenspan put and the current quantitative easing, and their inflationary outcomes. This indicates that despite certain inherent weaknesses, the gold standard may have been no worse than, and arguably superior to, fiat money.

The gold standard imparted a degree of inflexibility to using macroeconomic policies to stabilise growth, since money could not be created at will. Fiat money, however, suffers from the obverse problem that has seen policy makers succumb to moral hazards inherent in excessive policy flexibility. The gold standard at least delivered on price stability over the long term. Since the stock of gold is limited and finite, its value could not be eroded significantly. The stock of fiat money, on the other hand, is potentially unlimited and policy makers cannot be trusted to use it wisely.

A return to fiscal and monetary rectitude may well entail re-anchoring fiscal and monetary tools, and with it money itself, to gold (or some other natural material whose supply is limited) in some manner. This was underscored recently by Robert Zoellick, president of the World Bank.

How this re-anchoring should be done is not clear at this stage. However, the concept itself might not be entirely fanciful. The market response to the debasement of macroeconomic policies since the onset of the recent financial crisis seems to be to turn to gold as a safe haven—a status long occupied by the US dollar. The Rogers International Commodities Index (RICI) and gold prices represented by the World Gold Council (WGC) series that moved in tandem from 2000 right up to 2007 have diverged ever since. Gold prices have been moving steeply upwards, while commodities have been volatile.

Gold now seems to be behaving more like a currency than a commodity. Is this a classic illustration of the age-old Gresham's Law that bad money drives good money out of the market? The question is whether this is a temporary trend or a structural shift. Be it as it may, some long-term damage has been done. The gold standard and its variants have been around for millennia, outliving several disastrous monetary experiments. Fiat money has been with us for just four decades. Why should this time be different? The experience of the last four decades makes the historian fear for the future of fiat money.

Business Standard, New Delhi, 29 August 2011.

69

Drivers of the Gold Boom, Crash and ...

The steep rise and fall in gold prices in the recent past is quite dramatic, and reminiscent of the 1970s, which was also characterised by sustained economic uncertainty, a steep rise in the dollar price of oil and high inflation. The big difference between the 1970s and the recent past is that while inflation is currently subdued, huge liquidity injections by central banks have fuelled speculative fears regarding inflation going forward.

The gold bubble of the 1970s was pricked by the return of macroeconomic stability and growth, and decline in the dollar price of oil. The question, therefore, is whether the sharp fall in gold and oil prices is the harbinger of good times ahead and a return to normalcy for the global economy.

Seen thus, the sharp fall in gold prices is surprising because three fundamentals underlying aurum's recent bull run remain unchanged. First, sustained economic uncertainty had created generalised risk aversion and flight to risk-free assets. Gold, along with other hard currency treasury bonds, is perceived as a risk-free asset. Second, vast liquidity creation by central banks fuelled an asset boom despite a failing global economy on one hand, and inflationary fears going forward on the other. Gold is both an asset and a traditional inflation hedge. Third, rising gold prices attracted hedge funds seeking higher returns in an environment characterised by low yields in the risk-free segment, driving prices still higher.

These fundamentals have in no way changed, indeed, if anything they have been magnified over the recent past. First, the April edition of the International Monetary Fund's (IMF) *World Economic Outlook* is not at all upbeat about the prospects of a global recovery, having further downgraded its previous forward-looking growth forecasts.

Second, the Federal Reserve's massive monthly quantitative easing (treasury bond purchases) of $85 billion of treasury is now matched by Bank of Japan's monthly programme of $75 billion.

Third, while the deposit banking system is now better regulated than it was at the time of the housing bubble, including through the new Basel III capital provisioning and definition norms, the unregulated shadow banking system may actually be a beneficiary of this regulatory tightening.

So what could have happened to have taken the zing out of the gold market in such a dramatic manner, with prices falling by about a quarter in a matter of days? The gold market is not transparent, with an air of cloak and dagger about it. Unsurprisingly, a number of competing theories, including conspiratorial ones, are doing the rounds, involving major institutional players, namely central banks, bullion banks and hedge funds. Some argue, for instance, that the price drop is mostly on paper, since it is still difficult to procure gold in physical form without a premium on the market price. Distressed Cyprus is rumoured to be contemplating selling its gold reserves, to be followed shortly by other peripheral debt-stressed countries.

Central banks hold large gold reserve assets. Unlike their treasury assets, these do not yield any return. Central banks are, therefore, known to lease indeterminate volumes of these risk-free assets to bullion banks at around one per cent annual interest. Bullion banks, in turn, sell the gold in the London Bullion Market to invest in higher yielding, but risk-free, long-term treasury bonds. This is, however, not risk-free arbitrage since bullion banks need to buy gold back at the end of the period to return to central banks. If the price of gold appreciates sharply in the interim, they can book huge losses. It is, therefore, in the interest of bullion banks to keep gold prices low. However, any lumpiness in the amount of gold to be returned to central banks could drive up prices in the short term; alternatively, there is an incentive for bullion banks, and associated hedge funds (since the division is not water-tight) in these circumstances to try and drive down gold prices when large volumes are to be returned to central banks.

Alan Greenspan, erstwhile chairman of the US Federal Reserve (Fed), famously quipped in 1998 that central banks have a nobler objective in leasing gold, namely keeping gold prices down. Why the objective of central banks should coincide with those of bullion banks might appear strange at first sight, but there is a deeper macroeconomic objective. Since gold competes with treasury bonds as a reserve asset, low gold prices would, *ceteris paribus*, drive treasury bond yields lower. Seen thus, leasing gold by central banks becomes a monetary policy tool. Since central banks are currently pulling all levers—quantitative easing, credit easing, 'twisting' the yielding curve, etc.—it is entirely possible that some big, innovative central bank is driving down gold prices to keep treasury yields low without having to buy them.

The third major player in the gold saga is hedge funds, which include gold exchange-traded funds. Since gold is perceived as a risk-free asset, a large-scale shift of savings and investment from risk assets into gold is to be expected during a financial crisis. This should drive prices up. Any drop in prices would be absorbed by investors, but there should not be any need for fire sales arising from asset liability mismatches that are characteristic of a classic bubble prick. So, were large amounts of leveraged funds also going into gold hedge funds, despite wrecked balance sheets, private deleveraging and tighter financial regulatory norms following the global financial crisis? If so, even a modest falling trend in prices could have pricked the boom, leading to fire sales, just as what occurred during the recent housing and financial crisis, as short-term debt could not be rolled over. This line of reasoning is not out of the realm of the possible because shadow banking has still to be reined in.

Actions by central banks, bullion banks and leveraged hedge funds, singly or severally in varying proportions, rather any return to normalcy, are possible reasons for the recent sharp decline in gold prices. The more interesting issue, however, is whether this drop is a short-term correction, or the end of a dream bull run. This ultimately depends on the relative predominance of the three fundamentals described above that drove gold prices up in the first place. If the first two factors are more important, gold prices will rebound soon, as the real demand for the metal is actually going up with the market having virtually declared it as the hardest of hard currencies. And if prices rise again, it would not be long before hedge funds join the dance party once more.

Business Standard, New Delhi, 29 April 2013.

70

The Dollar Drag

The current global debate on monetary policy is centred on whether it should target financial stability in addition to the domestic business cycle. With relatively tight regulation of financial markets, where present concerns are more developmental than regulatory, the counterpart debate in emerging market economics (EMEs) centres is on reconciling two widely held economic policy formulations, namely the Mundell-Fleming's Impossible Trinity and the Taylor Rule. The problem has become all the more compelling in a rapidly globalising world where large, volatile capital flows lead to misaligned and volatile exchange rates that threaten macroeconomic stability. The recent currency crisis which constrained Brazil, Turkey, Indonesia and India into tightening policy rates amidst collapsing growth, makes the case for reconciling the Impossible Trinity with the Taylor Rule of monetary policy all the more compelling.

Ceteris paribus, if a country runs a current account deficit (CAD), its currency should depreciate against those of its trading partners. There are, however, two major circumstances, one emanating from the current account (the 'Dutch disease syndrome') and the other from the capital account ('southern cone syndrome') under which this reasoning does not hold. The latter is more germane here because large and volatile capital inflows into EMEs have become a far more frequent phenomenon as a result of loosening of financial regulation, innovation, globalization and monetary policy spillovers. Cross-border flows of capital to EMEs have increased manifold since the 1970s following the oil price hikes and export-led growth strategies adopted by several East Asian economies.

The first manifestation of this syndrome in developing economies was the wave of financial liberalisation which led to a debt-fuelled recycling of petrodollars by American banks in the 'southern cone' in Latin America.

While large capital inflows can sustain large CADs for some time, over the medium- to long-run, they tend to magnify external imbalances and lay the ground for external payments crises. There are also large capital flows into countries running account surpluses. Once the capital surge abates, and particularly in the event of a sudden stop, there is a likelihood of a sudden, rapid and accelerated correction in exchange rates, with the nominal exchange rate depreciating sharply, and the real effective exchange rate (REER) overshooting its neutral (long-term fundamental) rate. This can cause short-term macroeconomic instability, such as higher inflation, a loss in international confidence and credit downgrade that could compound the reversal in capital flows and even precipitate an external payments crisis.

What pushes capital into EMEs, and what triggers the sudden stops? While fundamentals and the prospects of higher returns are certainly contributory factors, it is now becoming increasingly clear that the major factor driving flows in and out of EMEs has little to do with the fundamentals of recipient countries but yields in the source countries—the US, in particular, which has the biggest and deepest financial market in the world. While the asymmetry in flows—particularly outflows—can to some extent be explained by differing fundamentals, the inflows and the outflows seem to come in waves, across a wide swathe of countries.

Large global imbalances themselves should not result in destabilising flows. They are nothing new, and capital account flows have traditionally been simply the counterpart of current account balances. However, the cocktail of loosening of financial regulation, innovation, globalization and the extant international monetary system have combined to open up a growing gap between gross capital flows and net flows that reflect current account balances. It is not entirely coincidental that the capital flows stopped in the southern cone in the early-1980s, in East Asia in the late-1990s, and across a broad sweep of EMEs since May 2013, followed a tightening of monetary policy by the US Federal Reserve (Fed).

With the integration of financial markets and globalization, the spillovers of US Fed monetary policies are only increasing because of the overarching dominance of the dollar in the international monetary system. Fed policies, therefore, hugely determine the direction and velocity of cross-border capital flows. No other central bank comes even close to exercising this kind of influence, even within its own borders.

Over the years, the dollar has effectively become the global reserve currency. As a result, US monetary policy has a determining influence on the direction and quantum of global capital flows. This, in effect, gives the issuer of the global reserve currency the flexibility to soak up capital when it needs it most, and to export it out when it suffers from excessive domestic liquidity. Through this mechanism, the US can fund literally unlimited amounts of external and internal deficits without being penalised by the markets as happens in the case of other countries. Open capital accounts, espoused by the International Monetary Fund (IMF), only facilitate this funding and magnify the 'exorbitant privilege' of the dollar.

It has long been argued, from the days of John Maynard Keynes, that the extant international monetary system has a structural flaw in that it lacks a mechanism, market based or otherwise, to induce surplus countries to adjust. This can lead to the persistence of large external imbalances that are potentially destabilising. Recent history however indicates that this is not entirely correct, as there is also little pressure on countries with reserve currencies, and especially the global reserve currency, to adjust even when they run large CADs, on account of the large external demand for their currencies. The latter is also consistent with the Triffin Dilemma, by which the reserve currency issuer is expected to run larger and larger CADs to meet the growing needs of global liquidity. This is manifestly not true in the cases of currencies like the Japanese yen and the Swiss franc. Both countries have run current account surpluses over the last decade and a half. Similarly, even while its currency was becoming important in the composition of the global portfolio of reserve currencies, the euro was running a roughly balanced current account position with the rest of the world. This is because it is really the dollar that is accepted as the *de facto* global reserve currency by markets, even though the IMF may have classified other currencies also as reserves.

In effect, the US Fed acts as the global central bank. Policy easing by the US Fed, both prior to and following the global financial crisis, led to a surge in capital inflows into emerging markets, appreciating their currencies. There were intervening periods of sudden stops, as US monetary policy changed course, resulting in sharp currency depreciation, sudden stops and external payments crises. This happened in the 1980s in Latin America, in the 1990s in East Asia, and is now affecting EMEs globally. International financial markets in EMEs appear to respond more to US Fed actions than to domestic economic fundamentals.

According to Impossible Trinity, a country can have only two of the following three: fixed exchange rate, monetary independence and free capital flows. A free monetary policy means that it is free to respond to the domestic business cycle. The Taylor Rule prescribes a rule-bound—as opposed to discretionary—monetary policy by which the central bank adjusts its short-term policy rate based on a mathematical formula using differentials between a country's potential GDP (gross domestic product) and actual GDP, and inflation target and actual inflation. The Taylor Rule and its variants are now used by almost all advanced-country central banks. The author of the rule, John B. Taylor of Stanford University, is of the view that it is relevant for developing country central banks also. Many developing countries have indeed started using the Taylor Rule.

In advanced economies, the Taylor Rule responds to the domestic business cycle. Monetary policy in developing countries, on the other hand, is constrained to respond to the external financial cycle, which distorts the application of the Taylor Rule. Thus, if domestic growth concerns warrant low interest rates, a sudden stop in capital inflows may induce them to keep interest rates unduly high to attract foreign capital, thereby magnifying the downturn in the business cycle. In other words, they end up trying to negotiate the Impossible Trinity. Raising interest rates at such times rarely works because the stops are frequently not country specific, and in any case, foreign investors are more concerned about capital losses than higher interest income.

Domestic debt in EMEs is backstopped by their central banks. External deficits denominated in international reserve currencies are not. The dependence on market support makes them susceptible to external payments crises in the event of market revolt if deficits are perceived to be excessive and unsustainable.

This threat of external payments crisis compels developing countries to frequently use monetary policy for managing external imbalances, in addition to managing the domestic business cycle. They need separate instruments, as part of a consistent policy framework, to target the external financial cycle so that their central banks retain monetary independence.

Financial Express, New Delhi, 7 February 2014.

71

How Emerging Markets Deal with Global Spillovers

Traditional development theory took a benign view of capital inflows into developing countries as these filled two critical developmental gaps, namely a savings-investment deficit and foreign exchange scarcity.

While developing countries continue to require large amounts of external savings to supplement their own to accelerate growth and development, a rapidly globalising world with large external imbalances, sophisticated financial markets and growing spillovers of US monetary policy also results in large, volatile capital flows leading to misaligned and volatile exchange rates, sudden stops and external payments crises that threaten macroeconomic stability.

There are three key ways in which emerging market economies, or EMEs, have dealt with global spillovers, although their sequencing and deployment have varied enormously across space and time. By and large, the macroeconomic response is usually the first line of defence in EMEs that have floated their currencies to varying degrees. This response includes greater exchange rate flexibility, coupled with adequate reserves that enable market intervention where required to deal with exchange rate misalignment and extreme volatility.

The second way is to use prudential measures to address financial stability concerns that may arise from failures and leakages from the first line of defence, such as domestic credit booms and asset-price inflation. Higher reserve requirements, countercyclical capital buffers, and capping loan-to-value ratios in the bubble sectors (such as housing) and foreign currency lending are some of the policy instruments that have been used. The G20 initiative to develop domestic currency bond markets and structural reforms that can increase the absorptive capacity of EMEs to direct capital inflows into investment in the real economy is part of the toolkit of this line of defence.

The third way is to impose short-term capital flow management measures (CFMs). This instrument has recently been recognised by the IMF as legitimate in extreme circumstances, and also endorsed by the G20 at their sixth Summit in Cannes. CFMs are putatively leaky, and more effective when imposed on inflows than on outflows. There are two broad types of CFM instruments: market-based controls which aim to increase the cost of the targeted capital transactions to discourage inflows, and administrative controls which impose outright restrictions on cross-border capital flows through prohibitions or explicit quantitative limits.

All three lines of defence create distortions of their own, and at best throw sand in the wheels. A point may arise when the three lines together are unable to stop the capital flow juggernaut, and an external payments crisis and loss of market access follows. There are three tried and trusted options available with developing countries to deal with this, namely bilateral and regional swap agreements, IMF funding and, as was done on a large scale during the recent financial crisis, liquidity and swap facilities with the US Federal Reserve (Fed), the issuer of the *de facto* global reserve currency.

What more needs to be done? There is need for streamlining the first line of defence, so as to limit the distortion of monetary policy by volatile capital flows on the one hand, and minimise recourse to short-term prudential and capital flow measures on the other. Ideally, only those prudential and capital flow measures should be in places that are desirable and sustainable over the long term.

Developing countries have found it impossible to use a single policy instrument—short-term interest rates—to simultaneously target both the domestic economic cycle and global spillovers (the external financial cycle) at the same time. According to the widely accepted 'Tinbergen Rule,' a policy instrument can be effective only if it has a single objective. They therefore need a new policy instrument that frees up monetary policy to target the domestic economic cycle.

The interest rate is clearly better suited to target domestic imbalances. Targeting a neutral real effective exchange rate, or REER, through market intervention, on the other hand, is clearly better suited to targeting external imbalances. This would, first, ensure that the nominal exchange rate remains closely aligned to fundamentals—i.e., it responds primarily to the current account and is not distorted by volatile capital flows that can be destabilising from time to time, even though they might at times make it easier to finance current account deficits (CADs) over the short term. Second, by sequestering excessive inflows during episodes of excessive inflows, it enhances the war chest for combating disorderly adjustment which can boost market confidence relative to EME peers. Such a policy/instrument is also entirely consistent with 1(iii) of IMF's Articles of Agreement that purports "to promote exchange rate stability."

A number of EMEs, such as India, have, as a matter of course, relied more on interventions in the foreign exchange market to manage volatile capital flows. However, they neither target it consistently, nor are they consistent in the use of instruments to achieve their target. A consistent, well-articulated and effectively communicated exchange rate and/or reserve management policy which protects monetary independence has still to be worked out by EME central banks. The use of separate instruments to target domestic and external balances by the central bank must be done within an overall framework of policy consistency that attenuates conflicting outcomes. There would, for instance, be no conflicting outcomes when there is a need to tighten monetary policy and sell foreign exchange reserves, or inversely when there is a need to loosen monetary policy and buy foreign exchange reserves. There could, however, be some conflict when there is a need to loosen monetary policy and sell reserves, and inversely when there is a need to tighten monetary policy and buy reserves. In the case of such conflict, the central bank would need to conduct sterilisation/liquidity provision operations alongside market intervention so that the monetary policy stance is not compromised.

Business Standard, New Delhi, 26 January 2014.

72

Pause and Reframe

As the country debates what its monetary policy framework should be, it is perhaps a good time to assess the stance, determinants and outcomes of the extant framework over the last decade through the prism of a framework used by central banks the world over, the Taylor Rule. John B. Taylor has argued that his eponymous rule is, *mutatis mutandis*, relevant for developing country central banks. While there are a number of variations of the Taylor Rule, including those by Taylor himself, a commonly used formula is as follows: policy rate = last quarter inflation plus 0.5 (last quarter GDP [gross domestic produce] minus potential GDP) plus 0.5 (last quarter inflation minus inflation target).

Two things are immediately apparent. First, monetary policy has been consistently very loose since 2003, both in periods of low and high growth. Second, since asset inflation seems to move in tandem with economic growth, this reflects optimism driven by sentiments surrounding growth prospects, rather than asset bubbles driven by loose monetary policy as in the US.

One can think of five possible reasons why monetary policy has been so loose over the past decade. First, the central bank may have been targeting alternative metrics of inflation, such as wholesale price (WPI) or core inflation. Wholesale prices are not used by other central banks for the conduct of monetary policy, however core inflation is used, but it is inappropriate for emerging markets because of its smaller weight in the consumption basket. Be that as it may, use of alternative metrics may qualify the extent to which monetary policy was loose but is unlikely to change the overall stance.

Second, the Reserve Bank of India (RBI) may have followed the precedent set by advanced country central banks in easing aggressively in response to downturns without commensurate tightening in the upturn. Central bankers are, after all, part of the exclusive Basel club. The consequence was asset inflation in advanced economies and persistently high CPI (common price index) in India.

Third, the RBI may have given preference to growth over inflation, perhaps prodded by the treasury, either directly or indirectly through fiscal dominance. Since fiscal policy was lax, there was little that the central bank could have done but accommodate it to prevent even greater distortions.

Fourth, since the source of inflationary pressures in India was on the non-core side, which is less amenable to monetary policy action, periodic modest rate-hikes have been unable to tame inflation, making monetary policy look unusually loose in retrospect. As Paul Volcker showed in the US, monetary policy has to be used as a sledgehammer if it is to tame inflationary pressures emanating from the non-core side.

The fifth explanation is that Indian monetary policy got trapped in the classic 'Impossible Trinity' by trying to simultaneously target the domestic growth-inflation cycle and the external financial-capital flow cycle. Thus, in the period 2003 Q3 to 2008 Q3, monetary policy was too loose with respect to the domestic growth cycle because the central bank was constrained in its response to huge capital inflows and the appreciating rupee.

The low growth period 2008 Q4 to 2009 Q2 during the global financial crisis was also a period of huge capital outflows and sharp depreciation of the rupee. With a large stockpile of foreign currency reserves, monetary policy now focused on the domestic growth cycle. The period of high growth in 2009 Q3 to 2011 Q2 saw the return of capital flows and rupee appreciation, constraining monetary policy to shift its focus back to the external cycle. In the recent period, 2011 Q3 to 2013 Q4, despite the rupee coming under pressure on account of capital outflows and sharp depreciation, the focus of monetary policy shifted back to the domestic growth cycle.

What lessons can be derived from the experience of the last 10 years for India's monetary policy framework going forward? First, the Taylor Rule is a single policy variable framework for responding to the domestic business cycle. However, cross-border capital flows are now increasingly driving business cycles, including asset prices, in emerging markets, exerting disinflationary or inflationary pressures through exchange-rate fluctuations. Since growth collapses just as the external cycle turns, central banks need to loosen monetary policy to stimulate growth but tighten it to prevent capital flight. They consequently find it impossible to use a single policy instrument, the short-term interest rate, to simultaneously target the domestic growth-inflation cycle and the external financial cycle. The latter is determined by the vagaries of monetary policies in reserve currency issuing countries and not by their own macroeconomic variables. According to the widely accepted Tinbergen Rule, a policy instrument can be effective only if it has a single objective. Developing countries therefore need to move beyond flexible inflation targeting to using a second policy instrument as part of a consistent framework to respond to the external financial cycle.

Second, while the financial regulatory structure may be robust enough to prevent loose domestic monetary policy spilling over into asset markets, the latter are nevertheless susceptible to spillovers from the monetary policies of advanced economies through capital flows. This warrants a suitable macro-prudential policy response. Third, and last, as long as there is fiscal dominance and a large weightage of food and fuel in the consumption basket, the credibility of any inflation targeting monetary policy framework will remain at risk, as these are not easily amenable to monetary policy actions.

The Indian Express, New Delhi, 24 March 2014.

73

Frozen in Time: World Bank, IMF

The Bretton Woods conference of 1944 put in place the institutional framework to rebuild the financial and economic system destroyed by the Great Depression and the War, spawning two of the most influential institutions of global economic governance of the post-war period, namely the International Monetary Fund (IMF) and the World Bank.

The international monetary system was repaired by pegging the dollar to gold, and other international currencies to the dollar. This system broke down in 1971 when the dollar went off the gold standard. In Bretton Woods Mark 2, major reserve currencies floated against each other, funding themselves from the market and backstopped by their central banks. Balance of payments (BoP) rises now became a structural feature of developing economies that were constrained to turn to the IMF during external payments crises when they lost market access.

East Asian economies, including Japan and China, leveraged Bretton Woods Mark II to grow at record levels by supplementing domestic demand with external demand by undervaluing/pegging their exchange rates against the dollar. IMF surveillance proved ineffective in preventing and correcting exchange rate misalignments. The consequential accumulation of large hard currency reserves by emerging market economies (EMEs) now reduced IMF's effective role as global lender of last resort (LOLR). Indeed, the larger EMEs, most notably China, provided the liquidity for a leveraged private consumption boom through a new shadow banking system in western economies that underpinned the record growth and apparent macro-economic stability during the 'Great Moderation.'

Bretton Woods Mark 2 broke down with the global financial crisis of 2008, as leveraged private consumption in advanced economies collapsed, signalling a permanent downward shift in demand and unwinding of global imbalances. It yielded to Bretton Woods Mark 3 with public debt taking over the burden of private debt to revive consumption. This however can be sustained over an extended period only by the US on account of the large international demand for dollars, and perhaps by Japan where public deficits can be funded by private surpluses. Market forces may force other countries to adjust, as in the case of peripheral Europe.

The World Bank was the second leg of the Bretton Woods system. It helped reconstruct the physical infrastructure of war ravaged Europe, following which its resources were redeployed in developing countries. At some point, it also shifted its focus from physical to soft infrastructure, with poverty alleviation rather than economic growth as its main focus even though its new constituency had a huge deficit in both physical and soft infrastructure, and both were necessary for a durable uptick in trend growth.

The resources of the Bretton Woods institutions ceased to grow significantly once the European project was complete, even as the developmental needs of emerging markets rose exponentially on account of accelerating growth. The World Bank's net disbursements of around $15 billion a year, of which half comprises concessional International Development Association (IDA) aid for poor countries, can finance only 2-3 major infrastructure projects each year. Its major shareholders clearly missed a trick, for they could have intermediated and redirected the global savings glut to fill the infrastructure gap in developing countries—the new engines of global growth as trend growth declined in ageing advanced economies. In the absence of this, capital flowed uphill from emerging markets to finance leveraged consumption in advanced economies, sowing the seeds of instability in global financial markets culminating in the recent crisis.

Even as World Bank lending was subject to supply constraints, the IMF was subject to demand constraints, making it duplicate some of the lending activities of the World Bank through facilities like the PGRF (Poverty Reduction Growth Facility). The crisis underscored the LOLR irrelevance of the IMF as countries that needed additional support to reassure markets turned instead to the US Federal Reserve (Fed) whose deep dollar pockets and nimbleness the lumbering IMF could not match. The Bretton Woods system was transformed from being growth enhancing and stabilising mechanisms to aid giving institutions for poor, developing economies.

The crisis provided a historic opportunity to adjust to the winds of change to make the Bretton Woods institutions relevant again. The G20 however failed to do so. It moved to substantially enhance the resources of the IMF by a factor of 4-5—not because these were inadequate to insure poor developing countries, for which IMF's resources were adequate, or for emerging market economics (EMEs) who were now self-insured, but because these were now required for peripheral Europe. Europe and the Euro zone now account for over 80 per cent of outstanding general resource amount (GRA) credits of the IMF. The big bazooka to resolve the European crisis, however, was always in Europe, as the embattled countries needed funding in euros, and not in any external currency. It was the European Central Bank's (ECB) 'whatever it takes' Outright Monetary Transactions (OMT) announcement, and not the IMF bail-out packages, that stabilised sovereign bond yields in Europe. Their requirements could have been easily funded without IMF intervention through amendment in their treaties that resolved flaws in the monetary union through a closer fiscal and monetary union. This would have freed up resources to enable the World Bank redirect global savings into financing the infrastructure gap to sustain high growth in the stuttering new engines of global growth.

The Bretton Woods institutions appear frozen in time because their governance structure has not adjusted to the tectonic changes in the global economy. The voting share of BRICS (Brazil, Russia, India, China and South Africa) is now equivalent to only about half their share in global GDP at market prices, and just over a third at purchasing power parity (PPP). Europe and the US also have a stranglehold over their top leadership. The unwillingness to cede voting share leadership to emerging markets is matched by an unwillingness to expand their resources on account of growing fiscal stress from ageing and declining growth.

As the Bretton Woods twins unravel, emerging markets endeavour to put in place alternative institutions, such as the Chiang Mai initiative in East Asia, the New Development Bank and the Contingency Reserve Arrangement of the BRICS. Whether these new institutions are nimble enough to address their developmental needs, and whether the rising economic powers can achieve the geopolitical co-operation to work collaboratively with each other in the manner the US and Europe did in the post-war period, however, remain to be seen.

Mint, New Delhi 15 December 2014.

VIII
Making Next Time Different
Reforming Global Finance

At last he rose, and twitched his mantle blue:
Tomorrow to fresh woods, and pastures new.

Lycidas, John Milton.

74

Regulatory Change at Risk

If Kenneth Rogoff and Carmen Reinhart are to be believed, policy makers have learnt little from the experience of financial crises over the last eight centuries. The same frailties, deriving from over exuberance and overleveraging, have surfaced time and time again, with surprisingly similar outcomes: banking crises, sovereign defaults, protracted downturns and a painfully long period of adjustment.

The financial collapse during the Great Depression in the 1930s laid the foundations of the post-war regulatory structure. The Glass-Steagall Act erected a firewall between tightly-regulated deposits-based banking that had access to liquidity buffers from central banks, and relatively lightly regulated investment banking dependent on capital markets without liquidity backstops.

The growing sophistication of the financial sector, and the 'irrational exuberance' deriving from the Great Moderation, gradually eroded this regulatory framework. Systemically significant financial activity migrated out of the regulated deposits-based banking system. Financial institutions became too big and interconnected to be allowed to fail. All this was facilitated by the repeal of the Glass-Steagall Act and the rise of universal banking. Despite repeated warnings from history, leverage was once again permitted to build up. Central banks lost sight of the fact that financial stability was the original mandate on which they were founded. They now focused almost entirely on output and inflation, targeting the business cycle while neglecting the credit cycle.

Reminiscent of the regulatory transformation in the wake of the Great Depression, the monumental collapse of the western financial system is leading to a fundamental reform of financial regulation under the watchful eyes of the G20. But will this time be any different?

Reforms agreed to so far, especially with regard to the new Basel III capital and liquidity standards, are impressive. But Basel III is still micro-regulatory and too focused on deposits-based banks. The retention of risk-weights and mark-to-market mechanisms may leave it still too pro-cyclical to control build-up of leverage in the absence of a robust unweighted leverage ratio. The shadow banking system, which vastly increased the money multiplier, and lay at the heart of the recent crisis, can only be reined in through macro-prudential regulation that would widen the perimeter of regulation. This has still to be done. Stronger regulation without widening the perimeter is likely to strengthen shadow banking. There are signs that this might, indeed, be happening.

Effective enforcement, supervision, harmonisation and monitoring have yet to begin. Cracks are also appearing in the global consensus on compensation practices, accounting standards, reining in rating agencies, financial transactions taxes, regulating Global Systemically-Important Financial Institutions (G-SIFIs) and the implementation of the new Basel III capital standards. With the collapse of major financial institutions, remaining SIFIs have become even more systemically important.

The rise of banking and joint stock companies was to facilitate tapping into individual savings for large, productive brick-and-mortar projects that accelerated growth, and hence, per capita incomes. These had crept ahead at snail's pace ever since the Neolithic Revolution and right up to the Industrial Revolution.

If banking intermediate savings for investment in the real sector, returns in the financial sector should be linked to productivity growth and returns in the real sector. But the financial sector generated returns far in excess of the real sector that enabled bankers to get outsized emoluments compared to real sector managers. This was possible because the banking sector, at some point, started intermediating for the financial sector itself. It became the engine of growth in advanced countries, as real sector activity started migrating to more productive emerging economies.

High returns were possible in the financial sector through a combination of leveraged investment in financial assets and loose monetary policy over an extended period. Much of this leverage was through the shadow-banking system. All this vastly inflated asset prices. Profits were booked not through actual trades that cleared the market, but on book profits calculated on index-based valuations on thin OTC trades. Since these returns were not based on productivity growth in the real sector, this was a bubble waiting to burst. These outsized profits, it turned out, were not—and could not be—funded out of returns in the real economy. It had to be eventually bailed out through taxpayer money.

Prior to the financial crisis, financial markets in developed countries were seen as models for developing countries. The ground reality, however, was that big emerging markets such as China were able to sustain high levels of growth despite less developed financial markets. Financial repression directed rising household savings into investment in the real economy. This repression also gave governments access to resources that enabled them to make the large investments required in physical and social infrastructure.

Developed countries, on the other hand, saw savings, investment and growth in the real sector decline since 1980s. This coincided with the ascendancy of the financial sector in their economies. Today's advanced countries too experienced sustained and steady growth when their banking sector was not as completely divorced from the real sector as now, when their banking sector was akin to that in India and China presently.

In developing countries like India, financial markets were regulated like public utilities on the unstated premise that there must be some underlying real sector exposure to justify financial activity. There were limits on borrowing for consumption, unless the level of borrowing could be sustained by discounting incomes from labour, or profits from productive activities in the real sector. Central banks in developing countries fixed one eye on financial stability, and there was always an element of macro-prudential regulation.

Stringent regulation, however, comes with a cost. It is a proxy for tax as it raises the cost of capital. Emerging markets, therefore, turned to the western model of light-touch regulation as a long-term objective to deepen financial markets to lower the cost of capital.

The priorities in emerging markets like India, before the crisis, were not deregulation but developmental, with the aim of deepening and developing new markets to sustain high rates of growth in the real economy.

Financial inclusion, high cost of capital, long-term funding instruments for infrastructure, development of liquid bond markets to improve monetary policy transmission, and financialisation of savings invested in physical assets such as gold so that they could be leveraged for productive investment, were inter alia, financial sector priorities in India before the crisis. Nothing has happened in Indian financial markets that warrant changing these priorities.

So, where do we go from here, now that the G20 is trying to harmonise financial regulation across major jurisdictions, including both developing and developed countries to reduce regulatory arbitrage across jurisdictions? Clearly, returning to the financial repression of the past is not an option, but neither is a return to largely self-regulated and self-correcting financial markets.

Historical experience indicates the existence of some kind of financial sector Kuznets Curve, where there is a close association between financial deepening and growth, but up to a point, beyond which risks multiply while growth and welfare benefits become ambivalent as the financial sector begins to feed on itself faster than on the real economy.

So, if this time is to be different, a fundamental philosophical shift is needed in the rules informing the regulatory framework of the financial sector. However, given the strength and reach of the financial sector lobby, including the 'group think' in, and intellectual capture of, financial institutions and centres, things may eventually turn out no different this time.

The Economic Times, New Delhi, 4 August 2011.

75

Basel III: The Norms are Not Suited for Emerging World Banking

There are fundamental differences between financial systems in advanced market economies (AMEs) and those in emerging market and developing economies (EMDEs). These differences, *inter alia*, explain why financial intermediation held up relatively well in these economies even as it froze in AMEs during the recent global financial crisis.

The biggest difference is that AMEs have increasingly moved towards reliance on short-term money and capital markets for funding, and money created against volatile financial assets and innovative products exchanged over the counter ('shadow banking'). EMDEs continue to be dependent on more stable deposit-based funding. This difference is critical.

Financial systems in both EMDEs and AMEs become vulnerable during downturns in the business cycle on account of deterioration in asset quality. Ever since deposit insurance was put in place following the banking panic during the Great Depression, and the central bank discount window became readily accessible, deposit-based banking is no longer susceptible to funding risks arising from financial panics and bank runs.

As long as their capital is calibrated to cover asset quality deterioration during business downturns, EMDE banks no longer face major funding risks other than a general decline in financial savings. At aleast as long as external currency-denominated deposits are kept within prudent limits through capital controls.

AMEs are, in addition, exposed to funding risks arising from financial panic characteristic of build-up of leverage in capital markets. This vulnerability has increased following the repeal in 1999 of the

Great Depression-era Glass-Steagall Act in the US that drew a firewall between deposit-based banks and those (investment banks) that rely on capital markets.

Basel II banking capital norms were calibrated to cover risks arising out of traditional deposit-based banking. They were not designed to cover funding risks emanating from sharp maturity mismatches and attendant difficulties in rolling over credit on account of financial panic that can result in rapid deleveraging, credit freeze and a breakdown in financial intermediation.

Financial panic has in some way or the other always been preceded by a considerable rise in leverage. The primary drivers of leverage in AMEs and EMDEs are strikingly different. Increasing leverage in AMEs in the period leading up to the global financial crisis was an attempt to increase returns on capital in an environment of low returns through increased trading of claims on real economy assets. This led to a rapid expansion of financial assets as a proportion of GDP.

High credit growth in EMDEs like India, on the other hand, was primarily to finance high rates of growth and investment in the real economy. The returns on capital in EMDEs are now significantly higher, as a result of which global production has long been migrating to these countries. These economies are much less financialised.

There was, of course, also speculative investment in certain asset classes, but margins on such credit were incrementally raised in response to the rising pace of credit expansion through conservative macro prudential financial regulation. This is a defining characteristic of EMDEs like India, where regulators have not hesitated to spot and prick asset bubbles, rather than simply waiting to clean up after they burst.

Following the recent global financial crisis, a slew of financial regulatory reforms are being contemplated under the aegis of the G20, Financial Stability Board (FSB), the Basel Committee on Banking Supervision (BCBS) and other standards-setting agencies to protect the integrity of financial intermediation.

Are these headed in the right direction? To the extent the western financial system, in which they park their excess savings, become safer, EMEs found it easy to sign up to the reforms as they also stood to gain. The impact of the ongoing reform on them so far has been relatively benign. Despite the general decline in cross-border claims on financial assets between advanced economies, capital flows to EMEs are back to pre-crisis highs. Indeed capital flows to EMEs appear to be more affected by monetary policies in advanced economies then by the regulatory rejig. While financial regulatory reforms are expected to be implemented across all jurisdictions, the immediate impact of most would be felt acutely in the relatively lightly-regulated AMEs, rather than in the more tightly regulated EMDEs. EMDEs clearly need to increase financial savings to accelerate growth and development, notwithstanding the fact that in recent years, capital was flowing uphill from EMDEs to AMEs. This was arguably a temporary and unsustainable phenomenon that may be about to change as the global economy rebalances.

The impact of the new Basel III banking capital adequacy norms, however, will be almost equal across both AMEs and EMDEs, even though the nature of risks in their financial systems is quite different.

AMEs need major regulatory changes that inoculate them more effectively against the risks their financial system faces. The challenge is to roll back some of the more extreme forms of financialisation that expose them to greater risk without commensurate impact on growth.

No amount of capital can be large enough to inoculate banks and other financial institutions against financial panic and bank runs. Sovereign and central bank bailouts would always be required in the case of big, systemically important financial institutions that cannot be allowed to fail. Such financial institutions need to hold higher amounts of capital and/or pay a special ('financial transaction') tax in normal times to at least partly compensate the general taxpayer for bail-outs.

Basel III, which seeks to enhance the quantity and quality of capital that banks need to hold, and the proposal to levy a 'financial transaction tax,' are to be seen in this light. While the rationale for tightening capital adequacy norms for the banking sector in AMEs is self-evident, the case for immediately migrating from Basel II to Basel III in EMDEs is not. The argument generally advanced against calibrating capital requirements to differential risks faced in AMEs and EMDEs is that this would result in regulatory arbitrage.

This is, however, not very convincing because capital would be migrating to a more regulated environment, which has additional costs. Regulation is a proxy tax, admittedly difficult to quantify. There is a danger that scarce savings in EMDEs might be pulled away from investment, necessary to sustain current levels of high growth, to cover non-existent risks in their financial systems precisely when their savings are falling.

Basel III constitutes a double whammy for countries like India. It would aggravate the growing savings—investment gap, manifest in a widening current account deficit. It would also widen the structural fiscal deficit as the government would need to cough up a substantial chunk of the additional capital by virtue of its large ownership of the banking sector. The cost of capital is already high in EMDEs on account of the savings-investment gap and tighter regulation. The enhanced capital requirements of Basel III are almost guaranteed to keep it high in the foreseeable future.

The moot point is why should EMDEs be pushed towards a regulatory framework calibrated to risks in AME financial systems. This would extract a high developmental cost through foregone growth. So where do we go from here? There are elements in Basel III that could be applied to Basel II, such as tighter definition of tier-I capital, and a countercyclical buffer in the event of build-up of excessive credit according to national circumstances.

A number of EMDEs, such as India, follow some variants of this macro prudential principle anyway. However, raising overall capital requirements, and especially the additional conservation buffer of 2.5 per cent, is not relevant for EMDEs at this stage.

There is, of course, no good reason to suppose that EMDE financial systems will remain where they are now. If some EMDEs see benefits in the development of innovative shadow banking, they could move towards lighter-touch regulation—strengthened by current regulatory changes in the pipeline—in which event these EMDEs could migrate to AME-type financial systems in future.

Financial Sector Assessment Programmes (FSAPs), mandated for all systemically important economies and jurisdictions, could periodically assess whether and when Basel II jurisdictions should migrate to Basel III.

The Economic Times, New Delhi, 24 September 2012.

76

An Economics to Fit the Facts?

The discipline of economics is by common consensus one of the major casualties of the recent global financial crisis. Fiscal multipliers and monetary policy have not performed as modelled, the much-programmed financial markets have not worked rationally, near term economic forecasts based on International Monetary Fund's (IMF) intimidating DSGE (dynamic stochastic general equilibrium) simulations have repeatedly failed, and there continues to be great confusion even over something as basic as measuring growth potential.

Barry Eichengreen ("An Economics to Fit the Facts", *Mint*, 16 May 2015) recently pointed to some drawbacks in the economics discipline as currently practiced. However, his empiricist pursuit of the holy grail of the perfect model through a new 'evidence based economics', which will fit all the facts is likely to meet the same fate as all those that preceded it. For example, IMF's new 'MAPMOD', which embeds the financial sector in the tried and failed DSGE model. Historians have been there and moved on. It is time that the younger discipline of economics did likewise.

Latter-day economists, it seems, have still to reconcile themselves to the humbling fact that their discipline is a social and not a natural science; that their subject matter consists of human behaviour for which there can never be any natural laws beyond some universal foibles, such as greed, generosity, jealousy, ambition, selfishness, thrift, pride, prejudice, love, hate, passion, profligacy, etc., personified in the classics of human literature. These classics remain evergreen because people have related to them across space and time as they distil the essence of what it is to be human. That is why we can relate more to Thucydides History of the Peloponnesian War that ascribed human actions to such foibles, than to Herodotus' more famous 'History' that ascribed it to divine intervention.

This is why we still relate to Mr Micawber's advice to David Copperfield in the Charles Dickens' classic: "Annual income twenty pounds, annual expenditure nineteen six, result happiness. Annual income twenty pounds, annual expenditure twenty pounds ought and six, result misery." This iron law of the consequences of leverage can scarcely be bettered. But it is too general a tool for model-building. Not all humans are profligate. This is why all model-building and universal laws relating to the human condition have floundered, most famously those devised by Karl Marx.

It could plausibly be argued that while individual behaviour can vary because of personality differences, macroeconomics is about aggregate behaviour that is more predictable and therefore programmable. To take an example from physics, while particle behaviour at the sub-atomic level is unpredictable, in the aggregate, the physical world functions according to natural, immutable laws. Might not the same apply to human behaviour? Is human behaviour in the aggregate rational and profit-maximising as Adam Smith assumed, or subject to some subconscious, almost Freudian, urges as recently underscored by behavioural economists such as Thaler and Sunstein?

There are, unfortunately, critical behavioural differences in response to similar circumstances across both space and time at the aggregate level. An increase in income can induce people in one part of the world to save more (think Angela Merkel's Swabian housewife), and others to spend more (think the stereotypical, credit-card-happy American housewife). Likewise, Asian societies behave like ants and save more than Latin American societies that behave more like grasshoppers. The response in the same place may be quite different in different periods, such as in pre-capitalist peasant societies that valued leisure more and cut back on production in response to higher prices. Even to this day, the French and Italians value leisure more than Americans and this is reflected in their economic behaviour. The same people behave quite differently in an economic boom and in a recession. Think 'ricardian equivalence', 'Minsky moment' and Keynes' 'animal spirits'. Data-dependent relationships, and even broader generalisations, derived from a specific time or place may not hold elsewhere or at other times.

To get around this problem, historians turned to the narrative as an analytical tool, because describing the way things happened turned out to be not very different from explaining why they happened. We need to recognise that similar facts need not result in similar outcomes across space and time.

In these circumstances, is it surprising that IMF's sophisticated models do not yield accurate forecasts of growth even in the next quarter, except in times of exceptional macroeconomic stability where future trends are a replica of past trends? In financial markets, where sophisticated model-building drives investment, interconnectedness and the critical role that confidence plays, can on their own gut any model, and they repeatedly have. The relationships between variables based on past data used to generate coefficients may not work going forward because there may not be any causal relationship between correlated data, and the correlation itself may not hold going forward. Models based on data derived from one area may not work in other areas.

The bottom line is that models and algorithms are useful, indeed desirable to avoid human error, where outcomes are dependent on physical and natural laws, such as flying aircraft or driving cars. The problem arises when algorithms are pushed to apply to areas, such as economics and finance, where outcomes are contingent on human behaviour. Economists consequently need to rely less on complex universally applicable models and incorporate a more nuanced understanding of human behaviour as they go about reinventing their discipline and rendering policy advice.

Mint, 10 June 2015.

77

Ring-fencing Wall Street

On 10 December 2013, the much acclaimed 'Volcker rule' was finalised by five US regulators: the Federal Reserve (Fed), the Securities and Exchange Commission, the Office of the Comptroller of the Currency, the Federal Deposit Insurance Corporation and the Commodity Futures Trading Commission. The rule was part of the Dodd Frank Act, which was passed in the wake of the global financial crisis. There are similar initiatives in the UK (Vickers Commission) and the EU (Liikanen Report). While the latter two are yet to be translated into legislation, the hotly contested but crucial rule-writing process for the Volcker Rule has been completed after three long years of deliberation.

The genesis of these three initiatives in key financial jurisdictions lies in the attempts to reinstate a Glass-Steagall-type firewall—which was in existence in the US since 1933, but repealed in 1999 by the Clinton administration—between deposit-based and investment banking.

Glass-Steagall restricted commercial banks, which had access to deposit insurance and liquidity buffers from the central bank, from underwriting or dealing in securities, and investment banks from accepting deposits. Like Glass-Steagall, the Volcker Rule is part of a slew of measures designed to maintain financial stability by insulating the critical economy-wide payments system from the kind of classic bank runs that haunted major advanced economies right up to the Great Depression, necessitating large taxpayer bail-outs.

This firewall was successful in preventing major bank runs in the post-war period until it was overtaken by financial innovation and 'light touch regulation,' which is based on disclosure rather than control. In retrospect, it is unsurprising that the collapse of this firewall led to the build-up of systemic risk in the financial system that boiled over with the run on Lehman Brothers, a systemically important, large investment bank.

The trigger for the crisis this time around was the shadowy investment, rather than depositary, arm of various banks. Fire-sales of assets led to prices spiralling downward. 'Shadow banks' did not access a stable deposit base for funding, but volatile short-term capital. This became difficult to roll over as credit markets froze. Shadow banks are not cushioned by the liquidity buffers of deposit insurance and central bank discount windows, which can prevent a liquidity problem from escalating into a full blown bank run.

By seeking to limit 'proprietary trading' (on the bank's own account) unrelated to customer needs and limiting the ownership or sponsorship of hedge/private equity funds to 3 per cent of tier-I capital, the Volcker Rule restricts the risky business activities of depository banks. This backtracking on universal banking is a major landmark in ongoing regulatory reform.

While the three models (Volcker, Vickers and Liikanen) will have to stand the test of another crisis to prove their efficacy, lingering concerns are already evident. The big question is whether the loss due to the passing on of the costs—of regulatory restructuring and the shrinkage of assets—to borrowers is commensurate with the gains in financial stability.

First, while Glass-Steagall prohibited an entity from undertaking both commercial and investment banking, the Volcker rule merely prohibits an entity that accepts public deposits from undertaking certain types of trades. Even as it prohibits proprietary trading, it allows hedging and market making. In practice, it is difficult for the regulator to distinguish between trades entered into for profit or for hedging, as financial innovation blurs such boundaries. The derivatives losses of J.P. Morgan caused recently by the 'London Whale' highlighted this difficulty. Its CEO, Jamie Dimon maintained before the US Congress that the trade was a hedge for its overall exposure. Would this trade have been disallowed under the Volcker rule? It is difficult to determine.

Second, the separation of banking from trading activities does not make commercial banking less immune to risky lending practices. The heart of banking lies in risk taking, and the biggest risk is credit risk. Every banker who buys risk into his balance sheet by extending a loan is within his right to seek options to mitigate the risk. Securitisation and derivatives are tools to do this. The problem lies not so much in these tools of risk mitigation as in credit assessment. If the underlying pool of mortgages were healthy—cash flows secured through expected stable labour incomes rather than through speculative positions on volatile asset prices—sub-prime defaults may have been contained, instead of boiling over on account of changes in monetary policy and the reversal in housing prices. Lax credit assessment and distorted compensation practices added fuel to the fire.

Third, would Glass-Steagall have prevented the financial meltdown of 2008? Institutions like Bear Stearns, AIG, Merrill Lynch, Goldman Sachs and Lehman Brothers, which all ran into trouble, were systemically important but not commercial banks. Deposit-taking commercial banks also had to be bailed out because of their holdings of the same illiquid securities through off-balance sheet investment vehicles. Investment in these securities was not restricted under Glass-Steagall. To the extent that the Dodd Frank Act empowers the Financial Stability Oversight Council to declare any financial institution—including investment banks, hedge funds, etc.—systemically important and bring it within the regulatory perimeter, it does address the problem of unregulated 'too big to fail' institutions. The problem is whether the Volcker Rule, and even Basel III, adequately firewalls depositary institutions against risks arising from shadow banking.

Lastly, the constructive ambiguities of the Volcker Rule constitute a legal minefield. It's an 882-page behemoth, appended to the gargantuan Dodd Frank Act, itself 828-page long, to be implemented by five separate agencies. Compare this to the 37-page elegance of the Glass-Steagall Act. In the legal battles that shall ensue, pitting regulators against Wall Street firms, there is little doubt who will have the highest-paid lawyers and psychiatrists—to prove intent—on their side.

The Indian Express, New Delhi, 23 December 2013.

78

Housing and Financial Stability

Housing is a financial asset. Unlike financial securities, it is has a direct utility value, like gold and other commodities. As such, it is can be a barometer of asset bubbles, and also of financial repression as savings flee financial securities when real interest rates turn negative. Housing markets are therefore central to financial stability.

As fixed assets, houses were traditionally considered non-tradable internationally. The proximate trigger for the greatest global financial crisis since the Great Depression of the 1930s, however, lay in the housing sector. A house in Arizona can now be financed by a municipality in Western Australia. As claims on ownership become eminently tradable, housing markets increasingly raise issues of global financial stability.

The few long-term house price indices that are available, such as those for the US, Canada, Australia and Norway, indicate that real house prices were quite stable since the series began in the 19th century right up to the 1970s, when they started rising and becoming very volatile. They rose dramatically from the end of the last decade of 20th century to peak just before the onset of the global financial crisis.

Who or what is to blame for housing bubbles? There are five prime suspects: international capital flows deriving from global imbalances, easy monetary and regulatory policies that lower yields and encourage risky credit, fiscal policies that promote house ownership, and the shift from the gold standard to fiat currency.

What are the takeaways for developing countries in general, and for India in particular?

First, house prices have risen sharply in urban India in recent years, the near term tapering notwithstanding. The NHB RESIDEX shows that residential housing prices in NCR (national capital region) have doubled since 2007. They rose even more steeply in Pune and Mumbai. They increased 3.5 times in Chennai. The moot point is whether the urban housing boom is a response to a real demand-supply imbalance, or whether it is a speculative bubble, driven by excessive liquidity, large capital inflows, financial repression on account of low real interest rates, and a booming informal or black economy.

Figure 78.1

Real US Home Prices (1890-2012)

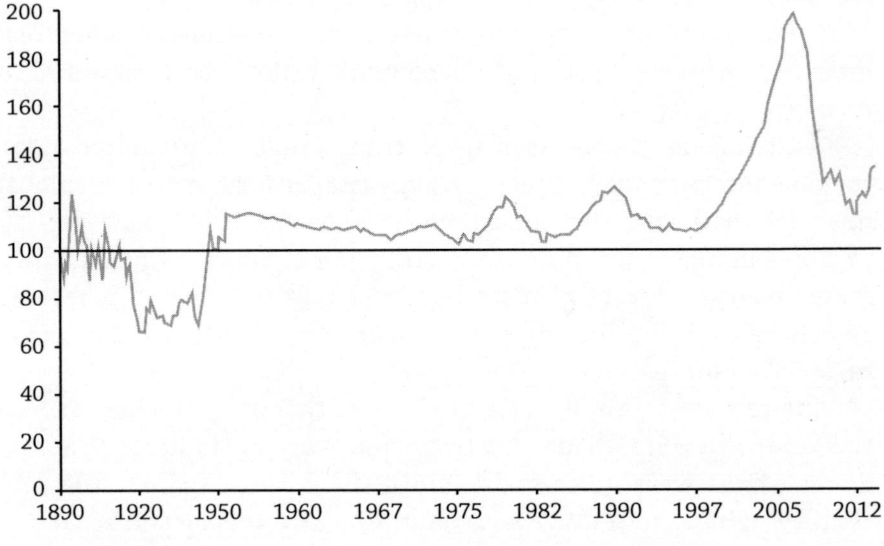

Source: Case-Shiller

What is a bubble? One way of looking at this is to compare rental incomes from investment in housing (2% currently) with the cost of prime borrowers (in excess of 10%). Investment in housing can only be repaid through capital appreciation. This was the original sin of the US subprime housing crisis. When housing prices declined, the financial edifice came crashing down.

Second, affordable housing is a bigger issue in developing countries because of lower median incomes and rapid urbanisation on one hand, and the steep rise in urban housing prices on the other. Low income households are vulnerable to being priced out of the market. The middle and upper classes have access to financial markets, while economically weaker sections are mostly financially excluded. Unsurprisingly, there is underinvestment in low income housing, regardless of overinvestment in middle and high income housing.

Third, what should be the policy response to address this imbalance? Lowering regulatory standards to enable the economically weaker sections access housing finance could result in a US type sub-prime that can threaten financial stability and entail taxpayer funded bailouts. The latter are also likely on equity considerations. Is it therefore more desirable to provide direct fiscal support through tax breaks and/or subsidies? The poor need access to shelter, which could be effectively done through income transfers for rentals until they are able to accumulate savings to own a house, when ownership could be transferred at subsidised prices, as in Singapore.

Fourth, monetary policy seems too blunt an instrument for promoting financial inclusion. Low interest rates can endanger macroeconomic and financial stability by fuelling asset bubbles, as in advanced economies. The Federal Reserve's purchase of housing mortgages on an epic scale in the wake of the crisis as part of its quantitative and credit easing policies to support housing markets may be spawning new bubbles and eventual taxpayer funded bailouts as the US housing sector is now virtually nationalised. On the other hand, if monetary policy is used to target asset bubbles it may deflate business cycles prematurely. This famously led Alan Greenspan, former Chairman of the Federal Reserve, to argue that central banks should not call asset bubbles but simply clean up after they burst. The GFC (global financial crisis) showed just how costly the clean-up can be. The debate over monetary policy targeting asset bubbles currently centres on finding new instruments, such as macro-prudential policies adopted by India in the run up to the GFC. The jury is still out on this, however, especially since some pro-cyclical features of the Basel II framework, such as mark-to-market, have been retained in Basel III.

Fifth, and finally, Indian housing markets are a mix of shadow and regulated banking finance. Registered housing prices grossly understate the market price. This makes it difficult to compile robust housing price indices. The data from BIS, Haver Analytics, the Global

Property Guide and Scotiabank used by the IMF to develop a new housing price index for emerging markets give very contradictory trends. This mix also results in a conundrum. In the event of a steep decline in housing prices, the shadow banking sector takes the hit. It is the shock absorber that shields the regulated banking sector from financial instability, with NPAs (non-performing assets) in the housing sector much lower than in other sectors.

Mint, New Delhi, January 2015.

79

Financial Regulatory Reform

Mid-term Assessment

Lax financial regulation and supervision took the major blame for the recent global financial crisis. This initiated the most far-reaching reform in advanced economies since the Great Depression under the watchful eyes of the G20, supplemented by national initiatives in major jurisdictions.

The G20 approach was comprehensive, logical and progressive. It was based on four pillars: first, agreeing to new regulations. Second, supervising their implementation across major jurisdictions to avoid regulatory arbitrage. Third, formulating resolution mechanisms to avoid taxpayer bailouts in case systemically important financial institutions (SIFIs) failed. Fourth, periodical stress testing the new structure for robustness.

There is notable progress on the first pillar through the new Basel III capital and liquidity standards for commercial banks focused on strengthening both the quantity and quality of capital, introducing new leverage and liquidity ratios, and improving risk management, governance, transparency and disclosure norms to insulate them from the activities of shadow banking that triggered the global financial crisis.

The progress on the second pillar is patchy beyond exchange of information.

The third pillar was addressed by the Financial Stability Board (FSB) that released guidelines and a list of global-SIFIs whom national regulators could subject to greater regulatory oversight. The Dodd Frank Act (DFA) in the US has put in place a framework to regulate any financial institution (FI) determined to be a SIFI and also for their orderly resolution, as required.

On the fourth pillar, the FSB has moved to strengthen the Financial System Assessment Programme of the IMF. Stress tests are now routinely used by national regulators.

Basel III

The quick international consensus on the new Basel III norms is remarkable, notwithstanding criticism from both sides of the ideological spectrum. Intense lobbying to dilute Basel III stringency is backed by the argument that since the economy is struggling to get back on its feet, the aggressive, regulatory push would only damage the recovery through accelerated deleveraging. The quick rebound of shadow banking to pre-crisis levels is also linked to the stringency of Basel III.

Critics of Basel III have underscored some additional concerns. First, it is ironic that although the source of the global financial crisis lay in shadow banking, it is commercial banking that has been fixed while regulation of shadow banking remains work in progress (WIP).

Second, Basel III continues to aid pro-cyclicality through the principle of mark-to-market (MTM), notwithstanding an element of counter-cyclicality introduced through revised capital ratios.

Third, although financial risk, asset inflation, bubbles and leverage are all correlated, Basel III does little to prevent build-up of leverage in the overall financial system. It does endeavour to 'disincentivise' commercial banks from taking risky debt through higher risk weights and also to rein in leverage through a new leverage ratio. The attempt to prevent systemic build-up of leverage is however feeble as high levels of leverage underlie the financialisation of advanced economies through rapid expansion of claims and reclaims of the same underlying asset between FIs, rather than through expansion of claims on real assets that expand the production frontier. Basel III fails to distinguish between good and bad forms of leverage or to contain total leverage in the system, which includes sovereign debt and shadow banking, at levels commensurate with economic growth. Fiscal policies that encourage debt over equity through asymmetric tax treatment are also unlikely to change any time soon.

Shadow Banking and the Volcker Rule

Recognising that sources of systemic instability in the financial system may remain outside commercial banking, the FSB is developing a framework for reining in shadow banking. It has released policy documents for strengthening oversight and regulation of shadow banks that may be finalised at the ninth G20 Summit in Brisbane, in November 2014. The G20 initiative on shadow banking however remains WIP.

New components of shadow banks like less leveraged real estate investment trusts, finance companies, business development companies, sovereign funds and private equity have emerged, while old instruments like ABCPs, SIVs and CDSs are now becoming extinct. Whether shadow banking in the post-crisis period is less destabilising than what it was prior to the crisis is however arguable. Be it as it may, given the experience with shadow banking during the recent crisis, and because it does not have the liquidity buffers of commercial banking to prevent runs and panics, regulators have agreed on the need for tighter control of shadow banks. Apart from DFA facilitating regulation of non-bank SIFIs, there are major national initiatives in the US (Volcker), the UK (Vickers) and the Euro zone (Liikanen) that ring-fence the 'shadowy' proprietary trading from the commercial banking arms of FIs.

Too Big to Fail (TBTF) and Resolution

SIFIs have assumed a special role by virtue of their size, complexity of operations, and the volume of transactions handled across a wide range of products, services and markets. They play a critical public utility role in the smooth functioning of financial markets and are therefore considered 'TBTF' as problems within a single SIFI can trigger system-wide crisis. The near collapse of the American financial system between 2007 and 2008 following the decision by the US Fed and Treasury to not bail out Lehman Brothers underscored this systemic fragility.

National regulators are now inclined to impose greater oversight and higher capital requirements for SIFIs. The FSB has stepped in with a list of Global SIFIs and to prepare a road map for recovery and resolution planning of G-SIFIs through the formation of crisis management groups. The US has a concrete road map vide the orderly liquidation authority (OLA) under the DFA. The OLA holds shareholders and creditors responsible for the losses of FIs so that taxpayers' funds are not used for liquidation purposes. This implies that the bank survives through bail-in by creditors rather than bail-out by taxpayers.

In order to facilitate orderly liquidation under DFA, all FIs classified as SIFIs are required to submit resolution plans ('living wills') to regulators. The 'living will' lays down the roadmap for its orderly resolution during liquidation. Several largest banks of the US have released their blueprints on how they could be dismantled after its collapse.

The robustness of OLA can only be tested in an actual financial crisis. There are several imponderables like probable knee jerk market reaction to the news, absence of cross-border resolution framework, failure of living wills when faced with market-wide crisis and the inherent difficulty in capturing all possible risks. Although these resolution mechanisms might minimise the likelihood of taxpayer bail-out, they also result in an implicit subsidy for SIFIs, lowering their borrowing costs relative to smaller banks. There are therefore fears that the implicit government guarantee enjoyed by SIFIs may result in riskier behaviour.

The SIFI problem is particularly acute in the European Union (EU) with several individual bank assets exceeding the size of their respective sovereign GDP (gross domestic product), making the SIFIs too big to be bailed out as their central banks do not have the power to print euros. This vicious loop between weak banks and weak sovereigns is impelling the EU towards a politically challenging single supervisor, single resolution and a harmonised deposit insurance system, and also lies behind the European Commission's backing for a Franco-German initiative to levy a Financial Transaction Tax to strengthen the fiscal hand of Euro zone governments. These issues also call for a stronger fiscal union.

The overall focus of regulatory reform has been on strengthening capital buffers and resolution mechanisms to avoid taxpayer bail-outs.

These buffers may be effective in business downturns, but may never be enough to deal with systemic risks of a financial crisis, when assets are marked down and markets are so dysfunctional that taxpayers may still have to step in. The payments system is so closely integrated with the financial system that together they can be considered a public utility underwritten by the taxpayer. It is arguable whether the financial system is now safer despite the new regulations, as the underlying source of heightened instability, namely financialisation of the economy to the extent that there is little correlation with economic growth, remains unaddressed. A new source of instability emanating from a monetary policy framework unresponsive to asset price inflation has accentuated the disconnect between the real economy (economic growth) and financial markets (asset prices).

To summarise, the G20 financial reform agenda is undoubtedly ambitious. But will this time around be different? Six years on, the outcome is mixed—WIP at best, and a tale of progressive dilution at worst on account of the putative incestuous relationship between the Treasury and Wall Street. By this I mean constant floor crossing of personnel between the two. The overwhelming concern is that as normalcy returns, business would be as usual. Basel III might be diluted. The moral hazards inherent in the banking emolument and credit rating systems remain unaddressed. Cross-border harmonisation and co-operation to obviate regulatory arbitrage remains weak. Shadow banking is back on its feet even as commercial banks struggle with new regulation. The issues of pro-cyclicality and over-leverage continue to haunt regulators. Banks today are bigger than what they were before the crisis due to mergers and acquisition (M&A). In the Euro zone, with its flawed monetary union, several banks are too big to be bailed out by their sovereigns, and no FI seems small enough to be allowed to fail because of inter-relatedness of the financial system. An unreformed monetary policy framework also continues to put financial stability at risk.

Financial Express, New Delhi, 12 June 2014.

80

Financial Regulatory Reform

EME Perspective

The ongoing G20 and Financial Stability Board (FSB) debates on reforming global finance have so far involved advanced economies (AEs). Emerging market economies (EMEs) have nevertheless willingly signed on to the reforms for three possible reasons.

First, the G20 co-opted them into the global high table of financial regulation through the restructured Financial Stability Forum (FSF), hitherto a preserve of AEs.

Second, most of these reforms would not be implemented immediately in EME financial systems that are still fundamentally different from those in AEs.

Third, EMEs stand to gain from a 'safer' financial system in AEs because as net savers, much of their own financial intermediation is routed through it. A shock in AE financial systems automatically transmits to EMEs through sudden stops and attendant currency crises that can derail their economies, as happened recently.

Financial panics are often preceded by escalating leverage with maturity mismatches. Drivers of leverage in AEs and EMEs are distinctly different. In AEs, the primary driver for leverage was consumption. Also, it was to increase the return on capital through increased trading of claims and re-claims on real assets in an environment of low returns. This led to rapid expansion of financial assets as a proportion to GDP (gross domestic product) through the shadow banking system. High credit growth in EMEs, like China and India, was linked to high rates of investment and growth through commercial banking. EMEs are far less leveraged and financialised, and their banking systems remain mostly deposit based.

Deposit insurance and central bank discount windows make EME financial systems less susceptible to financial panics and bank runs. Their central banks also deploy macro-prudential tools to ensure that financial bubbles are contained. Unsurprisingly, therefore, while EMEs were affected by sudden stops from abroad, their financial intermediation held up, even as it froze in AEs with their growing reliance on shadow banking.

The impact of the ongoing financial regulatory reforms on EMEs has been relatively benign so far. Despite the general decline in cross-border claims on financial assets amongst AEs, capital flows to EMEs are back to pre-crisis highs. This is perhaps aided by the long phase-in period for Basel III, and the preponderance of FDI (foreign direct investment) in these flows. Transnational corporations (TNCs), which drive these flows, never lost access to capital markets during the global financial crisis. Capital flows to EMEs have been more impacted by monetary policies in AEs than their regulatory reforms.

Unlike in AEs, EME concerns are more developmental than regulatory: increasing savings to accelerate growth; deepening the financial system to develop long-term funding instruments for infrastructure financing; absorbing large inflows of capital to counter the backwash from EMEs to AEs; and reducing the cost of capital and leads and lags in monetary policy transmission. AEs, on the other hand, need to roll back extreme forms of financialisation that expose them to greater financial risks without commensurate gains in economic growth.

Basel III is one area where the new regulatory norms will impact advanced market economies (AMEs) and EMEs almost equally at the same time. Indeed, EMEs are actually ahead of AEs in implementation. However, while banking capital needs to be strengthened in both AEs and EMEs, the rationale for tightening capital norms in EMEs is not self-evident. Capital norms in AEs need strengthening as financialisation of their economies has heightened systemic risks. In EMEs, on the other hand, additional banking capital was needed even under Basel II norms to address issues of rapid credit and economic growth. There is now a probability that migration to Basel III may divert scarce savings in EMEs away from critical investment needs to cover risks benchmarked to AE financial systems, keeping the cost of capital high in the foreseeable future.

Shadow Banking

Both AEs and EMEs have flourishing shadow banking systems. In China, it accounts for a little over 40 per cent of total financial intermediation, as against about 25 per cent in the US, UK and the Euro area. Despite superficial similarities, however, the driving force, structure and relationship with commercial banks are different in AEs and EMEs. This reflects the fundamental underlying difference that while shadow banking in AEs is a measure of their financial depth, in EMEs it is a measure of their financial repression, as they try to channelise household savings into providing low cost funds for investment and government developmental programmes.

The similarities are striking. First, there are strong linkages between commercial and shadow banking. Second, authorities have avoided regulating shadow banks to promote financial inclusion, including home ownership. Third, the growth of shadow banking stems from a demand for higher returns, in AE because of easy monetary policy and a global savings glut, and in EMEs because of low real returns on account of financial repression.

The differences are stark. First, the exposure of commercial banks to shadow banking was mostly off-balance sheet in AEs, whereas in EMEs it was direct because it was permitted, even encouraged, by regulators to promote financial inclusion. While sub-prime borrowers in the US may not have been credit worthy for housing finance, they were never excluded from the banking system as in EMEs.

Second, while shadow banking in EMEs channelised savings to risky borrowers at high rates of interest, in AEs shadow banking created money through a sharp increase in its velocity through repeatedly leveraging—'re-hypothecating'—the same pool of underlying assets. In other words, while shadow banking in EMEs was through vanilla credit instruments that converted savings into investment, in AEs it created money through innovative money market instruments.

Third, 'shadow banking' loans and mortgages in EMEs are refinanced by commercial banks, much like Fannie May and Freddie

Mac in the US. However, they are not securitised and taken off the balance sheets of both the loan originator and refinancing bodies through market sales. In India, the loan originator retains the loan on its balance sheet, thereby ensuring credit quality. Since these loans are backed by real assets, the threat of dispossession keeps loan delinquency low. Delinquency is also low because the borrower tends to declare a lower value for the asset to dodge taxes. This, ironically, makes the loan safer, as the borrower is constrained to bring in more equity from the shadow economy.

In view of these differences, neither the Financial Stability Board (FSB) initiative on shadow banking nor the 'ring-fencing' of the Volcker, Vickers and Liikanen kind is very relevant for EMEs at this stage. Shadow banking is an extension of regulated deposit-based commercial banking to remote areas and to address the credit needs of those at the lowest end of the socioeconomic spectrum where productivity levels are low, and who lack collateral to make them creditworthy. Shadow banking thus fulfils the role of traditional moneylending. In China, it currently also fulfils the role of development finance, as the government strains to keep banking credit in check without affecting growth.

Shadow banking in EMEs is closely monitored by regulators, something that is only now being attempted in AEs. Placing emphasis on opaque money markets, repo and securitisation markets—at the core of FSB's efforts to rein in shadow-banking—will not get such lending out of the shadows in EMEs, where productivity levels and property right frameworks need redressal.

Systemically Important Financial Institutions (SIFIs) and Resolution Mechanisms

EMEs have very few global SIFIs, except China which hosts Bank of China (BOC) and Industrial & Commercial Bank of China (ICBC). There are concerns regarding their health due to rapid credit off-take since the global financial crisis, because financial results are largely camouflaged and state controlled, and because of ICBC's growing presence abroad and links with global markets.

EMEs have a number of domestic SIFIs, mostly state-owned, such as the State Bank group in India, the Brazilian Development Bank (BNDES) in Brazil. Financial intermediation is regarded as a public utility which is committed to universal service through cross-subsidies. Less attention is consequently given to putting in place mechanisms for orderly liquidation to avoid taxpayer bailouts. Equity holders and taxpayers are mostly the same. Hence, it is difficult to envisage the need for any financial sector tax, when the cost of intermediation is already high, due to the public utility nature of financial intermediation.

EMEs have now realised that their exposure to G-SIFIs means that capital may flow out in the event of a crisis in their parent countries or banks. The global financial crisis led to a sudden stop of capital. Foreign banks in India exited certain areas under stress, although G-SIFIs like Citigroup, Deutsche and HSBC, never 'pulled the plug' on their emerging market operations as such, and even provided some support and resilience during the crisis. Several EMEs are nevertheless considering 'ring-fencing' mechanisms to ensure that problems with the parent does not lead to withdrawal of capital from overseas branches, by incentivising wholly owned subsidiaries over overseas branches.

To summarise, regulatory reforms in AEs hold little relevance for EMEs at this stage because their financial systems are fundamentally different. Financial systems in both need reform, but the challenges differ. EMEs have not actively engaged in the global debate on financial reform, but they now need to step up to the plate, after assessing its relevance and impact, instead of blindly assuming that their economies too should be financed on the lines of the 'gold standard' of AEs.

Financial Express, New Delhi, 13 June 2014.

Postscript

Towards a New Macroeconomics 101?

I

In its *World Economic Outlook* update of July 2015, the IMF projected global growth at 3.3 per cent in 2015 and 3.8 per cent in 2016. The forecast for 2015 is lower than the actual growth rates in the two preceding years. The world is however growing at roughly the 10 year average of 1994-2003 that preceded the boom of 2004-2007. The United States (US) unemployment rate has fallen below 6.0 per cent. Global capital markets have recovered to all time highs. The market volatility index (VIX) is low and stable. Sovereign borrowing spreads in peripheral Europe, with the notable exception of Greece, have fallen sharply. So is God back in his heaven and is all right with the world?

There are good reasons for believing that the underlying fundamentals, outlined in the piece "The Global Financial Crisis on its Sixth Birthday", have not substantially changed.

The International Monetary Fund (IMF), the Organisation for Economic Co-operation and Development (OECD) and the World Bank all lowered their forecasts for the global economy after the original *World Economic Outlook* of the IMF was published in April 2015. In recent years, it has become customary for the IMF to downgrade their own rather optimistic forecasts made in the earlier part of the year in the second half, as actual data comes in. The July 2015 forecast for global growth was 0.2 per cent lower than the projection made in April 2015, with "the distribution of risks to global economic activity still tilted to the downside," even as it retained its 2016 forecast at 3.8 per cent.

This is hardly surprising as several of the macroeconomic anomalies that helped ignite the global financial and economic crisis of 2008 and enumerated in the Preface not only persist but have in some cases been compounded by the emergence of new faultlines as argued in "The Great Stagnation and the G20".

Table 1

Global Growth

Period/Year	*World*	*AEs*	*EMDEs*
1994-2003	3.4	2.8	4.4
2004	4.9	3.1	7.5
2005	4.6	2.6	7.3
2006	5.3	3.0	8.2
2007	5.4	2.8	8.7
2008	2.8	0.1	6.1
2009	-0.6	-3.5	2.7
2010	5.1	3.0	7.4
2011	3.9	1.7	6.2
2012	3.4	1.2	5.1
2013	3.4	1.4	5.0
2014	3.4	1.8	4.6
Av. 2004-2007	5.1	2.9	7.9
Av. 2011-2014	3.5	1.5	5.2

Note : The crisis years of 2008-09 and the spurt in 2010 are excluded from the averages.

AEs: Advanced Economies; EMDEs: Emerging Markets and Developing Economies.

Source: IMF, *World Economic Outlooks*.

One: the spurt in 2010 that followed the deep recession of negative 3.5 per cent growth in 2009 excepted, growth in AEs since 2008 has been at around half the average of the preceding 15 years. The US, one of the better performing AEs, averaged just 2.0 per cent growth from 2011 through 2014. Its gross private investment as a share of GDP remains low by post war standards, and there is a puzzling decline in productivity. Growth in EMDEs is projected at 4.2 per cent in 2015, slightly lower than the pre-boom average. Their productivity also shows a declining trend. Their growth has declined four consecutive years since the sharp recovery in 2010. This decline, that has still to bottom out, has driven a coach and six through the decoupling hypothesis. Two BRICS, Brazil and Russia, are stuck in recession; both China and India, the dynamos of global growth engine, are stuttering.

Two: nobody realistically expects a return to the heady pre-crisis growth highs, despite the heroic efforts of the G20's flagship working group ("Framework for Strong, Sustainable and Balanced Growth") to push[1] global growth potential upwards through radical structural reforms. The German experience under Chancellor Schroeder indicates that in the absence of a fiscal cushion such harsh reforms will be politically very difficult to implement. The smart recovery of 2010 was followed by a sharp dip in the subsequent year. Any short-term spurt in growth needs to be sustained over a reasonable period to be credible.

Three, tepid as it is, growth in AEs continues to be based on extraordinary, crisis-level macroeconomic life support. Fiscal deficits have been rolled back. But policy rates, unusually low even in the pre-crisis period, have been stuck at the zero-bound for over half a decade, in Japan for almost two decades. Central banks assets, having quadrupled over the last decade, now stand at over $20 trillion. They are still growing. As the Federal Reserve winds down its asset purchases, the European Central Bank (ECB) is embarking on a fresh round of quantitative easing (QE). The continuing crisis in the Eurozone has trapped it in the vicious cycle of having to step in to buy the bonds of the weaker members to maintain financial stability. China, the remaining large economy, has recently joined the bandwagon in its usual peculiar manner. The real test of sustaining even current growth rates would be when the US Federal Reserve 'pivots' on its policy stance by raising interest rates. This changing stance hangs like the proverbial Sword of Damocles not only on the US economy but on the global economy as the Federal Reserve's monetary stance is increasingly the prime mover of cross-border capital flows.

Four: large liquidity injections by central banks in AEs through quantitative easing that were washed back as reserves of depository institutions continue to mostly remain with central banks. This indicates that the monetary policy transmission mechanism that

1. The G20 Framework Working Group agreed globally coordinated growth strategies at the ninth G20 Summit in Brisbane, Australia, in mid-November 2014, that could push up global GDP by another 2.0 per cent over what is currently projected five years hence.

normally translates such injections into credit growth through the money multiplier, remains broken. The money multiplier has fallen sharply.[2] The liquidity trap has not fully abated (Das, 2014). Uncontrolled leveraging, private and public, including liquidity injections by central banks, is casting a growing shadow on the sanctity of the fiat currency system that is less than half a century old. Nobody expects central banks to roll back their bloated balance sheets any time soon.

Five: private sector deleveraging notwithstanding, aggregate debt in AEs has not declined. While the private sector has been deleveraging since the crisis, this is more than fully compensated by public sector leveraging (Croxson *et al.*, 2012). Excessive leverage, it may be recalled, provided the gunpowder in the keg, later ignited by the US sub-prime crisis. This high level of leverage constitutes a major structural headwind to sustainable growth in AEs. Emerging economies have also levered up in the wake of unusually low foreign borrowing costs.

Six: fiscal deficits, that were rising prior to the crisis in response to demographic headwinds, rose sharply with the onset of the financial crisis. Going forward, these deficits will only worsen, when monetary policy normalises and interest rates on public debt rise. The increasing proportion of non-workers, and rising old-age welfare expenditures, are set to have a damaging fall out on both trend growth and public debt in AEs. The contrast with the post World War II period, which began with comparable levels of public debt, is depressingly stark. Demographic tailwinds and the demand from post war reconstruction helped AEs to grow out of high levels of public debt. In the aftermath of the Great Recession, deficits mostly continue to exceed nominal GDP growth despite fiscal correction. Public debt/GDP ratios are still rising, even as growth prospects are downbeat, and demographic headwinds gather force. Gross public debt in AEs, on average, now stands at over the 90 per cent threshold that has damaged growth in the past (Reinhart and Rogoff, 2011). It is difficult to see AEs growing out of such high levels of debt at current levels of growth without

2. Federal Reserve data.

an extended period of financial repression that penalises savers and creates macroeconomic instability.

Seven: the grand G20 financial regulatory reform initiative notwithstanding, it is still far from clear whether AE financial systems are now significantly less risky than what they were before the crisis. Basel III retains a fair degree of pro-cyclicality through retention of the mark to market mechanism.[3] Shadow banking has bounced back at the expense of the more tightly regulated components of the financial system (Tett, 2011; Chassany and Sender, 2013; Alloway and Fleming, 2013; Foley, 2013; Tett, 2014; McLannahan, 2015; Indap, 2015). An unrepaired monetary framework continues to fuel asset booms. Financial stability in the Eurozone is contingent on continued ECB interventions. AEs are no less financialised after the crisis than what they were prior to it.

Eight: demographics apart, there were other structural headwinds to sustainable high growth in AEs. Some of these have strengthened since the crisis erupted. Labour participation rates, real wages and household demand continue to stagnate. Income inequality too continues to rise. These headwinds were suppressed by leveraged consumption on the back of an unsustainable asset boom during the 'Great Moderation', facilitated by financial innovation and lax regulation.The current recovery is not based on income growth generated by investment in the real economy. It relies on the wealth effect of life-support policies. Just as it was in the run up to the global financial crisis. Symptomatic of this is the rise in US housing prices in a sector that has become virtually nationalised since the crisis broke (Timiraos, 2013; Foley, 2013a). It is the rise in US household wealth that appears to be driving the US economic recovery (Feldstein, 2014). New booms, such as the automobile sub-prime credit boom in the post crisis period (Silver-Greenburg and Corkery, 2014), may similarly stimulate demand in the same manner. But without a sustained rise in real labour incomes these will eventually come to grief, just like the sub-prime housing boom before the crisis. The real test of recovery would be when economic growth is driven by rising real

3. "Transcript: Sheila Bair",*F orbes Magazine*, 2 February 2010. See also, Kay (2013).

sector investment and personal income growth, and with life support withdrawn.

Nine: a durable solution to the domestic demand constraint clearly lies in demand rebalancing. Although global imbalances have indeed abated since the crisis, this is likely because of lower aggregate demand rather than on account of structural changes in the global economy. The stimulus in both the US and China focussed on consumption and investment respectively. This exacerbated, rather than corrected, extant imbalances. AEs need to become more productive, competitive and consume less. China's rebalancing outcomes are predicated on far reaching institutional and political reforms to break the inertia of its current model of growth over-reliant on investment.

Even as external imbalances have abated, new internal imbalances in AEs have only compounded the demand problem. Growth has become more dependent on public expenditure and unorthodox monetary policies. This twin rebalancing—external and internal—requires far-reaching and rather harsh structural reforms. AEs need to be more competitive. Emerging markets need to rely more on domestic demand as the ignition of the engine of growth is turned on.[4]

Ten, the unresolved crisis in the Eurozone, including possible 'Grexit', continues to threaten global financial integrity. There is a real danger of contagion from Greece to other vulnerable peripheral countries, and also large economies such as Spain, Italy and even France. Markets have laid bare major design flaws in the Eurozone that leave it exposed to financial instability, trapping the ECB from exiting QE. The modest recovery in the Eurozone is predicated on market expectations that the ECB would walk the talk on its 'whatever it takes' resolve to forestall any crisis in the periphery. The market is absorbing peripheral bonds because of an implicit ECB guarantee. Not because it sees better economic prospects going forward. The

4. A return to a high global growth trajectory of 4-5 per cent on a sustainable basis may well hinge on the outcome of changes afoot in the two large, populous and once dominant, ancient civilisations, namely China and India, what Roach (2010) has described as the 'Next Asia'. In China these changes revolve around demand rebalancing and addressing the big debt overhang, and in India, which is already largely domestic demand led, on far reaching structural reforms that can help it realise its growth potential which is comparable to that of China.

ECB is within its powers to buy sovereign bonds to ensure financial stability. However it is still far from clear that when push comes to shove, Germany would agree to sovereign bail-outs, not provided under existing treaty arrangements, without an effective fiscal and banking union that rolls back sovereign rights. A *de facto* banking and fiscal union alone can stabilise the European Monetary Union in a durable manner. The triumph of Euro-sceptics in recent elections, and the Greek referendum, has further queered the pitch for deeper integration. This was always going to be politically challenging. Ironically, even as policy makers struggle to deal with the problem of financial institutions that are too big to be allowed to fail, an interconnected world ensures that small bubbles like the in the sub-prime housing segment in the US, and a small economy like Greece, can also threaten global financial stability.

Eleven: and finally, the world has still to evolve a suitable governance model to more effectively harness the efficiency gains from global integration and to mitigate potentially destabilising negative spillovers on individual economies. Transnational corporations are the most dynamic forces leveraging these gains. But they are in uneasy equilibrium with nation states. The two increasingly come into conflict inter alia because of dispersal of tax bases, free cross-border movement of factors of production, and intellectual property right (IPR) regimes.

Domestic inflation, interest rates and exchange rates are now increasingly determined by cross-border spillovers rather than by domestic macroeconomic balances. The global economy is now behaving like an integrated national economy, but the persistence of nation states ensures that policy making is fragmented and un-coordinated, with sub-optimal economic outcomes. The cross-border policy coordination necessary to harness the efficiency and welfare benefits of globalizing tendencies appears to be weakening—both within the G20 and the EU. The G20, that at one stage seemed ready to supplant the G7 and bridge the trust deficit fracturing extant institutions of global economic governance, itself appears to be running out of steam in tandem with the diminishing economic prospects of emerging markets. A flawed design for monetary union threatens to undermine years of painstaking efforts to knit Europe into an integrated entity. Even as a globalizing world struggles to forge new institutions of governance to harness its efficiency and welfare enhancing benefits, the anachronistic nation state refuses to fade away. (Stephens, 2013).

The failure to address these weak fundamentals is ultimately a reflection of the failure of macroeconomics 101 to address the mounting anomalies discussed in the Preface. There was no credible intellectual or policy response prior to the crisis. Instead, they were pushed under a splendid new carpet called 'The Great Moderation', or the end of business cycles. Perhaps more searching questions were not asked, and necessary policy adjustments and structural reforms not deemed necessary or urgent, because global growth and asset prices were at a record high and consumer price inflation was within target: A 'Goldilocks Economy' if ever there was any!

The carpet was blown away by the global financial crisis. The slow and halting recovery that followed bared the awkward pieces beneath. If policy makers continue to struggle to stabilise their economies this is at least partly because the new macroeconomics 101, which could form the basis of such a response, is still to be written. Economists and policy makers need to now pick up these pieces and arrange them neatly on the shelves in the form of a new macroeconomics 101 in a shift to this new paradigm.

The reader may justifiably ask that it is easy enough to flag anomalies and weak fundamentals, but what remedies or alternative formulations does the author suggest?A fair question. The chief economist of the IMF organised three conferences to rethink macroeconomics, with few tangible results. Only fools would dare to tread where even angels fear to go. A constructive critique must nevertheless at least lead towards solutions and answers.

It seems apparent that underpinning these growing anomalies are inter alia the disruptive forces of globalization, the ageing of societies, the persistent neglect of the nitty-gritty of financial markets, and a rather simplistic conception of human behaviour as economics tried to re-invent itself as a natural science.

II

Globalization expands the reach of markets. Along with rapid technological innovation that has defined human societies since the industrial revolution, it enhances human productivity, and can be harnessed to vastly advance human welfare. There have always been cross-border flows of goods, services and people, but it was the technological revolution associated with the Industrial Revolution that up-scaled such flows exponentially. This is an ongoing and dynamic process. According to recent research by the McKinsey Global Institute, global flows of goods, services and finance increased 1.5 times between 1990 and 2012. During this period, global output more than doubled. These flows are expected to triple from their current level by 2025 and are estimated to enhance global GDP by 15-25 per cent (Manyika *et al.*, 2014).

These globalizing forces are redefining trade, production systems, growth, and the grease that intermediates them, namely the financial system. The rise of global production chains attest to the continuing robustness of the microeconomic insights of classical economists on the efficiency and productivity enhancing impact of trade. At the macroeconomic level, however, they are rendering extant metrics of measuring bilateral trade balances and trade policies irrelevant. Most consumable products are no longer made in one country. Components, technological patents and investments are sourced from different parts of the globe.

With exports becoming increasingly import-intensive, political constituencies favouring tariff walls have faded away, and those advocating depreciation declining, talk of 'currency wars' notwithstanding. Petroleum exports comprise a major share of India's export basket even though it has a large energy deficit and imports large amounts of crude oil. Protection can no longer be captured statistically through tariff-based formulae on which trade economics has long relied. Trade metrics are now shifting from bilateral balances to value added measures.

The sharp increase in the volume of international trade in goods and services allows countries to grow at rates inconceivable in the past, and also to counter business cycles, by importing demand.

Stagnant wages are themselves a byproduct of the globalization-technology interface. Automation and the much greater mobility of capital relative to labour is shifting the factor advantage in manufacturing back towards capital as it did in the early stages of the Industrial Revolution. Even as rising tide of globalization has tended to lift all boats it has reversed the flattening of income inequality in the Kuznets curve.

Over the last couple of decades large emerging markets undergoing a phase rapid productivity growth, such as China and India, have entered the global labour market for goods and services. The exponential increase in trade flows has had a disinflationary impact on consumer price inflation. This allowed countries with stagnant real wages and rising inequality to nevertheless improve standards of living. In a word, globalization lay behind the anomalies of the 'great moderation'.

In addition to the redefining growth potential, globalization along with rapid advances in information technology and automation is also transforming the structure of the growth process in a fundamental manner. Received macroeconomic wisdom accorded pride of place to manufacturing in the growth process. However, with automation manufacturing is becoming more robotic, services more labour intensive in comparison and, with advances in information technology, almost as tradable as merchandise goods.

As manufacturing, and indeed several services such as 'driving' and 'flying' become more automated, old manufacturing and service jobs are destroyed, creating new jobs through a process that Joseph Schumpeter described as 'creative destruction'. Jobs are becoming increasingly portable geographically. The driver of a car on the street in New York could conceivably be replaced by an operative directing traffic from a computer screen in Bangalore. The old driving or flying job could therefore be 'bangalored'. Welcome to the new 'Gig' economy.

Such structural changes open up possibilities of new models of development and economic organisation not foreseen by earlier generations of economists, such as Nicholas Kaldor, who gave pride of place to manufacturing in economic transition (Manyika and Roxburgh, 2011; Manyika *et al.*, 2012; Eichengreen and Gupta, 2011;

Tett, 2014a). For instance, automation enables extended participation of older workers in economic activity. While this has given rise to the phenomenon of heightened 'youth unemployment', it also makes it easier to re-negotiate long-standing and generous social compacts underlying the current welfare state that have become fiscally unsustainable. This is because the Gig economy also has the potential of making older AEs more competitive with younger ones, enabling them to supplement their falling domestic demand with external demand to prevent aggregate GDP growth from turning negative. This however entails rebalancing the current pattern of global demand which is dependent on consumption growth in AEs.

The new macroeconomics may also need to align the debates on rebalancing and climate change. The global economy grew very slowly right up to the 18th century. It accelerated at an unprecedented rate over the last three centuries following the spread of the Industrial Revolution and the welfare effects of fast expanding international trade. Rapid growth sustained over such an extended period is however resulting in anthropogenic climate change that threatens human existence if mitigating and preventive steps are not undertaken going forward. This requires capping the overall rate of increase in human consumption, and therefore growth.

But climate change negotiations are deadlocked on the issue of burden sharing. It goes without saying that the equitable way of staggering environmental change is by dampening consumption growth in countries with high per capita incomes that have contributed to most of the existing stock of greenhouse gases, to compensate for the inevitable increase in emissions from developing countries to the point that per capita incomes converge, a process already underway.

But this shift in consumption growth is necessary not just for equity but also for the global rebalancing of demand required to raise global growth and incomes. It is developing countries that have the highest growth potential. Globally coordinated strategies on adaptation to and mitigation of climate change would spawn and scale up new 'green' technologies that can be new engines of growth in AEs that retain their technological edge.

The forces of globalization have also broken or severely blunted tried and trusted policy tools used in macroeconomic management to stabilise business cycles ever since the Great Depression and the Keynesian Revolution. This was especially so after Paul Volcker's dogged and aggressive use of monetary policy to slay stagflation. Fiscal multipliers were found to be very variable, ranging from negative to positive values. It was nevertheless assumed that macroeconomic policies were effective tools for stabilising business cycles.

"We are all Keynesians now," the legendary Milton Friedman famously remarked even as he dethroned fiscal policy to put monetary policy in the pole position in the conduct of macroeconomic stabilisation policies. Fiscal policy was deemed too destabilising and political to be nimble, especially in the exit phase. Discretionary policies fell out of fashion. Fiscal policy was mostly limited to automatic stabilisers with seamless and automatic entry and exit.

Over time monetary policy also became rule bound, exemplified by the Taylor Rule that told central bankers what the policy rate should be, using the deviation between actual and potential growth, and between actual and targeted core consumer price inflation. The equation had a constant of 2.0 per cent, for reasons that are not entirely clear, other than historical. This meant that if growth was at full potential, and inflation on target, the predicted policy rate, based on successful FED interventions in the past, should be current inflation plus the constant.

In the wake of the global financial crisis economists and policy makers are no longer so sanguine about the effectiveness of macroeconomic policy tools. Aggressive policies have been unable to lift growth back to pre-crisis levels. Indeed, the dogged, protracted use of what were designed to be short-term policy tools is generating fresh sources of instability in the form of unsustainable public debt and new asset bubbles.

Part of the problem lies in measuring growth potential. The global economy grew at an average of 5.0 per cent between 2003 and 2007, compared to 3.5 per cent in the 10-year period prior to this, and 3.0-3.5 per cent since the height of the crisis. If 5.0 per cent was above trend, why was consumer price inflation within the central bankers' comfort zone? If 5.0 per cent was indeed the growth potential, why has aggressive, including unconventional, macroeconomic policies, been unable to restore growth to this level?

The convenient solution to the conundrum is to argue that potential growth has declined since the crisis. But why then is IMF advising policy makers to persist with highly stimulative monetary policy?

The measurement of something as basic as potential growth, which policy makers rely on to formulate macroeconomic policies, needs to be reworked because globalization has undermined well-established paradigms on which the metrics were based. Such as the relationship between consumer price inflation and growth, or Okun's Law that postulated a close relationship between employment and growth.

These disconnects were a major source of instability in the recent past on account of a monetary policy framework based on inflation targeting even though its assumptions were being undermined. This framework is still mostly in place. Indeed, these disconnects have only widened in the post crisis period through highly accomodative and unconventional monetary policies.

Macroeconomic policy tools have been blunted by rising cross-border trade and capital flows, in turn the outcome of rapid advances in technology and innovation. This blunting was evident prior to the global financial crisis, undermining the Taylor Rule, but went largely unnoticed. Indeed, it may have deluded central bankers into overestimating potential growth. As a result, policy rates were so low that they contributed to inflating the asset bubble underlying the recent global financial crisis. Global production chains are further blunting these tools as currency depreciation now increasingly cuts in both directions.

Consumer price inflation, central to extant monetary policy rules, is no longer the reliable canary in the goldmine that can assist policy makers in measuring growth potential. This is because core consumer price inflation is no longer simply domestically driven. Rapid productivity shifts, especially following the entry into the global market of large developing countries like China for goods, and India for services, has kept core consumer price inflation in check. As a result, excessive liquidity is diverted instead to asset markets that are less tradable across borders. But asset price inflation is not an input into the Taylor equation.

Sharp increases in cross-border capital flows prevent central bank interventions at the short end of the yield curve from being transmitted to long-term interest rates. It is the latter that matter for savings and investment, and therefore for economic growth. Alan Greenspan famously observed that the US Federal Reserve was losing control of long term interest rates because of large and volatile capital flows.

Developing countries, such as India, too adopted variants of the Taylor Rule. Their problems were even more acute, as their transmission channels were already blunt on account of relatively illiquid bond markets and administered interest rates. They therefore continued to use control of monetary aggregates alongside short-term interest rates as policy tools. The control of inflation in such economies is arguably more attributable to the impact of international trade than to monetary policy. Inflationary pressures in their economies stem from the non-core side, namely commodities like oil, and food where various trade barriers still exist in international agreements. In India this is reflected in the periodic sharp divergence between wholesale and consumer price inflation. These supply side constraints do not respond easily to monetary policy.

Large capital flows have blunted their tool-kit even further. They distract central bankers in developing countries from a single-minded focus on the domestic business cycle. At any point in time monetary policy is usually a trade-off between higher growth and lower inflation. But they often found themselves trapped by the 'impossible trinity', constrained to use monetary policy to counter the destabilising impact of volatile capital flows.

III

Demographic transition is perhaps the most profoundly underestimated force undermining macroeconomics 101. The ageing process, that strikes at the very roots of the welfare state and the social contracts on which social democracy rests, has just begun in

AEs. It is just a matter of decades when its impact is felt across the globe.

If one were to take a telescopic view of the link between demography and growth, human history can be broadly divided into five stages. In the beginning, human populations were sparsely distributed during the hunting gathering phase that lasted right up to the end of the last ice age around 10,000 BC. Population densities never exceeded 1-2 persons per square mile. Survival was a full time profession for everybody. There was no such thing as division of labour or economic growth.

This began during the second stage with the Neolithic Revolution and the discovery of agriculture. This facilitated generation of a 'surplus' over and above what was required for daily survival, leading to the beginnings of the division of labour. Technological change, its dissemination, and consequently productivity shifts, were however slow and measured in centuries. Aggregate GDP therefore grew at very low rates over an extended period, and worker productivity even more slowly. Economic growth was more a function of population increase than productivity growth. Birth rates were high, but so were death rates, resulting in a large, young, dependent population that consumed but did not contribute to economic activity. The constraints on economic growth were therefore on the supply rather than demand side. War, famine and pestilence led to periodic sharp declines in both population and output, followed by long periods of slow recovery. This pattern that persisted right up to the 17th century.

The third stage began in the 18th century with the Industrial Revolution. This was characterised by a continuing technological revolution that facilitated rapid population growth—a sharp fall in death rates through improvement in public health, with the birth rate adjusting only slowly—through upward shifts in human productivity. A virtuous cycle of rapid supply and demand growth ensured that both aggregate and per capita GDP, and with it standards of living, grew at unprecedented rates.

Macroeconomics 101 is a child of this third stage. It now needs to adjust to the next stage where birth rates first approach the replacement rate, leading to a levelling off of population growth, and then fall below the replacement rate, leading to population decline. It needs to be recognised that humans are the only animals where beyond a certain point prosperity leads to demographic decline rather than to rapid expansion of the species. Several European countries and Japan have entered the fourth stage, characterised by a sharp decline in aggregate GDP growth. The slow recovery from the global financial crisis must be seen not simply against the backdrop of a balance-sheet recession (as opposed to simply a down turn in the business cycle) but also through the prism of ageing. The demographics underlying the recovery from the Great Recession of the first decade of the 21st century are very different from those of the Great Depression of the 1930s.

Beyond the fourth stage lies a possible fifth stage, where productivity growth may be inadequate to prevent negative aggregate GDP growth, although per capita GDP would continue to grow at robust rates. A shrinking working population is leading to a large, but this time old, dependent population that consumes but has traditionally contributed little to economic activity. In a closed economy, this would lead to lower growth because of problems on both the supply and demand side. While these constraints are substantially mitigated in an open, globalized economy, attempts to overcome demand constraints through leveraged consumption are not sustainable in the long run. Indeed, this was one of the underlying causes of the recent global financial crisis.

Figure 3

Demographic Transition: Stylised Growth and Productivity Shifts

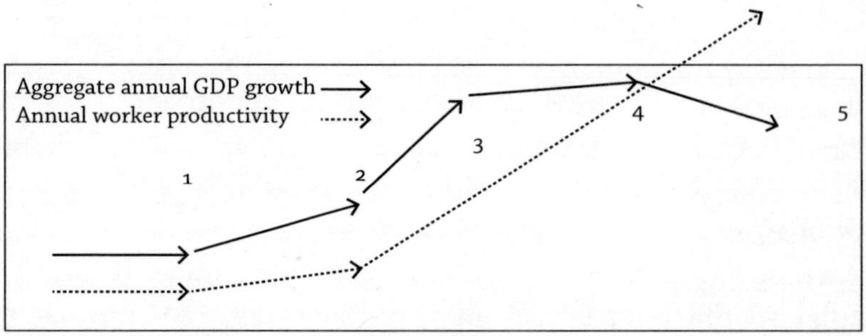

The peculiarity of the fourth and fifth stages is that per capita worker hourly productivity does not decline. However aggregate production may decline because of a shrinking work force. Indeed, the productivity potential may well rise with technological advancement. The new macroeconomics 101 therefore needs to change its metrics of measuring growth.

The ageing process can work itself through the economic system in surprising ways. For instance, while the impact on fiscal policy and growth is widely agitated, the likely impact on financial markets, monetary policy and indeed on inequality going forward need fuller consideration. There has been much talk about rising inequality (Piketty, 2014) on account of the increasing returns to capital relative to labour in a globalizing world. But as the world ages, and the number of workers falls, the returns to labour would rise as the proportion of those buying assets (workers) would shrink as sellers (retirees) increase. It is entirely possible that we have only seen the tip of the ice-berg called 'savings glut'. This would tend to keep the cost of capital and interest rates low, and workers would need to save more and more for retirement, especially since the State's fiscal capacity would be weakened by a shrinking tax base. This process may already have begun. Would this then reverse the current trend of relative returns to capital and labour? What would this imply for income inequality and tax policies going forward?

IV

Perhaps the most puzzling failure of macroeconomics 101 lay in its persistent neglect of financial markets which were fast becoming a hotbed of innovation. While considering the strong positive correlation between financial depth and growth as its Ark of the Covenant, it did not get into the nitty-gritty of financial markets that came to be dominated by mathematicians, physicists and other rocket scientists, who rather mysteriously contrived to generate outsized returns that the real economy could not match. Some of this rubbed off on macroeconomics 101 which started deploying complex models and equations, such as the Dynamic General Stochastic Equilibrium model.

But more of this later. Let us dwell for the moment on the finance-economy nexus. Financial intermediation played a critical role in the Industrial Revolution by aggregating individual savings through innovations like joint stock companies and banks for the large investments required to attain the economies of scale necessary for rapid improvements in productivity. Without such innovations in financial markets, the Industrial Revolution could not have been sustained.

There have been several financial innovations since, such as stock, commodities and futures exchanges, investment banks, structured finance, derivatives, shadow banking, dark pools, high frequency algorithmic trading, over the counter markets, etc., some beneficial, often destructive. But the underlying fundamentals of finance remained the same as John Kenneth Galbraith (1993) presciently observed several years ago, "even as the investing public is mesmerised by the great financial mind, finance does not lend itself easily to innovation as the underlying fundamentals are unchanged".

What are these fundamentals? All credit is secured against some asset, and no matter how much it is sliced and repackaged, at the end of the day it must generate adequate income to both service and repay the original credit.

As returns to capital fell in AEs in tandem with declining trend growth consequent on demographic transition and loss of competitiveness, they became increasingly financialised in an attempt to raise returns through leverage.[5] The financial sector turned on itself. It started cannibalising, instead of being an intermediator that aggregated and re-directed savings into productive investment. Investment in financial assets no longer reflected investment in the real economy. It became a conduit for trading in claims on real assets. It facilitated consumption growth through the illusion of wealth created by inflation in asset prices on account of rising levels of leverage. Meanwhile labour incomes, the traditional source of

5. There is a danger of this model being replicated in emerging markets. The Shanghai stock index rose by 140 per cent between June 2014 and June 2015 at a time there was great unease in markets regarding a structural slow down in the Chinese economy. Indian stock markets were also undeterred by similar fears.

consumption growth, stagnated. Under extant national income accounting methodology consumption is counted as growth. But what if consumption becomes less dependent on income growth and more on leverage? The financial sector turned into a behemoth as it pulled resources from other sectors of the economy, much in the manner of the Dutch Disease syndrome (Cecchetti and Kharroubi, 2013), making investment in the real economy less attractive and lucrative than investment in financial assets.

One could go further and argue that there is evidence to show that the relationship between financial depth and economic growth may well be non-linear, more like a Kuznets curve—positive up to a point, beyond which the correlation is broken even as risks increase (Solow, 2013; Haldane, 2010).

The searching question that was not asked was how could consumer demand growth in AEs have been so robust as to drive the global economy to unprecedented levels of growth above 5.0 per cent per annum in the absence of rising real incomes? It was this financialisation that lay behind the 'goldilocks economy', named, fittingly enough, after a fairy tale, a fantasy far removed from the real world succinctly described by the hardnosed Micawber in Charles Dickens' *David Copperfield*: "Annual income twenty pounds, annual expenditure nineteen [pounds] nineteen [shillings] and six [pence], result happiness. Annual income twenty pounds, annual expenditure twenty pounds ought and six, result misery."

What makes David Copperfield a literary classic is that it contains those little gems about the human condition that transcend space and time. Happiness, according to Micawber's world view, derives from savings, which can be used in lean times, when income is short of expenditure. Misery is a descending debt spiral. No prudent banker, or person, would lend to anyone in chronic deficit, or without adequate savings to service and repay the debt. Formerly you had to convince a banker to lend to you. Bankers now started coming to the doorsteps of persons with 'No Income, No Job or Savings (NINJA)' to lend.

Fairy Tales and Classics are distinct from Fables which, to quote the online free dictionary, are a "short narrative making an edifying or cautionary point and often employing as characters, animals that speak and act like humans." The fable of the *Ant and the Grasshopper*, along with its variant by Martin Wolf (2010; 2010a), chief economic commentator of the London based *Financial Times*, illustrates this quite nicely.

The scientific study of ants (myrmecology) indicates that they form an ideal society. They were the first innovators of many of our most fundamental activities, way before we even perfected hunting, or farming or algorithms. They make up a significant portion of the earth's biomass. The ant brain is the largest among insects as they have 250,000 brain cells—human brains have 10,000 million—and their combined weight outweighs that of humans.

Ants are tireless, thrifty workers who work through the year, even through the joyous spring time and summer, when both food and sunshine are plentiful, saving enough for consumption during the lean winter when nature is short on both sun and food. Grasshoppers, in contrast, prance around leisurely and make merry through the summer, without a care in the world. Cometh the harsh winter, and they perish. Unlike the ants, they have not stored food for the winter. The ants would not give them any. The ants, aware of their profligate ways, rightly fear that grasshoppers do not have the capacity to return what they borrowed. The moral of the fable? Idleness brings want.

The original fable focusses simply on the annual flows of savings and consumption. In a modified version, Martin Wolf introduced the stock dimension. Since ants produce more than what they can consume, over time their stock of savings pile up. They now need to work even harder to build new storage to park their growing stocks. The utility value of these assets keeps declining.

Along come the locusts—the financial capitalists—with an ingenious technological alchemy—structured finance—through which ants are persuaded to park their surplus/savings with them at a reasonable return instead of having to work harder and harder to build extra storage for their growing stock of savings whose value keeps falling.

As ants convert their savings from the physical to the financial form, this drives down interest rates as the market supply of financial assets goes up. This in turn enables the locusts to lend the money borrowed from the ants to the grasshoppers—who have no income or assets of their own—to purchase assets. This drives up the price of assets. Since grasshoppers have no income or assets of their own, they can only service and repay the loan only so long as the price of their leveraged asset keeps rising and interest rates remain low. Of course, they now have more than enough for purchasing and consuming the surplus goods produced by the ants right through the year.

The ingenious locusts were well aware of the risks involved. The grasshoppers had no income of their own to repay their loans. They could do so only as long as asset prices kept rising, just like in a Ponzi scheme. The locusts therefore did not wish to keep such dodgy debt on their books longer than necessary. Structured finance was designed to convert such dodgy loans given to NINJA grasshoppers into triple A assets. These were to be sold back to the ants by slicing and dicing—or securitizing—the receivables from grasshoppers into new asset pools that were sold to ants over and over again. This way more and more of the ants savings could be channelled to the grasshoppers.

And so the party went on round the year, in both summer and winter. The ants toiled on industriously as before, but instead of having to constantly expand their nest to store their ever-growing savings they handed them over to the locusts in exchange for easy-to-store Triple A rated paper. Through this mechanism the grasshoppers pranced about as usual in the summer, but now had plenty to consume over the severe winter as well.

We all know what happened next. The Federal Reserve stopped the music by raising interest rates. Housing prices fell. The unsustainable bubble collapsed. With no source of income except that based on rising asset prices, grasshoppers started defaulting on their loans. The value of their loans now exceeded the price of the underlying asset the loans had financed. The ants now realised their folly. Their savings had been converted into worthless paper. The only way they could cut their losses was to continue giving money to the locusts to be channelled back to the grasshoppers for servicing their loans. In any case, they no longer had the storage space to accommodate the large surpluses given to the locusts. It is to be noted that even though both ants and grasshoppers were devastated, the locusts, who merely lived off fees and managerial expenses charged from both, continued to flourish in both good times and bad.

To understand why the locust's seductive financial alchemy was doomed to disaster we need to delve deeper into the relationship between financial markets and the economy. The economy's production frontier expands when the surplus of income over consumption, or savings, goes into productive investment. This alone can create the value to make saving worthwhile. This can be done directly by savers themselves, as equity, and/or through lending to those who invest. This is where the ants erred in judgement in the Martin Wolf variant, as they were inveigled by the wily locusts into extending credit for investment in financial assets for consumption vide appreciation in their prices, rather than for investment in value addition that alone could service and repay the credit no matter in what direction asset prices moved. The NINJA grasshoppers could service their debt only as long as asset prices kept rising. They had no other source of income.

Over time, the financial system in AEs seems to have turned rogue, taken over by locusts, or investment bankers. Banking ceased to be a conservative profession that rationed scarce credit and allocated it to investment with the highest value addition. It acquired a new aggression in marketing loans and opaque instruments to those that earlier generations of bankers would not have considered creditworthy as these were intended for final consumption rather than productive investment (Turner, 2014).

The nature of financial intermediation changed, as it increasingly leveraged not for value addition but for purchase of claims and reclaims on the same pool of underlying productive assets (Singh and Aitken, 2010). This inflated their prices, converting them into volatile financial assets that expanded consumption rather than production (Das, 2013). Intermediaries that were expected to subsist on a percentage cut from the profits of the real economy for services rendered notched up profits that exceeded those of brick and mortar businesses that were the source of all value addition in the economy. The surge in credit and liquidity was mostly through a new, lightly regulated shadow banking system that bypassed the regulatory framework put in place in the post war period to prevent another financial crisis of the kind that led to the Great Depression of the 1930s. Shadow banking had the same asset maturity mismatches as commercial banking, but without the liquidity buffers and central bank backstops to prevent financial panic. It is unsurprising therefore that the financial crisis this time around emanated from a financial panic and electronic run on shadow banking rather than from a conventional bank run characterised by long queues in front of commercial banks.

Central banks also played a role on account of a broken policy framework focussed on short term flows associated with the business cycle while ignoring long-term stocks associated with the financial or credit cycle (Jen and Yilmaz, 2013). This resulted in loose monetary policy. By an accounting identity aggregate savings in a closed economy always equal aggregate investment, with the interest rate as the equilibrating device. Thus, real interest rates and returns on assets tend to decline when there is an increase in savings relative to investment, and vice versa. Misaligned interest rates are likely to result in unsustainable imbalances and bubbles in the form of over-investment or over-consumption, and a shortage of savings. The upward pressure on interest rates, however, was suppressed by the forces of globalization—the ants were in Asia, and the grasshoppers in Trans-Atlantica.

Investment can take the shape of either equity or debt, both of which are serviced through the value added by the underlying investment over time, i.e., through economic growth. It is, therefore, self-evident that it is real sector activity that creates the value that services, in an ultimate sense, the returns. These returns are from both the financial and non-financial sectors. Returns in the financial sector, however, can, and do frequently vastly exceed the underlying growth rate of the economy. This can only happen when the growth in aggregate leverage exceeds the growth in aggregate income. Fractional banking was designed to keep uncontrolled money creation through leverage in check. Money creation through the shadow banking system, where most of the leverage now occurred, was not subject to the restraints on fractional banking.

Excessive liquidity is expected to boil over into inflation. However, as disinflationary forces deriving from rapid productivity shifts and globalization kept consumer price inflation stable, excess liquidity mostly spilled over into asset prices, in the process creating several new classes of financial assets, such as commodities, oil, housing, and a whole range of securitised paper. The buying and selling of these assets several times over yielded returns far in excess of the underlying value addition in the real economy.

Unlike real economy assets that need human labour and real goods, on which there are finite constraints, financial assets can be created at the click of a mouse. A financial bubble, therefore, can be far more devastating than a real economy bubble based on over-investment in, say, factories producing cars. There are limits to how many cars can be used, so a point will arise when car inventories will pile up, the profits of car companies start declining and fresh investments dry up. In a financial bubble, however, a vicious cycle of growing leverage and rising asset prices can keep demand expanding almost indefinitely till the 'Minsky' moment arises and confidence drops, resulting in falling asset prices, rising defaults, a crisis in the payments system, deleveraging and an economic recession—the classic ingredients of a financial crisis.

There are therefore two distinct economic cycles, the business cycle, and the financial cycle. The first cycle is about short-term real economy flows. The second cycle is about long-term debt and equity financial stocks (Borio, 2012). Mainstream macroeconomics, with its dominant 'short-term' Keynesian paradigm tends to focus on short-term demand management of the business cycle through counter-cyclical monetary and fiscal policies. It mostly ignores the 'long-term' financial cycle. In the long-term, Lord Keynes famously remarked, "we are all dead".

The long-term financial cycle occupies pride of place in the Austrian School of economics. According to the Austrian School, the business cycle is driven by the temporal interplay between savings and consumption. An increase in savings relative to consumption results in lower interest rates and higher investment. This increases the production frontier of the economy, leading in turn to higher future consumption. The oscillation between higher savings/investment and consumption is what drives the business cycle.

There is little role for macroeconomic policy in such oscillations[6] as structural faultlines cannot be corrected through short-term policies that simply prolong the underlying problem. Business cycles should be allowed to play out. If central banks set interest rates below the equilibrium rate this can result in an unsustainable credit bubble, or a rapid upswing in the financial cycle, where investment zooms despite a decline in demand. This leads to a build-up in the stock of debt that ultimately lead to a financial crises and an associated 'balance-sheet' recession.

In an open economy business cycles can be substantially mitigated. Investment cycles can be extended through greater reliance on external demand. Consumption cycles can be prolonged by importing capital and goods and services. This is precisely what happened in China, on the one hand, and in the US on the other. To the extent this imbalanced global growth is based on leverage it merely replicates the domestic financial cycle. The credit boom in AEs in the run up to the global financial crisis was consumption rather than investment driven as envisaged by proponents of the Austrian School, but the underlying dynamic was the same. According to the Bank for International Settlements (BIS) school of thought, instead of supporting growth over the short-term by prolonging the credit cycle through macroeconomic stimulus, the financial cycle should be allowed to play out through deleveraging for a return to sustainable growth over the medium to long-term.[7]

Savings are central to both the Austrian and Keynesian models. However, while according to the former savings are what drives economic growth, according to the latter while savings may be good for each individual, if everybody were to save, the 'paradox of thrift' would lead to a reduction in demand, and thereby a downturn in the business cycle. In such an event stimulative fiscal and monetary policies should be used to revive growth. The stage of the financial cycle, or the state of the balance sheet, of the economy is irrelevant.

6. The use of macroeconomic policies to counter a decline in growth unrelated to the business cycle, such as that caused by demand and supply, and including external, shocks may not however be inconsistent with the economic model of the Austrian School of thought.

7. Bank of International Settlements, *Annual Report 2013-14*.

Both philosophies have some validity. But they also have their shortcomings. There is presently a glut of savings, but this is not resulting in expansion of the production frontier. Macroeconomic policies have been unable to persuade people to spend or to invest, with the extraordinary stimulus in major economies coordinated by the G20 staggering the deleveraging and endangering financial stability through a continuing disconnect between asset prices and economic growth. It would also be evident that these two macroeconomic paradigms, in some sense fundamentally in conflict, need to be reconciled through a new macroeconomics 101. The short-term and the long-term need to be unified, as the long-term is nothing but stringing together the short-terms.

It is now also increasingly clear that the institutional homes of the two paradigms are also different. The Keynesian philosophy is strongly entrenched in the IMF, whose approach has informed the G20 policy response to the global financial crisis. Judging from various papers and speeches emanating from it, it would appear that the institutional home of the Austrian School currently lies in the BIS, which is critical of the extraordinary stimulus that is counteracting the deleveraging essential for a return to sustainable growth.

Some of the work coming out of BIS suggests that the G20, IMF and central banks are making a monumental mistake by preventing the financial cycle from playing out through highly stimulative macroeconomic policies. These simply replace private leverage with public. Interest rates far below the equilibrium rate are sowing the seeds of another financial crisis. The efforts of the G20, the Basel Committee of Banking Supervision and the Financial Stability Board to rein in global finance through regulatory reform is hobbled by this failure to rein in leverage in the financial system. It has spectacularly failed to reverse financialisation of AEs and to tether financial intermediation to the real economy.

V

Finally, let me turn to the science of economics itself. There appears to be a widely held presumption, more implicit than explicit, that the science of economics is subject to some universal, natural laws. Ever since econometrics was coopted into economics, economists have become the awesome rocket scientists of the social sciences, complete with calculus, regressions, algebra, complex equations and econometric models that very neatly fit real life data retrospectively. But not prospectively, which is the litmus test of a physical science. Recent selections of the Nobel Prize Committee have over the years only served to amplify their rocket scientist status.[8]

The application of mathematics, algorithms and complex statistical techniques has no doubt vastly enriched economics, as they have indeed other social sciences as well (Temin, 2014). They

8. Frederich Von Hayek, one of the early recipients of the Nobel Prize for economics (1974) had sounded a note of caution in this regard in his acceptance speech, "The Pretence of Knowledge": "the still recent establishment of the Nobel Memorial Prize in Economic Science marks a significant step in the process by which, in the opinion of the general public, economics has been conceded some of the dignity and prestige of the physical sciences....We have indeed at the moment little cause for pride: as a profession we have made a mess of things..It seems to me that this failure of the economists to guide policy more successfully is closely connected with their propensity to imitate as closely as possible the procedures of the brilliantly successful physical sciences—an attempt which in our field may lead to outright error. It is an approach which has come to be described as the "scientistic" attitude—an attitude which, as I defined it some thirty years ago, "is decidedly unscientific in the true sense of the word, since it involves a mechanical and uncritical application of habits of thought to fields different from those in which they have been formed." ...Unlike the position that exists in the physical sciences, in economics and other disciplines that deal with essentially complex phenomena, the aspects of the events to be accounted for about which we can get quantitative data are necessarily limited and may not include the important ones. While in the physical sciences it is generally assumed, probably with good reason, that any important factor which determines the observed events will itself be directly observable and measurable, in the study of such complex phenomena as the market, which depend on the actions of many individuals, all the circumstances which will determine the outcome of a process, for reasons which I shall explain later, will hardly ever be fully known or measurable. And while in the physical sciences the investigator will be able to measure what, on the basis of a prima facie theory, he thinks important, in the social sciences often that is treated as important which happens to be accessible to measurement. This is sometimes carried to the point where it is demanded that our theories must be formulated in such terms that they refer only to measurable magnitudes. It can hardly be denied that such a demand quite arbitrarily limits the facts which are to be admitted as possible causes of the events which occur in the real world. This view, which is often quite naively accepted as required by scientific procedure, has some rather paradoxical consequences. We know: of course, with regard to the market and similar social structures, a great many facts which we cannot measure and on which indeed we have only some very imprecise and general information. And because the effects of these facts in any particular instance cannot be confirmed by quantitative evidence, they are simply disregarded by those sworn to admit only what they regard as scientific evidence: they thereupon happily proceed on the fiction that the factors which they can measure are the only ones that are relevant," *http://www.nobelprize.org/nobel_prizes/economic-sciences/laureates/1974/hayek-lecture.html*

have, for instance, helped to uncover patterns and relationships, *viz.*, between the Black Death (plague) and the Industrial Revolution. These techniques however have been most useful while uncovering relationships after events have unfolded. It should have been clear that the same model or equation that very neatly fitted historical data was applicable to a particular conjuncture and was rarely robust in predicting future outcomes.

While correlations were relatively easy to uncover working with historical data, causal relationships were not clear. The coefficients deduced rarely worked prospectively for predictive purposes necessary for policy interventions. As a result, it is difficult to forecast something as basic as the growth rate in the current year or even quarter, particularly during times of economic instability. For the model to be robust prospectively, for predicting future outcomes, all other relationships would need to remain the same. *Ceteris Paribus* is a critical caveat in econometric models, but this is a condition which rarely holds in the social sciences in the manner it does in the physical sciences.

Because conditions in the physical sciences can be replicated prospectively[9] their predictive value is robust. Their models have very exacting standards for acceptance. In physics just one apple needs to fly upwards instead of falling to the ground to disprove the theory of gravity. In the social sciences, on the other hand, future outcomes are unpredictable as they are the result of human choices that can vary across space and time with respect to the same parameter. The models that fit past data therefore rarely work prospectively. Their predictive value is limited. While this should have served as a warning signal to economists, the tragi-comic fact is that so far this has done little to deter them. Staistical models are being further refined using even more complex equations to fit the new facts.

9. This is not to say that physical scientists understand the working of the real world in its entirety. This is always work in progress. At the level of fundamental particles—Quantum Physics—the pattern can also seem random and unpredictable. But the 'Heisenberg uncertainty principle' does not come in the way of useful macro-level predictions that can successfully land a module on Saturn's moon through projections far into the future.

The recent global financial crisis inflicted collateral damage on economics' status as a rocket science, as hardly any economist saw it coming. If they did, like the IMF, the crisis did not unfold in the manner envisaged. Once the crisis set in, IMF's future-looking, quarterly, forecasts had to be revised significantly every subsequent quarter, often involving a sign change as well. Economists at the London School of Economics have been struggling to answer a question asked of them by Queen Elizabeth almost six years ago as to why none of them saw the credit crunch coming. In the physical sciences this is equivalent to failing to spot a large asteroid heading straight to planet earth.

Economics, it now appears, is buffeted by the same unpredictable winds of cultural differences and human choices that vary across time and space just like any other social science. The rational, profit-maximising and predictable homo-economicus of neo-classical economics that has made economics a dismal science, is simply not the rather excitable homo sapiens-sapiens of the real world. Economics is not as dull as it is made out to be. On the contrary!

What is the difference between rocket science and social science? Tomes have been written on the subject. There is a simple 'prediction' or 'apple' test derived from the great philosopher, Karl Popper (1934), who had a simple test derived from Newton's epiphany observing apples falling to the ground. Later Einstein's theory of relativity treated gravitation not as a force but as a curvature of space and time around a body. However, the theory of gravity continues to lay claim to universal validity within the terra firma. You can, on its basis, predict that every apple will eventually fall to the ground, if not picked. The flipside of the prediction is that it needs just one apple to head skywards instead of falling to the ground to disprove the theory of gravity. You can also, on the basis of such predictions, work out the precise calculations to land a space probe on Titan several years after its launch.

The predictions of economists, like those of other social scientists that have dared to make them, having no reliable gravitation to go by, mostly go awry. This is because they are based on models that capture relationships between past data. Whereas in the physical sciences the relationship between the same data set is true both retrospectively and prospectively, because physical laws are immutable, there are no such laws for human behaviour. Future outcomes are dependent on present and future human actions that are not programmable. This conflates the difference between 'why' things and 'how' they happen, which is why the narrative method is central to the social sciences.

The narrative method is superfluous in the physical sciences because the same pattern is replicated again and again. Water always boils at 100 degrees at what is defined as normal temperature and pressure. No matter what. But patterns in human affairs are never replicated, howsoever similar they might appear to be on the surface.[10] In economics a simple change in behaviour can alter the price of a financial product. Therefore, forecasts in social science disciplines, such as economics, are robust only in times of great stability when current trends can simply be projected into the future during times of little change and great stability. That is, rarely. The logical corollary is that they usually go haywire in times of change and instability. That is mostly. The repeated and sharp revisions of recent IMF forecasts on economic growth every three months, and the eventual outcomes, tabulated below bear testimony to this sobering fact.

Yet the underlying theories and models seem to survive amongst their adherents. They continue to be used for predicting the future and for policy purposes as if they were natural laws. Old models are now being made more complex, like IMF's new MAPMOD that incorporates developments in the financial sector for growth projections. The search for the perfect, evidence based model that fits the facts continues. There are two disciplines one can think of that continue making predictions that are repeatedly disproved in the real world, and yet continue to claim a wide following. One is astrology, and the other is theology. The growing popularity of models also perhaps lies behind the decline of the sub-discipline of economic history whose stars waned in tandem. But these stars are now in the ascendant.

---

10. This provoked Karl Marx to famously remark that ""Hegel remarks somewhere that all great, world-historical facts and personages occur, as it were, twice. He has forgotten to add: the first time as tragedy, the second as farce." *The Eighteenth Brumaire of Louis Bonaparte* (1852).

Table 2

IMF's WEO Forecasts in Retrospect

	2008			2009			2010			2011			2012			2013		
WEO	*Wd*	*Ad*	*Em*	*Wd*	*Ad*	*Em*	*Wd*	*Ad*	*Em*	*Wd*	*Ad*	*Em*	*Wd*	*Ad*	*Em*	*Wd*	*Ad*	*Em*
Apr-08	3.7	1.3	6.7	3.8	1.3	6.6	4.8	2.7	7.1	4.9	3.1	7.0	4.9	3.0	7.0	4.9	2.9	7.0
July Update	4.1	1.7	6.9	3.9	1.4	6.7												
Oct-08	3.9	1.5	6.9	3.0	0.5	6.1	4.2	2.0	6.7	4.8	2.9	6.9	4.8	2.8	6.9	4.7	2.5	6.9
January Update	3.4	1.0	6.3	0.5	-2.0	3.3	3.0	1.1	5.0									
Apr-09	3.2	0.9	6.1	-1.3	-3.8	1.6	1.9	0.0	4.0	4.3	2.6	6.1	4.9	3.0	6.8	4.9	3.0	6.8
July Update	3.1	0.8	6.0	-1.4	-3.8	1.5	2.5	0.6	4.7									
Oct-09	3.0	0.6	6.0	-1.1	-3.4	1.7	3.1	1.3	5.1	4.2	2.5	6.1	4.4	2.6	6.4	4.6	2.5	6.6
January Update	3.0	0.5	6.1	-0.8	-3.2	2.1	3.9	2.1	6.0	4.3	2.4	6.3						
Apr-10	3.0	0.5	6.1	-0.6	-3.2	2.4	4.2	2.3	6.3	4.3	2.4	6.5	4.5	2.4	6.6	4.5	2.4	6.6
July Update	3.0	0.5	6.1	-0.6	-3.2	2.5	4.6	2.6	6.8	4.3	2.4	6.4						
Oct-10	2.8	0.2	6.0	-0.6	-3.2	2.5	4.8	2.7	7.1	4.2	2.2	6.4	4.5	2.6	6.5	4.6	2.6	6.6
January Update				-0.6	-3.4	2.6	5.0	3.0	7.1	4.4	2.5	6.5	4.5	2.5	6.5			
Apr-11	2.9	0.2	6.1	-0.5	-3.4	2.7	5.0	3.0	7.3	4.4	2.4	6.5	4.5	2.6	6.5	4.5	2.5	6.5
July Update				-0.5	-3.4	2.8	5.1	3.0	7.4	4.3	2.2	6.6	4.5	2.6	6.4			
Oct-11	2.8	0.1	6.0	-0.7	-3.7	2.8	5.1	3.1	7.3	4.0	1.6	6.4	4.0	1.9	6.1	4.5	2.4	6.5
January Update							5.2	3.2	7.3	3.8	1.6	6.2	3.3	1.2	5.4	3.9	1.9	5.9
Apr-12	2.8	0.0	6.0	-0.6	-3.6	2.8	5.3	3.2	7.5	3.9	1.6	6.2	3.5	1.4	5.7	4.1	2.0	6.0
July Update							5.3	3.2	7.5	3.9	1.6	6.2	3.5	1.4	5.6	3.9	1.9	5.9
Oct-12	2.8	0.1	6.1	-0.6	-3.5	2.7	5.1	3.0	7.4	3.8	1.6	6.2	3.3	1.3	5.3	3.6	1.5	5.6
January Update										3.9	1.6	6.3	3.2	1.3	5.1	3.5	1.4	5.5

Although most economic models are robust only while explaining past relationships, they can nevertheless serve as useful general guidance for present and future actions and policies. The present, after all, has grown out of the past. The danger lies in elegant, seductive models and mathematically precise models that distract or lull us from detecting new dynamics undermining old relationships or acknowledging the wide variations in human behaviour across time and space.

Economics for, like other social sciences, has very powerful tools to understand the world and give insights into our future. If history is amongst the oldest of human disciplines, trade, exchange, markets, money, income, surplus distribution, investment, consumption, etcetera—the stuff economics is made of—are known to exist in most primitive human societies. Several ancient texts such as Kautilya's *Arthashastra* and Ibn Khaldun's *Muqaddimah* deliberated these matters over the ages, long before the classical economists of the 17th century. Rather, this is a plea for rescuing the discipline of economics from the jaws of rocket scientists and handing it back to the humanities where it originally belonged.

One can empathise with economists because, unlike those social scientists who simply seek to understand the real world, economists in addition endeavour to change it. Like Karl Marx. Its practitioners however need to appreciate to a greater extent the limitations of a social science that is shaped by the enormous variability of human behaviour across space and time. This makes it difficult to forecast the future. They need to fold this nuanced understanding into the new macroeconomics 101, as this matters greatly for the design of economic policy.

Human behaviour can be very variable across time and space. Some time ago a number of studies of traditional peasant societies found that peasant rationality seemed to differ from capitalist rationality. The production response to price changes was quite different from what one expects under a capitalist system of profit maximisation (Thorner *et al.*, 1966; Shanin, 1971; Wolf, 1966). However, instead of mainstreaming peasant studies into economics, they were banished to social anthropology. Even today, countries such as France and

Italy seem to value leisure more than Americans. This is reflected in differences in economic behaviour, and hence in their response to the same macroeconomic policies.

Human behaviour can vary across space. It would be clear from the fable of the ant and the grasshopper that they behaved quite differently. Asians, with their high saving rates are the ants of the developing world. Latin American countries with their low saving rates are the grasshoppers. There are both ants and grasshoppers in Europe as well. North Europeans are the ants and southern Europeans the grasshoppers. Angela Merkel, the German Chancellor, is wont to refer to the Swabian housewife,[11] an ant that would save any extra penny given to her by way of stimulus. The American housewife is perhaps a Grasshopper in comparison, more likely to spend two pennies for every additional penny received. Economic research has found that it is very difficult for policy makers to influence long-term saving behaviour because it is, to a large extent, culturally determined. The response over the short-run is also very likely different, with the ants responding to low interest rates by saving and investing more, and the grasshoppers by borrowing and consuming more.

Keynes assigned a critical to animal spirits, or sentiment, in economic activity. However mainstream economic theories are based on the conception of human behaviour envisaged by neoclassical economists who saw people as rational actors coolly weighing costs and benefits and optimizing personal outcomes. More recently, behavioural economists like Thaler and Sunstein (2008), who lean more on psychology, a halfway house between the social and natural sciences, have argued that people rely on a set of instincts, biases, and cognitive shortcuts to make decisions. They have attempted to uncover such instinctive behaviour through real life experiments. Such experimentation forms the basis of policy recommendations to achieve intended outcomes.

Behavioural economists have had some notable successes, such as reducing speeding outside schools, and spillage in men's urinals. They have been so influential in recent years that they were drafted

11. "The German Mentality. Hail the Swabian Housewife",*The Economist*, 1-7 February.

by President Obama in the design of his "Making work pay tax credit", part of the 2009 stimulus bill. This was one of the least noticed tax cuts of all time. Rather than coming as a check from the government with the sum written on the dotted line, the tax credit was disbursed in a steady dribble on the advice of behavioural economists to counter Ricardian equivalence and improve fiscal multipliers. But this did not help improve fiscal multipliers (Sahm *et al.*, 2012). Why? Perhaps because the same people behave differently in normal times and in financial crises. The experimental research that formed the basis of the policy recommendation was done in normal times. The same person's saving and spending behaviour will be very different when he sees his wealth growing, and when he sees it shrinking, where the prospects of retaining his job look uncertain, and Ricardian equivalence looms large.

This is however only part of the huge public policy problem we are confronted with. The same experiment may have yielded very different results in Swabia. It is also entirely possible that humans may adjust to shortening parallel lines and painted fly images and speeding and spillages may resurface in future. Ultimately the assumptions regarding the predictability of human behaviour in behavioural economics appears not to be philosophically very different from those of the neoclassical economists.

To take one final example, high levels of debt during the boom preceding the financial crisis enhanced consumption. But high levels of debt in the post crisis period are depressing consumption and prolonging the recovery. Such variations in human behaviour from one context to another are also the reason why the outcome of research on fiscal multipliers is inconclusive, contradictory and confusing (Barro, 2012; Cogan *et al.*, 2009; Ilzetzki *et al.*, 2011; Delong and Summers, 2012; Romer and Bernstein, 2010; Sahm *et al.*, 2011).[12]

In a nutshell, in sharp contradistinction to the assumptions of both neoclassical and behavioural economics, human behaviour can vary enormously across both space and time. This makes uniform, or

12. *World Economic Outlook*, October 2008, Chapter 5; *World Economic Outlook*, October 2010, pp.165-66;*World Economic Outlook*, October 2012, Chapter 1, Box 1.1, pp.41-43.

one size fits all economic policy recommendations, very difficult. The narrative is equally, if not more, important as theoretical abstractions in the social sciences. Explaining why things happened the way they did is often indistinguishable from how they did.

VI

This is a postscript—additional remarks following the main corpus—not a concluding chapter or summary. Let me nevertheless, at the very end, attempt a tour *de force* that distills, rather than summarises, the central themes scattered across various chapters of what is an omnibus more than a book per se.

We live in a world that is fast globalizing across every conceivable frontier. The process of globalization began the moment the first humans ventured out of their original home in the African continent more than a million years ago. The world nevertheless remained mostly poor, local and decentralized right until the end of the Middle Ages, with human migrations mostly a one-way street.

The proximate roots of the globalizing world that we are familiar with were planted from the middle of the last millennium with technological advances, especially in maritime transportation, and the enlightenment in Europe. These forces shaped the Great Age of Discovery, the Industrial Revolution, the emergence of the Nation-State, the Great Divergence that saw the passing of the mighty Asian agrarian empires, and European colonialisation of the globe.

These developments accentuated age-old European rivalries that spilled over globally, briefly kept in check in the post Napoleonic period by Britain's global dominance. This was in turn based on its head start in industrialisation that marked the second stage of globalization. Britain presided over an uneasy peace in Europe in the 19th century through the Concert of Europe, the original institution of global governance. This peace was shattered towards the end of the nineteenth century with the emergence of a new power that could not be accommodated within the extant balance of power.

Trade and markets, intermediated by scarce, precious items that served as a medium of universal exchange, or money, existed since the dawn of human societies. Mostly local and neighbourhood phenomena till recently, these were globalized through the growing need to transport large volumes of goods quickly across vast distances to connect distant markets. Innovations in technology and finance, and the massive productivity gains that followed, led to rapid improvements in the quality of life, demographic shifts, and new forms of economic (large factories, banks, joint stock companies) and social organisation (capitalism, socialism, urbanisation). The asymmetric spread of these forces lay behind the Great Divergence.

The third stage of globalization followed two devastating global wars. It coincided with the passing of the gold standard as fiat currency opened up new fiscal, monetary and financial possibilities. Macroeconomic policies were honed through the battle with inflation and fiscal excess that saw the emergence of central bank independence and rule bound monetary policy such as the Taylor Rule.

The emergence of the dollar as the de facto global reserve currency was double-edged. On the one hand it facilitated a system of global economic governance dominated by the US, the new global hegemon that replaced Britain in the post-war period. On the other hand, it also ushered in the Great Age of Convergence. Former colonies in Asia aggressively leveraged external demand to supplement their modest domestic demand to grow at rates unprecedented in history. The Great Convergence challenged extant institutions of economic global governance that become dysfunctional. They failed to adjust to tectonic shifts in economic balance underway.

The same inertia was also evident in the relatively young discipline of economics. Economic and financial crises were a recurring feature in history, but these were local in a localised world. A globalizing economy led inexorably to global crises. The Great Depression was the first global economic crisis. Unsurprisingly, modern macroeconomic analysis and policies—macroeconomics 101—and institutions of global economic governance, beginning with Bretton Woods, developed in response to the first global crisis.

Much of the original tools of economic analysis and policy took closed economies centred on the Nation-State as their point of reference, including those fashioned in the wake of the Great Depression. These tools were however being blunted, and macroeconomics 101 undermined, as globalization seamlessly entered a frenetic fourth stage through the rise of information technology. Instead of refashioning its tools through a greater appreciation of the nuances of the great range of human behavior across space and time, the relatively young social science tried to break loose from its moorings in the social sciences. Complacently stereotyping human behaviour it endeavoured to reinvent itself as a rocket science by incorporating tools from the physical sciences, such as advanced mathematics.

The failure of the discipline, and along with it of policy makers, to respond adequately to mounting anomalies with respect to macroeconomics 101 perhaps explains why a crisis in the small sub-prime segment of the US housing market rapidly morphed into the second global economic and financial crisis, with few seeing it coming.

It was through this blunted macroeconomic toolkit, fashioned in a different era, that a nascent institution of global economic governance mounted what was by all counts a spectacular and unprecedented coordinated policy response to the global financial crisis. The response may have prevented a sharp decline in economic activity and deflation on the scale of the Great Depression. But the G20 was unable to prevent the Great Recession which is now almost as protracted as the Great Depression, with the slowest recovery on record in the post war period. Indeed, the protracted use of what are essentially term tools have created distortions that have queered the way for their exit.

The global economy is still not out of the woods. Aggressive macroeconomic policies can revive cyclical downturns but not structural downward shifts in demand. Demand was already weakening because of rising inequality, stagnant real wages, falling labour participation rates and demographic transition. It was however propped up by an extraordinary credit boom generated by easy monetary policy, lax financial regulation and external imbalances. Central bankers were deluded by the structural fall in inflation through a combination of technological innovation and globalizing forces that kept productivity growth ahead of consumption growth. In the post crisis period they have engineered yet another asset boom even as the real economy flags. The rise and rise of leverage in the aftermath of the demise of the gold standard may be undermining the short reign of fiat money.

The current mantra of the IMF and G20 to return to a higher growth trajectory comprises a cocktail of structural reforms, infrastructure investment and public demand. Paul Krugman has long argued that fiscal policy was not aggressive enough. But public debt in AEs now exceed levels they can realistically be expected to grow out of without higher taxes, inflation, financial repression and ultimately lower growth. Can the outcome of a public credit boom be very different from that of a private credit boom?

The G20 and the IMF are nudging countries to drive up global growth through the 'Brisbane Action Plan', the centre-piece of the Leaders' Declaration at the Ninth G20 Summit in November 2014. But we have had St. Petersburg and Los Cabos Action Plans before. The appetite for deep-seated land, labor and product market reforms seems weak. There is also no fiscal space left to cushion the social impact of what are politically challenging reforms. Lower growth alone may not spur democracies into animated action. Such reforms are more contingent on domestic political appetite than on non-binding plurilateral commitments.

A more realistic goal is to restructure advanced economy lifestyles and metrics to adjust to lower growth. This would address the twin imperatives of rebalancing global demand and mitigating climate change. Consumption levels in advanced economies are already so high that were developing economies to ape them we are all done for. Over the short term this might dim high growth prospects in developing countries overly reliant on OECD economies for demand. With rebalancing of demand, however, their long-term growth prospects would remain good. With structural reforms advanced economies could push their own growth rates higher on the coat-tails of this demand rebalancing.

AEs would do well to remember that right up to the Industrial Revolution growth averaged below one per cent per annum, mostly through demographic expansions periodically audited by Nature in red pencil, rather than through sustained productivity growth. Low aggregate growth over extended periods, minus the froth and red pencil, need not mean low per capita growth, and should not be scoffed at. Such adjustments might also make these societies happier, with more time for leisure and family and friends. Ironically, this option might make capitalism converge more towards Karl Marx's vision of the (communist) future!

In the Preface, I listed a number of macroeconomic anomalies in evidence prior to the crisis. The failure to address these within a new macroeconomic framework perhaps explains why a number of persistent faultlines remain in the way of stabilizing the global economy in the post crisis world.

The objective of this book was never to draw the contours of a new paradigm, an endeavour far beyond the capabilities of this author, but to flag issues regarding the existing one. It would nevertheless appear that the forces of globalization-technological innovation, ageing, financialization and a simplistic conception of human behaviour have undermined the extant paradigm of macroeconomics 101. Macroeconomic policies, in any case, can simply help stabilise business cycles; they cannot be a substitute for adjustments to structural changes in the economy necessary to return to a high growth trajectory.

These forces contain pointers to the new paradigm needed to repair extant monetary, fiscal and trade policy frameworks. Central banks need to be concerned even when inflation and growth are within target. Large macroeconomic imbalances can compromise financial stability as predicted pressures on interest and exchange rates may be countervailed by large cross-border capital flows. New metrics need to be mainstreamed for measuring trade (value added), growth (per capita and adjusted for quality of life), leverage (productive), fair value (clearing markets), and intellectual property protection (recouping investment). The nitty-gritty of financial markets also need to be mainstreamed in the new paradigm. The Keynesian and Austrian School paradigms need to be reconciled and conflated. Financial intermediation needs to be tethered to the real economy by, inter alia, revisting old paradigms relating to financial depth and repression.

On a more philosophical plane, both finance and economics need to stop pretending that they can ever be natural sciences driven by immutable natural laws. They are social sciences driven by the vagaries of human behaviour that vary sharply across space and time. Such a nuanced understanding of human behaviour would make macroeconomics 101 lean more on history, sociology, anthropology, psychology and political science and less on the physical sciences like mathematics and physics. The macroeconomics of the brave new globalized world of the 21st century awaits its Adam Smith. And a new classic, perhaps with the simple and elegant caption—Human Wealth—to put Humpty Dumpty back on the wall again.

References

Alloway, Tracy and Sam Fleming (2013). "Shadow Banks Reap Fed Rate Reward", *Financial Times.* 11 November.

Barro, Robert (2012). "Stimulus Spending Keeps Failing", *The Wall Street Journal.* 9 May.

Borio, Claudio (2012). "The Financial Cycle and Macroeconomics: What have we Learnt?", *BIS Working Paper* No 395. December.

Cecchetti, Stephen G. and Enisse Kharroubi (2013). "Why Does Financial Sector Growth Crowd Out Real Economic Growth?", The Joint Institute for New Economic Thinking-Federal Reserve Bank of San Francisco Conference *Finance and the Welfare of Nations.* San Francisco. 27 September.

Chassany, Anne-Sylvaine and Henny Sender (2013). "Finance: Forced into the Shadows", *Financial Times.* 6 June.

Cogan, John F. , Tobias Cwik, John B. Taylor and Volker Wieland (2009). "New Keynesian versus Old Keynesian", *Government Spending Multipliers,* February.

Croxson, Karen, Susan Lund and Charles Roxburgh (2012). "Working Out of Debt", *McKinsey Quarterly.* January.

Das, Satyajit (2013). "Post-crisis Policies Promise Chronic Stagnation", *Financial Times.* 11 September.

———. (2014). "Quest to Trigger Inflation has Failed", *Financial Times.* 5 March.

DeLong, J. Bradford and Lawrence H. Summers (2012). "Fiscal Policy in a Depressed Economy". 20 March.

Eichengreen, Barry and Poonam Gupta (2011). "The Service Sector as India's Road to Economic Growth", *NBER WP* 16757.

Feldstein, Martin (2014). "America's Move to Faster Growth", *Project Syndicate.* 27 May.

Foley, Stephen (2013). "Warning Lights are Flashing in America's Credit Markets", *Financial Times.* 2 August.

———. (2013a). "Fannie Mae's $59 bn Dividend Lifts Hopes of US Taxpayer Profit", *Financial Times.* 9 May.

Galbraith, John K. (1993). *A Short History of Financial Euphoria.*

Haldane, Andrew (2010). "The Contribution of the Financial Sector: Miracle or Mirage?", Speech at the *Future of Finance* conference. London. 14 July.

Ilzetzki, Ethan, Enrique G. Mendoza and Carlos A. Végh (2011). "How Big (Small?) are Fiscal Multipliers?", *IMF Working Paper* WP/11/52. March.

Jen, Stephen L. and Fatih Yilmaz (2013). *The Slow and Agonizing Passing of Inflation Targeting*. SLJ Macro Partners. 14 July.

Kay, John (2013). "*The Market is not the Best Place to Set a Fair Price for Assets*", *Financial Times*. 16 July.

Manyika, James and Charles Roxburgh (2011). *The Great Transformer: The Impact of the Internet on Economic Growth and Prosperity*. McKinsey Global Institute. October.

Manyika, James Jeff Sinclair, Richard Dobbs, Gernot Strube, Louis Rassey, Jan Mischke, Jaana Remes, Charles Roxburgh, Katy George, David O'Halloran and Sreenivas Ramaswamy (2012). *Manufacturing the Future: The Next Era of Global Growth and Innovation*. McKinsey Global Institute. McKinsey Operations Practice. November.

Manyika, James Jacques Bughin, Susan Lund, Olivia Nottebohm, David Poulter, Sebastian Jauch and Sree Ramaswamy (2014). *Global Flows in a Digital Age: How Trade, Finance, People, and Data Connect the World Economy*. McKinsey Global Institute. April.

Piketty, Thomas (2014). *Capital in the Twenty-First Century*. Translated by Arthur Goldhammer. Harvard University Press.

Popper, Karl (1934). *The Logic of Scientific Discovery*.

Temin, Peter (2014). "Economic History and Economic Development: New Economic History in Retrospect and Prospect", *National Bureau of Economic Research Working Paper* 20107. May.

Reinhart, Carmen and Kenneth Rogoff (2011). "A Decade of Debt", *Discussion Paper* 8310. Centre for Economic Policy Research. April.

Roach, Stephen (2010). *Stephen Roach on the Next Asia: Opportunities and Challenges for a New Globalization*.

Romer, Christina and Jared Bernstein (2010). *The Job Impact of the American Recovery and Reinvestment Plan*. 10 January.

Sahm, Claudia R., Matthew D. Shapiro and Joel Slemrod (2011). *Check in the Mail or More in the Paycheck: Does the Effectiveness of Fiscal Stimulus Depend on How It Is Delivered?* 14 June.

———. (2012). "Check in the Mail or More in the Pay Check: Does the Effectiveness of Fiscal Stimulus Depend on How it is Delivered?", *American Economic Journal: Economic Policy* 4(3): 216–50.

Shanin, Teodor (ed.) (1971). *Peasants and Peasant Societies*.

Silver-Greenburg, Jessica and Michael Corkery (2014). "In a Sub-prime Bubble for Used Cars, Borrowers Pay Sky High Rates", *The New York Times*. 19 July.

Singh, Manmohan and James Aitken (2010). "The (sizable) Role of Rehypothecation in the Shadow Banking System", *IMF WP* 10/172. July.

Solow, Robert M. (2013). "How to Save American Finance from Itself. Has Financialization Gone Too Far?", *New Republic*. 8 April.

Stephens, Phillip (2013). "Nations are Chasing the Illusion of Sovereignty", *Financial Times*. 6 June.

Thaler, Richard H. and Cass R. Sunstein (2008). *Nudge: Improving Decisions about Health, Wealth and Happiness*.

Tett, Gillian (2011). "Shadow Spreading across International Banking", *Financial Times*. 27 June.

———. (2014). "Tranquil Markets are Enjoying too much of a Good Thing", *Financial Times*. 29 May.

———. (2014a). "Digital v Human: The New Debate", *Financial Times*. 28 March.

Thorner, D. , B. Kerblay and R.E.F Smith (ed.) (1966). *A.V. Chayanov: The Theory of Peasant Economy.*

Timiraos, Nick (2013). "Five Years Later, Fannie Mae, Freddie Mac Remain Unfinished Business", *The Wall Street Journal.* 6 September.

Turner, Adair (2014). "Too Much of the Wrong Sort of Capital Flow", Conference on *Capital Account Management and Macro-prudential Regulation For Financial Stability and Growth.* Centre for Advanced Financial Research and Learning, Reserve Bank of India. New Delhi. 13 January.

Wolf, Eric (1966). *Peasants.*

Wolf, Martin (2010). "The Grasshoppers and the Ants: A Modern Fable", *Financial Times*, 25 May.

———. (2010a). "The Grasshoppers and the Ants: Eucidating the Fable", *Financial Times,* 1 June.

Index

U

V

W